IGNITED

JACI WIGHTMAN

IGNITED

HOW CHRIST CAN LIGHT OUR INNER FLAME

(AND KEEP IT LIT!)

CFI
An imprint of Cedar Fort, Inc.
Springville, Utah

Paperback ISBN 13: 978-1-4621-4584-3
Ebook ISBN: 978-1-4621-3163-1

Published by CFI, an imprint of Cedar Fort, Inc.
2373 W. 700 S., Suite 100, Springville, UT 84663
Distributed by Cedar Fort, Inc., www.cedarfort.com

Library of Congress Registration Number: 2023941151

Cover design by Shawnda Craig

Edited by Liz Kazandzhy
Typeset by Liz Kazandzhy

Printed in the United States of America

10 9 8 7 6 5 4 3 2 1

Printed on acid-free paper

To Mom, Dad, Todd, Mindi, and Brad

May a future day find us gathered at the Lord's feet,
bound together in the love of an eternal family.

Other Books by Jaci Wightman

Aren't You Tired?: Embracing the Lord's Call to Enter His Rest

A Princess Story: The Real-Life Fairy Tale Found in the Gospel

Body Image Breakthrough: Learning to See Your Body and Your Beauty in a Whole New Light

Contents

Acknowledgments. ix

Introduction 1

1 When Our Flame Blows Out. 5

It's Not Just a Story—It's a Journey

2 A New Twist on an Old Tale 17
3 The Seduction of Our Desires 31
4 Our Fallen Heart. 43
5 Those Unbreakable Chains 59

Continuing in Eve's Footsteps

6 Fig Leaf Fashion 79
7 Hide and Seek 103
8 Our Pointing Finger 125

The Secret of Our Heartlight

9 If You Only Knew 145
10 Christ in Us. 161
11 Prone to Wander 181
12 The Invitation 203
13 Awake to Grace 225

A Soul Ignited

14 Lighting Our Inner Flame 243
15 Infused with Joy. 265
16 Abiding in His Love. 281

Epilogue: Come Home 303

About the Author 310

Acknowledgments

I'll let you in on a little secret. This was my very first manuscript, which I started over fifteen years ago. That's a long time to work on a book. So you can probably guess this isn't just another project for me—this one is my baby. Simply put, if I could pick just one message to share with the world, this would be it. It's that life-changing and important to me.

The crazy thing is, this particular message didn't start out in book form at all. Back then, I never even imagined myself as an author—I was just a weary soul searching for answers. As my quest for those answers progressed, I kept a three-ring binder with the scriptures, quotes, and lessons the Lord unveiled along the way. Then one day it struck me that my binder was divided into sections that resembled chapters, and put together, those chapters revealed an incredible journey. That moment lit a fire in me to do everything I could to get the message out of that binder and into the hands of those who needed it as much as I did.

Thankfully, over the years I've had a great deal of help with this project. The Lord brought many powerful mentors into my life—some who still lived on the earth and even more who'd already passed on (many of whom are quoted in this book). These giant souls opened up a whole new world to me. I'll never be able to adequately express the different ways these teachers and authors blessed my life through their profound testimonies of Jesus Christ.

In addition, several of my loved ones left an indelible mark on this work. My sister-in-law, Desi Wightman, spent more than a year offering her wonderful editing skills and thoughtful suggestions, which made my awkward words come alive in a fresh, new way. My husband's parents, Philip and Pat Wightman, endured multiple manuscripts and provided valuable insight. And my children (who were teens and pre-teens when this journey began) graciously allowed me to immerse myself in writing from time to time and didn't complain when I did some of my mothering while sitting in front of a computer.

Of course, this journey wouldn't have been possible without the presence of my wonderful traveling companion—my husband, Greg. His blend of wisdom, humor, patience, and love made the rough roads more bearable and provided great strength for me to lean on. Truly, there's no one else I'd rather have by my side throughout the eternities.

I'm also incredibly grateful for the untold hours of dedication from the faithful team at Cedar Fort. This will be our fourth book together, and I've never had a single complaint. The Lord has truly used their efforts to make my message into what it needed to be—and really could never have been without them.

Finally, and most importantly, this work simply would not exist without the love and influence of my Savior. To me, Jesus Christ no longer seems like a mystical figure from long ago. Instead, He's become very real to me—so real, in fact, that He's taken His rightful place as the light and life of my soul and the joy of my heart. For this, I join my words to those penned by the Psalmist: "I love the Lord . . . for [He] hast delivered my soul from death, mine eyes from tears, and my feet from falling" (Psalm 116:1, 8). I will praise His name as long as I have breath (see Psalm 150:6).

Introduction

In the pages ahead, we've got quite an adventure waiting for us. But before we jump in, you need to know that this isn't just a book—it's a journey I've gone through myself, a quest so significant and paradigm-shifting that it has completely transformed my entire life. Because this process has had such a dramatic impact on me, I've been driven over the last fifteen years to capture the details in written form. Again and again, I found myself jotting down notes at a stoplight or typing away at 3 a.m. when I couldn't sleep. It's been quite a challenge to take something intangible and make it come alive on the page so others could read and understand it.

Now that it's finally in print, what I want more than anything is for others to experience what I've experienced, or as Alma said, to "[taste] as I have tasted, and . . . [see] as I have seen" (Alma 36:26.) But for that to happen, I need to warn you that this isn't going to be a quick and easy read. You won't be able to speed through it in a few days and move on to something else. Well, I guess you could *try* that approach, but if you do, you'll miss the whole point of going on this quest. To really get the most out of this journey, you need to slow down and personalize it. Internalize it. Do all you can to make it your own.

I say that because many of the issues we're going to discuss took me months—and often much longer—to work through in my mind and heart. I had to study, pray, ponder, and journal, and then study and pray some more. It required, as Elder David A. Bednar has described, "spiritual, mental, and physical exertion and not just passive reception."[1] So if you're going to take this journey seriously, you've got to do more than just read about my experience—you've got to be prepared to do some work of your own along the way.

The secret of this expedition is simple. You're the one who determines where the paths will ultimately lead. Yes, you can casually skim through these pages, but all that will do is keep you stuck in the same old rut, struggling with the same old issues you've battled for years. Or you can leave your comfort zone behind and walk with me down some new roads. Better yet, you can dive in with all the passion, strength, and courage you can possibly muster.

The choice is up to you.

To help facilitate this powerful, life-changing process, the structure of this book will follow a very specific pattern. After reading and processing the ideas in each chapter, you'll encounter two additional sections: "Readings & Reflections" and "Response."

In the "Readings & Reflections" section, you'll have the chance to explore that chapter's gospel topic in greater depth. I included several scriptural verses and passages you can study, and there are also some questions you can answer either in a personal journal or in the provided space within the book. This personal application is what will make this journey more relevant to your life and your individual circumstances. As you work through each section, take time to ponder and reflect on the things you're learning. Meditation is a wonderful way to slow down and let the truths you're studying sink deep into the recesses of your mind and heart.

You'll then finish with the "Response" section. This is your chance to find a way to express your thoughts and feelings about the things you're learning. You may decide to record some new insights in your

---

1. David A. Bednar, "Seek Learning by Faith," *Ensign*, Sept. 2007, 64.

journal. You may write a blog post or share an idea on social media. Or you may start a conversation with a friend or family member. The possibilities really are endless. I'm praying that the "Readings & Reflections" and "Response" sections will help you explore and own the eye-opening truths you'll discover along the way.

With that said, if you're not sure you have the time or energy to devote to such an in-depth journey, all I ask you to do is turn the page. I'm hoping our introductory chapter will be enough to convince you to join me and take your first bold steps into the great unknown.

1

When Our Flame Blows Out

I'm guessing you've felt it before. Maybe you're experiencing it right now. It's that feeling of emptiness inside—like your inner pilot light has gone out and you just can't get it relit. You may describe it as a sense of hopelessness or restlessness. You may feel apathetic, listless, or even numb. Or you may feel like you're just going through the motions—like your heart has checked out and you can't get it back in the game. However you describe it, this feeling is a gnawing *soul hunger*. Deep down you know there's a void, but you're not sure where it came from or how to make it go away.

Like it or not, this void seems to plague all of us at some point, and it leaves us scrambling to find a way to fill the emptiness and reignite that lifeless inner spark. But try as we might, we find our soul hunger to be both stubborn and unpredictable. At times, it refuses to budge even if we take that much-needed vacation or get that raise we've been asking for. It continues to plague us no matter how much we eat, watch, play, scroll, or self-medicate. Helpless to pull ourselves out of the abyss, we may conclude that our inner pilot light has a life of its own and that we don't have any control over the height of the flame.

Would you be surprised to learn that Isaiah captures this soul hunger in the pages of the Old Testament? Funny how an ancient text can describe exactly what we go through in today's modern world. He wrote, "Ho, every one that thirsteth, come ye to the waters, and he that hath no money; come ye, buy, and eat; yea, come, buy wine and milk without money and without price. Wherefore do ye spend money for that which is not bread? and your labour for that which satisfieth not? hearken diligently unto me, and eat ye that which is good, and let your soul delight itself in fatness" (Isaiah 55:1–2)

First, the prophet calls out to the thirsty, and we know he's not talking about a big drink of water. He's addressing those of us whose *hearts* are in need—whose souls are parched, drained, and in desperate need of refilling. Whether that void is a lack of love, joy, peace, or even just patience to get through the day, Isaiah invites us to find the "waters" that can truly satisfy our relentless inner thirst.

Next, Isaiah speaks to those who have "no money," and again, we know he's not talking about dwindling Israelite bank accounts. He's beckoning to those of us whose *hearts* are destitute or bankrupt. We're talking about much more than just having a bad day (or even a string of bad days). These are the seasons when we're living in mental, emotional, or spiritual poverty. When we feel absolutely no hope and no desire to continue on. Thankfully, Isaiah offers the answer to everything our impoverished soul is so desperately searching for.

The prophet then takes a dramatic turn. After addressing the thirsty and the bankrupt, he calls out to those of us who *do* have money to spend—only we're spending it on things that don't really satisfy. I'm sure we've all been there a time or two. Maybe we tried to fill our soul hunger with a nicer car, a new pair of shoes, or some epic concert tickets. Maybe we tried remodeling the house, grabbing that new bestseller, or downing yet another bag of M&M's. We convinced ourselves we'd finally be happy if we could just have ________ (fill in the blank). But regardless of how much money we spent, our inner void still continued to haunt us. Again, Isaiah holds the key to our heart's insatiable need.

And what about the prophet's last category—those who "labour for that which satisfieth not"? What kind of work could he be talking about? Perhaps he's speaking to those of us who try to fill our emptiness by throwing ourselves into as many activities and responsibilities as we possibly can. We load our to-do list with an endless array of busyness and service in an attempt to create a meaningful and fulfilling life. But for some reason, we continue to struggle with anxiety and burnout. We try to shake ourselves out of it, but nothing really does the trick. We're left to wonder if the path we've chosen really leads to fulfillment or just a lot of extra stress and exhaustion.

No matter which of Isaiah's scenarios fit our lives, I believe we're all looking for the same end result: a way to ignite that inner spark. To escape the feelings of emptiness or numbness or restlessness and feel *alive* again. But often that just feels impossible. Despite all our efforts, the void won't seem to budge, so we end up settling for survival mode where we try to scrape together what little happiness we can find through our favorite hobbies, escapes, and coping mechanisms.

But what if there's more waiting for us in the gospel of Jesus Christ?

What if there's an answer we haven't even begun to comprehend? One that will change our lives—and hearts—forever?

To find it, we have to return to the end of Isaiah's passage. You see, his goal in these verses wasn't just to describe the spiritually thirsty and emotionally bankrupt, or to call out the weary spenders and worn-out laborers. I believe that was just a setup to reveal the greatest secret of all: that there *is* a way to satisfy our soul hunger. It comes through what Isaiah calls a glorious feast of "fatness"—an abundant offering of food and drink for our soul. Others have joined him in this call to the banquet table, including Book of Mormon prophets like Jacob (see Jacob 3:2) and Alma (see Alma 5:34). Through their inspired words, we're summoned to a plentiful buffet that will obliterate our inner hunger. In short, it will satisfy every lingering craving of our soul and every unfulfilled longing of our heart.

Perhaps most striking of all is a verse where Christ Himself speaks of the results of this glorious feast. After providing the sacrament as a representation of His atoning sacrifice, Jesus makes this staggering promise that's simple yet mind-blowing at the same time: "He that eateth this bread eateth of my body *to his soul*; and he that drinketh of this wine drinketh of my blood *to his soul*; and *his soul* shall never hunger nor thirst, *but shall be filled*" (3 Nephi 20:8; emphasis added).

Notice what the Lord doesn't say in this verse. He doesn't say that every time our soul is empty, He'll be there to fill us up again. No, He reveals a much greater promise than that. With astounding clarity, the Savior instead declares that once we truly learn to feast on Him—meaning we learn to fill ourselves with His incredible light and power and love—*our soul will never feel hungry, thirsty, or empty ever again*! It's a miracle that goes far beyond what most of us are currently experiencing. Can you imagine what it would feel like to have your heart filled so full that you never live in a state of deprivation? To have your flame so lit up that you never spend another moment feeling numb or lifeless inside? It truly is a mind-blowing possibility.

One way to capture this idea is by asking yourself what your soul is hungering for right this very minute. Are you battling nagging feelings of insecurity or a lingering sense of loneliness? Are you plagued by worry or fear or worn down by the stress of your daily routine? Are you thirsting for a greater personal awareness of the Lord's love or peace in a difficult family relationship? If so, Christ is telling you that He can *fully satisfy all those longings*. Not only that, but He can do so in such a way that your needs *stay met,* no matter what's going on in your daily life. Through Him, your restlessness can be calmed, your impatience quieted, your fatigue lifted, and your irritation soothed. Through Him, your sadness can be comforted, your anxiety relieved, your anger dissipated, and your emptiness filled. It's one of the most amazing gifts available through the power of His Atonement.

However, obtaining such a gift is no small task. The only way we can receive it is to seek it "with all [our] heart and with all [our] soul" (Deuteronomy 4:29). In other words, it's going to require a journey. You could call it an adventure, a quest, or even a pilgrimage. It's a trek that will lead us to an astonishing summit—to a place where our inner blaze will shine *continually* rather than just sparking or sputtering every once in a while.

Of course, like any adventure worth its salt, we're going to face some challenging trails before we can reach those blessed heights. The first section of our journey will help us understand the dynamics of our heart and why we experience that emptiness and hunger in the first place. And the middle section will help us identify the things that have kept us from experiencing the kind of lasting inner fire we've been longing for. But if you'll continue to travel with me, the road will eventually lead us to the secret of our *heartlight.*

I want you to get used to that word because you're going to hear it a lot, especially in the latter part of our quest. Put simply, heartlight is the term I'm going to use to describe the flame Jesus Christ can light deep inside our heart. The best part is, it's a light that actually *stays* lit—*every single day for the rest of our lives.* I promise, once you experience this incredible heartlight for yourself, every sacrifice you've made along the way will fade into nothingness as your soul explodes in a brilliant burst of light, passion, energy, and love. It truly is everything our weary, burned-out hearts could ever hope for.

So tell me—are you willing to endure the rigors of this journey to learn the secret of your heartlight? Would you like to leave your emptiness behind and experience an inner flame that glows with more brightness than you ever thought possible? Do you want to fill your hungry soul by feasting on all the "fatness" Lord has prepared for you?

If so, it's time to lace up your figurative hiking boots. We're about to embark on the expedition of a lifetime.

Readings & Reflections

Have you ever thought much about the idea of your soul hungering and thirsting just like your body does? What do you think that looks like for you personally? How does this hunger manifest itself in your everyday life?

To read more about the feast the Lord can provide for our soul hunger, look up several of the verses referenced in this chapter. For instance, take some time to study 2 Nephi 9:50–51; Jacob 3:2; and Alma 5:34. Now add Proverbs 13:25; Enos 1:4; Alma 42:27; and 3 Nephi 12:6. What thoughts and impressions are you left with?

Let's return to Isaiah's passage and make it more personal. As you read it again, notice the four areas pointed out in this chapter:

"Ho, every one that thirsteth, come ye to the waters, and he that hath no money; come ye, buy, and eat; yea, come, buy wine and milk without money and without price. Wherefore do ye spend money for that which is not bread? and your labour for that which satisfieth not? hearken diligently unto me, and eat ye that which is good, and let your soul delight itself in fatness" (Isaiah 55:1–2).

Now prayerfully evaluate the ways you've felt or experienced each of the areas the prophet mentioned. For instance:

- When has your inner man felt thirsty?
- When has your inner man felt bankrupt or destitute?
- When have you spent money on that which couldn't satisfy?
- When have you poured your labor into something that didn't bring lasting rewards?

Finally, how do you feel about the idea of "[letting] your soul delight itself in fatness"? It's a feast of rich spiritual food for the soul. If you're not sure if you've ever experienced such a thing, what do you imagine that would feel like? How would you want it to feel?

RESPONSE

In what ways are you feeling prompted to respond to the concepts found in this chapter? It could be as simple as a journal entry or as significant as a deep personal conversation with a loved one. Simply ask yourself: what would help me continue to process these ideas and truly make them my own?

It's Not Just a Story—It's a Journey

"And ye shall seek me, and find me, when ye shall search for me with all your heart."

(Jeremiah 29:13)

2

A New Twist on an Old Tale

Our quest begins with a step into an age-old story, one most of us know extremely well. Come with me in your imagination to the Garden of Eden. Throughout our journey, we're going to travel alongside Adam and Eve in an attempt to see through their eyes and walk in their footsteps.

Only this time, there's a catch. I want you to take all the familiarity you have with this story and set it aside for a while. If it's alright with you, I'd like to use the characters of Adam and Eve to represent something entirely different from what we're used to. By giving the account an interpretive twist, it will help us view our own life's journey in a whole new light. After all, that's the cool thing about a figurative story: by playing with the meaning and symbolism, it deepens what the Lord is able to teach us through one simple tale.

To speed things up, let's bypass the creation of the earth and start at the point where Adam arrives on the scene. We'll get our first glimpse of Adam by looking at Genesis 5:2. Referring to the creation of man, it reads, "Male and female created he them; and blessed them, and called *their* name Adam, in the day when they were created" (emphasis added). Notice that *their* name was called Adam—both male and female. That's because the Hebrew word *adam*, which is translated as both "Adam" and "man" in Genesis, means not only "man" but also "human being, people, or humankind."[2]

Because the word Adam can signify both men and women, I want to use his character to symbolize something that's part of every single one of us. For our telling of the story, Adam will represent our *outer self*, meaning our physical body and its various senses and appetites. I know that may sound odd, but remember, for this particular quest, we're trying to think outside the box.

Because Adam will characterize our body throughout this journey, let's consider the crucial role he plays in our mortal experience. Through our Adam (or our body), we use our senses to take in the many sights, sounds, and wonders of life. Through him, we breathe, see, hear, laugh, walk, and run. We've often heard it said that we shouted for joy in the premortal world when offered the privilege of receiving a physical body. To inherit this gift is something we waited for eons of time to do. Do we truly appreciate the joy of having a body? No matter the condition of your health, take a minute to ponder the blessings you've inherited through this incredible gift.

Now that the figurative character of Adam is taking shape, I next want to introduce you to a new view of Eve. Let's focus first on the specifics of her creation, remembering to look at the account in a unique and metaphorical way. For starters, the scriptures tell us that God took a rib from inside of Adam to make her (see Genesis 2:21). Because of this, Adam describes her as "bone of my bones, and flesh of my flesh" (Genesis 2:23). He also calls her "the mother of all living" (Genesis 3:20).

So, if Adam represents our outer self during our journey, then Eve—who's made from a rib—must personify something *inside* of us—something so personal that it feels like "bone of [our] bones, and flesh of [our] flesh." What could that be? I'd like to propose that for

---

2. James E. Strong, *The Strongest Strong's Exhaustive Concordance of the Bible* (Grand Rapids, MI: Zondervan, 2001), 1468.

the short time we'll travel together, Eve will characterize our *heart*—our innermost thoughts and desires, our hopes and dreams, and our deepest passions, yearnings, and feelings.

If you think about it, there are some striking similarities between Eve and our heart. Like we said, Eve was called "the mother of all living." A mother is one who nurtures, supports, and inspires. I'd like to suggest that our heart does that very same thing for us throughout our entire lives. Our Eve actually holds great power to guide our choices, nurture our relationships, and provide the motivation for much of what we say and do. Life on earth wouldn't even be possible without our heart. The scriptures tell us, "It is not good that the man should be alone" (Genesis 2:18). I know we often interpret this statement as alluding to the marriage covenant, but the concept can also apply to our current journey. Having a body is not enough. Our outer self must be joined with our heart to give full meaning to our mortal experience.

With our main characters introduced, I want to throw in another little detail as we begin to study the essence of our Adam and our Eve. The last verse of Genesis 2 tells us that when the two were created, "they were both naked, the man and his wife, and were not ashamed" (verse 25). I know it may seem odd to apply this to our personal lives, but symbolism is given in the scriptures for a reason. Notice that the verse tells us two things in particular: first, when Adam and Eve are created, they are naked, and second, they aren't bothered by it in the least. How could we fit this information into our unique view of the story?

Think about it: to be naked is to be completely and utterly exposed. There's not a thing about us that's hidden or covered. Everything—and I mean *everything*—is out in the open. As much as that may make us squirm, it's actually a perfect way to describe the relationship we human beings have with our God. Not only can He see everything about our Adam, meaning everything we do in our outward life, but our Eve is also fully open and exposed to His view. As the Book of Mormon reminds us, "he knows *all* the thoughts and intents of the heart" (Alma 18:32, emphasis added; see also Hebrews 4:13). He sees not only every action we take but also every feeling, yearning, dream, longing, and desire we hold deep inside our heart. In short, we truly are utterly naked before Him.

While that prospect may seem unsettling to some, remember that Adam and Eve didn't feel that way in the beginning. They weren't ashamed of their nakedness at all. The verse implies they were completely comfortable with this relationship of openness, at peace with the idea that God knew them and loved them so openly and intimately. It's a very important detail in the narrative, one we're going to study more as our journey continues.

But for now, I want to pause and put all the different parts of the story together. When we look at it through this unique and metaphorical lens, the account truly captures who we are, both inside and out. Standing side by side, Adam and Eve beautifully showcase what it's like to be alive. The problem is, mortality often feels so routine that we lose sight of this marvelous wonder. So let's take a minute to contemplate the amazing blessing it is to be living in this world.

Having come from premortal life where we'd never experienced a physical body before, let's first revel in all the amazing things our Adam can do. We can gaze on a dazzling sunset or stroke the soft fur of a pet. We can hear the intricacies of a symphony or smell the aroma of freshly baked bread. We can sing and play, walk and talk, and laugh so hard it hurts. Having a body truly is an exhilarating thing to experience. But the magic of mortal life involves much more than just employing the senses and functions of our physical body. Our Adam has been joined with our Eve, a companion who possesses the capacity for exquisite pleasures all her own.

For example, consider the euphoric feelings that swell inside your heart when you fall head over heels in love. Or imagine the exhilarating thrill you feel when a long-held dream suddenly comes true. Or think back to a Christmas in your youth when you experienced such joy and happiness that you thought your heart would explode from the intensity of it all. The depth of feeling that comes through our heart can be more powerful than we even have words to describe. For this reason, we need to slow down and take a closer look at Eve.

Just like a woman, the heart is a mystery, and I want to make sure we understand her a little better before we move on.

If you run a digital search on the standard works, the results reveal a whopping 1,475 verses that include the word *heart*. That's right—over *1,400* verses. In contrast, a search on the word *body* (our Adam) only brings up 297 verses. Eve certainly gets a lot of attention in the word of God. So if the Lord places such a huge emphasis on the heart, I think it's time for us to do the very same thing.

For starters, I want you to reflect on the various needs, desires, and attributes hidden inside your heart. What is it you long for? When are you the happiest? What makes your inner man sing with joy? Ponder your heart's most powerful yearnings and most influential passions. Do you even know what they are? If it's been a while since you took a good long look deep inside, then take a minute to do so now. Deep down, what's driving your everyday life? Underneath the hustle and bustle of all your activity, who is your Eve, really?

In my own personal study and reflection, I've found three core desires that seem to best characterize our Eve. See if you relate to the following picture of the basic needs living inside our hearts.

First, our Eve wants to feel *alive*.

I think the best way to capture this attribute is to look at a few of the things our hearts love to do. Why do some of us enjoy a winning football game so much that we whoop and holler and jump up and down like a little kid? Why would a friend of mine get so lost in a novel that she drove with it on her lap and read at every stoplight? Why do some of us spend hundreds of dollars to see a beloved singer in concert? What is it we're so drawn to in these scenarios?

I'd like to suggest that through these kinds of experiences, our Eve seeks to rise to higher heights—to feel powerfully and passionately *alive*. Our heart longs to feel energetic. Engaged. Filled to overflowing with enthusiasm, vitality, and *life*. It's that inner blaze we were talking about earlier. We want it burning as brightly as it possibly can. We'd love it if our heart could "mount up with wings as eagles" (Isaiah 40:31) just like Isaiah described. Like I said, if our lives aren't that exciting in the moment, we'll seek this exhilaration by diving into a good book, going to a favorite concert, or cheering our heads off at a football game.

However, it's not enough just to feel alive. As each test and trial comes, we also want to be strong and victorious—to display the inner strength needed to rise above every challenge, tackle every inadequacy, and defy every intimidating fear. And if we're not feeling all that strong or capable, we're even more captivated by the fiction hero or movie character who will live it for us through their individual stories.

I want you to take a minute to think through this attribute of Eve. What is it that makes your heart come alive? What fills you with energy and vitality? And what do you do when that feeling is missing? If you're honest with yourself, would you say you're really *living* or just sitting on the sidelines? Are you going through the motions, or are you experiencing each moment in a way that you feel really, truly *alive*? Consider the different ways this need has been met (or unmet) in your own personal experience.

Second, our Eve longs to have *joy*.

Notice that I used the word *have* in that sentence. That's because we don't just want a little happiness here and there. Our Eve is searching for *lasting* contentment—to live in a state of unrelenting joy and fulfillment. After all, isn't that what the "plan of happiness" is all about? President Russell M. Nelson made this very point in a 2016 general conference talk:

"Clearly, Lehi knew opposition, anxiety, heartache, pain, disappointment, and sorrow. Yet he declared boldly and without reservation a principle as revealed by the Lord: 'Men are, that they might have joy' (2 Nephi 2:25). Imagine! Of all the words he could have used to describe the nature and purpose of our lives here in mortality, he chose the word *joy*!"[3]

And yet with all the difficulties and challenges we face, doesn't true happiness often feel beyond our reach? It may even feel like every time we grab hold of it, it slips right through our fingers. Evaluate

---

3. Russell M. Nelson, "Joy and Spiritual Survival," *Ensign* or *Liahona*, Nov. 2016, 82; emphasis in original.

your personal experience for a minute and then tell me: if you look underneath all your daily busyness and responsibilities, are you happy? Really . . . are you? Is your Eve truly satisfied and content? What is it that brings you happiness? What does the word *joy* mean to you? What does it feel like? When was the last time you experienced true joy? No matter our daily circumstances, this desire seems to lie at the very center of our Eve's existence.

Finally, and perhaps most importantly, our Eve has an irrepressible need for *love.*

I'm sure you'd agree that one of our heart's strongest yearnings is to experience deep and meaningful love throughout our entire lives. To fulfill this longing, we seek to be valued and cherished—even *treasured* for who we are. We want others, as they get to know us, to be drawn to what they see. This desire drives us continually, whether it's with our family, our friends, or our search for a lifelong companion. It even impacts our relationship with God.

I love the way theologian Dr. Gerald May captures this attribute of our Eve:

> There is a desire within each of us, in the deep center of ourselves that we call our heart. We were born with it, it is never completely satisfied, and it never dies. We are often unaware of it, but it is always awake. It is the human desire for love. Every person on this earth yearns to love, to be loved, to know love. Our true identity, our reason for being, is to be found in this desire. . . .
>
> If you pause and look quietly inside, you may be able to sense something of your desire for love right now in this moment. Sometimes it is wonderful to touch this deep longing; it can seem expansive and joyful. At other times it can be painful, lonely, and even a little frightening. Whether it feels good or bad, its power and depth are awesome. When the desire is too much to bear, we often bury it beneath frenzied thoughts and activities or escape it by dulling our immediate consciousness of living. It is possible to run away from the desire for years, even decades, at a time, but we cannot eradicate it entirely. It keeps touching us in little glimpses

> and hints in our dreams, our hopes, our unguarded moments. We may go to sleep, but our desire for love does not. It is who we are.[4]

Pretty profound words, don't you think? Using May's quote as a foundation, pause and take some time to assess how this need has been met in your own life. As he pointed out, has your search for love been lonely or even frightening at times? Has it brought you expansive joy, pain, or likely a mixture of both? Have you ever buried this desire or run from it, only to have it rise up again in those little "unguarded moments"? No matter how our need for love has played out in our lives, it will always play a huge part in who we are deep inside.

So, there you have it: our heart's three most poignant and pressing desires. What do you think? Do you agree with my assessment? Like me, does your Eve carry a deep inner longing to experience life, joy, and love? I know these aren't the only desires that exist deep inside us, but they certainly are three of the strongest. In fact, it almost seems that if our Eve feels alive, loved, and happy, all our other wants and needs will simply fall into place. These three characteristics really are crucial components in this complex journey we call mortality.

Surprisingly, if we go back to the Genesis account, we'll find a perfect example of the key role our heart's desires play in our everyday lives. In chapter 2, we're told that Eve was created as a "help meet" (Genesis 2:18) for Adam. Again, I know this statement seems directed specifically to the marital relationship, but if you think about it, you'll see that the phrase "help meet" can also characterize the strong motivational force of our heart. Like we talked about earlier, our Eve "helps" our Adam in that our heart provides the inner drive that fuels everything we outwardly say and do.

To illustrate, let me take you to our home many years ago on a busy spring Saturday. In typical Idaho fashion, the weather was very cold and windy, but it was past time for the garden to be planted, so our entire family grudgingly bundled up and headed out to work. Later that afternoon, as I stood in my kitchen looking at the indoor

---

4. Gerald G. May, *The Awakened Heart: Opening Yourself to the Love You Need* (New York: HarperOne, 1993), 1–3.

mess that we'd neglected with all our outdoor work, I sighed as I wondered how I was going to rally the troops for even more chores after such a miserable morning. Unfortunately, I knew what to expect since most Saturdays I met plenty of moaning and groaning over the housework.

It was then my husband suggested we treat the kids to the latest *Chronicles of Narnia* film at the movie theater if they finished their chores. The minute I mentioned a movie, my children suddenly experienced a radical change in their attitude and behavior. They immediately dragged out the vacuum, the bathroom cleaner, and the dust rags. They straightened messy rooms and picked up piles of toys, all the while continuing to ask, "Is there anything else I can do, Mom?" I laughed, secretly wondering if we could afford to go to a movie every Saturday.

More than anything, I was reminded of how much our Adam's behavior changes once our Eve's desire is ignited. Out of the blue, things that used to feel like drudgery don't seem so terrible anymore. Rather than moaning and groaning, our Adam is suddenly willing to climb mountains, ford rivers, and scale rocky cliffs. That's because the *satisfied desire of the heart*—or the *promise* of that satisfaction—is a very strong motivating force. When our Eve is convinced a certain path will bring life, joy, or love, there are no limits to what our Adam will pursue. Simply put, the core desires living in our heart are the reason why we do what we do every single day.

Because our Eve holds such a significant place in our lives, I want you to watch her closely as we continue our quest. As we navigate each twist and turn on our journey, she has a great deal to teach us about the dynamics of our mysterious "inner man" (Ephesians 3:16).

Readings & Reflections

Read 1 Samuel 16:7, then ponder this quote from Elder Marvin J. Ashton:

> When the Lord measures an individual, He does not take a tape measure around the person's head to determine his mental capacity,

nor his chest to determine his manliness, but He measures the heart as an indicator of the person's capacity and potential to bless others.

Why the heart? Because the heart is a synonym for one's entire makeup. We often use phrases about the heart to describe the total person. Thus, we describe people as being "big-hearted" or "goodhearted" or having a "heart of gold." Or we speak of people with faint hearts, wise hearts, pure hearts, willing hearts, deceitful hearts, conniving hearts, courageous hearts, cold hearts, hearts of stone, or selfish hearts.

The measure of our hearts is the measure of our total performance. . . . If our works and the desires of our hearts are the ultimate criteria of our character, how do we measure up? What kind of heart should we seek? For what kind of heart should we pray?[5]

Take a minute to ponder Elder Ashton's questions:

- How do you tend to measure your heart?
- What kind of heart do you seek?
- Have you ever prayed for a certain kind of heart?

Turn to Psalm 37:4. How do you think this verse applies to our heart's three core desires? In what ways do you think the Lord is involved in fulfilling these fundamental human needs?

5. Marvin J. Ashton, "The Measure of Our Hearts," *Ensign*, Nov. 1988, 15.

Look up Doctrine and Covenants 56:15. Does it ever feel like your heart is "not satisfied" like it says in this verse? Which of Eve's three longings do you think that applies to the most?

I love this story from Elder Dieter F. Uchtdorf that shows the powerful motivation and influence that can come through the strong desires of the heart:

> We were in the American-occupied part of Germany, and in school I had to learn English. Somehow I could not learn it. To learn Russian was difficult, but English was impossible. I even thought my mouth was not made for speaking English. My teachers had a hard time. My parents were desperate. And I knew English was not my language.
>
> I agonized through those school years, helped and encouraged by kind and understanding English teachers, but I just couldn't do it. It wasn't my thing!
>
> At this time, my dream in life was to become a pilot. Almost daily I rode my bicycle to the airport. I could picture myself in the cockpit of an airliner or even in a military jet fighter. This was definitely my thing!

> I eventually learned that to become a pilot, I needed to speak English. Suddenly, the resisting condition of my mouth changed. I was able to learn the language. Why? Because of a strong motive![6]

Over the years, how has your life been influenced by the core desires of your heart? What role has your Eve played in the various actions of your Adam?

What about right now? How are your heart's desires affecting your work, your Church service, your family, or the way you choose to use your leisure time?

6. Dieter F. Uchtdorf, "Making Choices for Eternity," *Ensign*, Oct. 2002, 28.

Response

In what ways are you feeling prompted to respond to the concepts found in this chapter?

3

The Seduction of Our Desires

Returning to our story, it's time to catch our first glimpse of the infamous Garden of Eden. It's a paradise overflowing with abundance for Adam's physical senses and Eve's inner soul. As our path begins to wind through the lush beauty of this new world, things soon take an interesting turn. We hear Adam and Eve being told of two specific trees in the garden: the tree of life and the tree of knowledge of good and evil (see Genesis 2:9).

Regarding these trees, God instructs the couple, "Of every tree of the garden thou mayest freely eat: But of the tree of the knowledge of good and evil, thou shalt not eat of it: for in the day that thou eatest thereof thou shalt surely die" (Genesis 2:16–17).

You probably know what happens next. Whether you grew up in the Church or not, the story of Adam and Eve has been depicted in countless ways over the centuries, so most of us know the details pretty well. In short, God says don't eat the fruit or you'll die, Satan shows up on the scene and tempts the couple, and they eat the fruit. Then God returns, Adam and Eve confess what they've done, and He casts them out of the garden.

But rather than getting stuck in the same old familiarity with this part of the story, I want to continue looking at the narrative with new eyes. Since the focus of our journey is on the heart, we need to examine how the adversary tempts *Eve* in particular. I believe this will provide some powerful insights that will help us learn more about our own inner man.

For instance, have you ever noticed that in the two scriptural versions we have of this story, there's absolutely no mention of the snake tempting Adam? Think about it. In both the Genesis and Moses accounts, the serpent avoids Adam altogether and zeroes in on Eve like a heat-seeking missile. Why do you think that's the case? In the scriptures, why is it Eve—not Adam—who draws the adversary's attention? While there may be many ways to answer that question, I believe one reason is that Satan understood the powerful influence Eve had on Adam. The enemy knew if he could convince *her* to consider his temptation, he'd have a much better chance of getting *him* to partake.

The same principle also holds true for our hearts. Satan knows he can't make our Adam do anything that our Eve doesn't want to do. Because of our agency, we can't be *forced* to do evil, so the adversary must first trick and persuade and seduce our hearts into actually *wanting* whatever temptation he's offering. Simply put, he knows the influential power of our Eve's desires. Just like the story of my kids and the *Narnia* movie, he understands how much things can change once our heart is convinced something will meet our core needs of life, love, and joy. So he's going to focus all his efforts on the desires and passions living inside our heart. In the words of Christian philosopher Dallas Willard, the adversary "governs through images, through ideas, through feelings and fears. From this complex arena of our minds and hearts come most of our actions, so this is the arena where Satan focuses his work."[7]

Let's look at the way he did this with Eve in the garden. The scriptures use one specific word to describe his motivation and method.

---

7. Dallas Willard, *Life Without Lack: Living in the Fullness of Psalm 23* (Nashville, TN: Thomas Nelson, 2018), 82; emphasis added.

The book of Moses says Satan "sought . . . to *beguile* Eve" (Moses 4:6; emphasis added). Paul also taught that "the serpent beguiled Eve through his subtilty" (2 Corinthians 11:3), and Abinadi lamented "that old serpent that did beguile our first parents, which was the cause of their fall" (Mosiah 16:3). Eve even used this same word herself, admitting to God that "the serpent beguiled me, and I did eat" (Genesis 3:13).

When I went to the dictionary for more insight on the word *beguile*, the first definition centered on the idea of deceiving or tricking someone.[8] I think we can all agree that deception was a major motivating force behind Satan's plan. But when I saw the second definition, warning bells started going off in my head. To beguile can also mean to *charm* someone—to attract, entice, or seduce them. To capture their imagination. To engage their interest. To bewitch, delight, or captivate them.[9] Or, to put it in a way that fits our current journey, to beguile someone is to *win over their heart's deepest and most poignant desires.*

Seen in this light, it appears that Satan's goal wasn't just to trick Eve—it was to charm her so powerfully that she'd actually *want* the forbidden fruit. To entice her so seductively that she'd desire it and crave it and long for a bite. How did he do such a thing? By opening her eyes to all the delicious benefits and rewards she'd get from partaking—to show her how satisfying it would be on multiple levels.

And his plan worked. Notice what we're told in verse 6: "And when the woman saw that the tree was *good for food*, and that it was *pleasant to the eyes,* and a tree to be *desired to make one wise*, she took of the fruit thereof, and did eat, and gave also unto her husband with her; and he did eat" (Genesis 3:6; emphasis added).

In this one simple verse, we can see how Eve's desire was ignited. I like the way the Good News Translation of the Bible translates verse

---

8. *Dictionary.com*, s.v. "beguile," accessed Apr. 1, 2023, https://www.dictionary.com/browse/beguile.

9. I used a combination of several online dictionaries to come up with my own characterization of *beguile* here.

6: "The woman saw how beautiful the tree was and how good its fruit would be to eat, and she thought how wonderful it would be to become wise." In other words, she was enchanted. Charmed by the fruit of the tree. Beguiled by its delicious and tempting appeal. She got to the point where she *wanted* it, and that led her to take a big, juicy bite. Then she went straight to Adam to convince him to partake as well.

Elder James E. Talmage captured the seduction of Eve's desires in his book *The Articles of Faith*. After describing how "Satan . . . sought to beguile the woman," he pointed out that "the woman was *captivated* by these representations; and, *being eager* to possess the advantages pictured by Satan, she disobeyed the command of the Lord, and partook of the fruit forbidden. She feared no evil, for she knew it not."[10]

While there's more that could be said about Eve's motive, our main concern is what this scenario teaches us about our own individual hearts. It's no secret that the adversary also tries to beguile each one of us. He does all he can to charm us and seduce us and enchant us in an effort to win our heart's most powerful desires. Unfortunately, the advantages found in different kinds of forbidden fruit can captivate our hearts just like Eve in the garden. Let me share one simple story from my past to show how this fruit really can appear to offer us the love, life, and joy our heart is so desperately searching for.

The setting was my junior year of high school. Like most teenagers, I'd heard endless Young Women lessons, general conference talks, and youth firesides on the importance of choosing wisely when dating. Still, I'll admit that I often wondered what all the fuss was about. For goodness' sake, who would even *want* to date someone with lower standards? It seemed like a no-brainer—like unappetizing fruit that would be very easy for me to avoid. I had no idea how quickly my feelings would change in just a few weeks' time.

Soon after school started that year, I noticed a young man crossing my path several times a day. I assumed we had similar schedules and didn't think much more about it. But as often happens when you run into someone a lot, the conversations eventually began. To

10. James E. Talmage, *The Articles of Faith*, 12th ed. (1924), 59; emphasis added.

my surprise, our friendship developed so quickly that it felt like we'd known each other forever. In fact, I enjoyed his company so much that I found myself seeking him out as often as I could throughout the day. Without even recognizing it, my Eve was growing very attached to the way this boy made her feel.

It was only after we began dating outside of school that I realized the situation I'd gotten myself into. As it turned out, this young man's habits and standards on the weekends were, to say the least, very different from my own. But because I'd never encountered that side of him at school, it caught me unawares. Immediately, I knew the only way for me to maintain my gospel values was to discontinue our relationship. To turn and walk away.

But for some reason, I couldn't get my heart to go along with that particular plan. No matter how hard I tried to repress my feelings for this boy, they continued to haunt me. Yes, my Adam knew what he "should" do, but my Eve kept trying to pull me in the opposite direction. To put it plainly, this young man made me feel so loved, alive, and happy that my heart began to rationalize all kinds of reasons to continue the relationship. Because my Eve was so reluctant to turn away from someone who meant so much to her, my only recourse was to pray for help and strength like I'd never prayed before. Needless to say, it was a very difficult year.

The thing that shocked me the most about the whole situation was that even after it became clear what I needed to do, my heart simply did *not* want to do it. It almost felt like my Eve had betrayed me—like she'd launched a full-scale assault on the strength of my will. In the end, I learned that it's very easy to resist forbidden fruit when your Eve thinks it's rotten and disgusting, but it's a whole different situation when she sees it as the most appealing delicacy in the entire world.

Has the adversary ever turned the tables on you like that? Rather than tempting the physical senses of your Adam, has Satan ever made a beeline straight for your Eve? You may not have even seen it coming, but suddenly you find your heart longing for something you know you shouldn't even want. Such rebellious feelings leave us dazed and confused as we try to figure out why we'd even consider forbidden fruit in the first place. I mean, we know we shouldn't want it—we know it won't be good for us—but we end up longing for it and craving it and dreaming about what it would be like to partake.

Now, here's where we really get into trouble. Once our heart begins to contemplate all the benefits of tasting the forbidden fruit, we're not usually content to stop at that point. What our Eve wants most is to convince our Adam to partake (see Genesis 3:6). These are the moments when our Eve urges our Adam to watch that inappropriate movie, to share that juicy piece of gossip, or to do more online shopping even though our credit card is almost maxed out. Her desires won't truly be fulfilled until our body experiences the intoxicating taste of the fruit, so she pushes and prods and mentally obsesses until he finally gives in. I believe the adversary loves nothing more than watching our Eve pressure our Adam into taking the plunge. Again, that's the reason Satan works so hard on our heart in the first place—because he knows that once our Eve's desire is ignited, our inner longings are going to *help him* convince our Adam to partake.

However, let's say that we muster the courage to resist our heart's tempting thoughts and feelings. Let's say that despite our rebellious inner desires, we still manage to keep ourselves from gossiping, overspending, or watching something we shouldn't. Couldn't we count that as an impressive triumph? Couldn't we pat our Adam on the back for having the fortitude to reject the fruit our Eve was holding out to him? While that may sound like it makes sense, the reality is that it's already too late. Satan has already won. I say that because even though we kept our Adam from committing certain sins on the outside, our Eve still harbored sinful feelings on the inside. As a result, we've already partaken of the forbidden fruit.

The Lord pointed out this very scenario in the Sermon on the Mount when He taught that sin can be committed not only through our Adam but also through our Eve. For example, the Savior doesn't applaud us just because we never followed through on the temptation to have an affair. Instead, He says that if any indulging of that temptation arose in our imagination, we've "committed adultery . . . already in [our] heart" (Matthew 5:28). Similarly, He doesn't congratulate us just because we've never attacked or killed another person. If we simply got "angry with [our] brother" in our heart, we still stand "in danger of the judgment" (Matthew 5:22).

"I don't care if you only *thought* about it," He might say as we lay out all our excuses. "If you partook with your heart, it's the same as if you partook with your body. You still took a bite of sinful fruit." In the words of Elder Jeffrey R. Holland, "[Christ] said not only should we not break commandments, but we should not even *think* about breaking them. And if we do think about breaking them, we have already broken them in our heart."[11] That's a pretty shocking statement if you ask me. *To the Lord, it is just as real and serious for our Eve to partake as it is for our Adam.*

Once we begin to look at life through this lens, we can suddenly see all kinds of ways our heart chooses to partake. For instance, our selfish impulses promise to give our Eve exactly what she wants right when she wants it. Our lust—not just for sex but for any number of things—engulfs our heart in an exciting glow of anticipation. And our judgmental tendencies convince our Eve that she's better than those around her. Even the thought of forbidden fruit like this can fill our heart with an enticing sense of satisfaction. So we can see why the Lord was so serious about the thoughts and feelings of our heart—not just our outward behavior—when it comes to our experience in mortality.

With that said, it's time for us to face a difficult truth: at one time or another, we've all chosen to eat some type of forbidden fruit. Not only has our Adam given way to physical temptation, but our Eve has been charmed and enticed as well. In fact, the seduction of our heart's desires has played a huge part in every sinful decision we've made. And because we've made this choice to partake, we face the same consequence God gave to Adam and Eve.

It's called *the Fall*.[12]

---

11. Jeffrey R. Holland, "The Cost—and Blessings—of Discipleship," *Ensign* or *Liahona*, May 2014, 7; emphasis in original.

12. For more on this, see "Fall" in *True to the Faith: A Gospel Reference* (2004), 56.

Stop and let that sink in for just a minute. This is no longer just a story; no longer an ancient narrative about two people who lived in a garden thousands of years ago. The Fall is very real, and it also applies to you and me. Because we've partaken of forbidden fruit with both our Adam and our Eve, we experience the very same outcome that they did.

So what happens to us as a result of the Fall? If you remember, God answered that question in the very beginning. When He first told Adam and Eve about the fruit, He specifically warned them that "*in the day* that thou eatest thereof *thou shalt surely die*" (Genesis 2:17; emphasis added). But here's the crazy thing: the couple didn't physically die the moment they partook. They didn't fall down lifeless at His feet. Yes, we know their bodies became mortal in that moment, which meant they would eventually experience physical death. But the Father said death would come *in the very day* they took that bite. What in the world was He talking about? Could it be that we're missing a very important detail in the story?

Thankfully, Alma helps us with this perplexing question. He taught that "the fall . . . brought upon all mankind a *spiritual* death as well as a *temporal*" (Alma 42:9; emphasis added). Notice that there are two kinds of deaths that affect us because of the Fall. Our temporal death is the one that affects our Adam. It causes our bodies to age and subjects us to illness, pain, weakness, disease, infirmity, and eventually physical death. But there's another death that comes upon every single one of us, and this one affects our Eve. Alma simply called it spiritual death (see 2 Nephi 9:12; Helaman 14:16; Doctrine and Covenants 29:41).

Now, this is the point where things get a little more complicated. Temporal death is easy to understand as we see ourselves and others grow old; battle sickness, pain, and weakness; and ultimately die. But what happens to us when we die spiritually? Because this death affects our spirit or inner man, what exactly happens to our Eve? Could this have been the death the couple experienced the very day they chose to eat the fruit? To explore these questions in greater depth, join me as we turn the focus of our journey to exactly what took place with the fall of our heart.

Readings & Reflections

Read Colossians 2:4, 18. Who else can beguile besides the devil? How do you think Satan has used the influence of others (like he did with the serpent) to entice you and seduce your heart?

Can you recall a sin you've committed that first started with a desire in your heart? Think about how appealing that temptation felt at the time. How could a desire that felt so right turn out to be wrong?

Read through Philippians 2:21 and Doctrine and Covenants 1:16. In these verses, what does it mean to "seek [our] own" and "[walk] in [our] own way"? How do you think this applies to Eve's partaking of the forbidden fruit? Why are we so driven to do what we *want* to do?

Study Mosiah 15:1–9, focusing especially on verses 2, 5, and 7. What was it that made Jesus Christ different from us when it came to yielding to Satan's temptations? What gave Him the power to withstand the enemy's attempts to beguile?

If you want to go deeper with the topic of desire, President Dallin H. Oaks offered us two wonderful talks on the subject. One is "The Desires of Our Hearts" from the June 1987 *Ensign*, and the other is "Desire" from the April 2011 general conference.

Response

In what ways are you feeling prompted to respond to the concepts found in this chapter?

4

Our Fallen Heart

You know, the heart is an incredibly popular subject. Just for fun, I typed the word *heart* into Amazon's search feature. Would you believe there are over 50,000 books with the word *heart* in the title? I found the same result in the music category. Really, this popularity shouldn't be all that surprising because most of us rely on our heart as our inner compass—as our basis for making decisions and navigating our way through life. Our heart seems to be the one unwavering anchor we can count on in this complex and confusing world.

Yet if we turn to the Book of Mormon, we'll find a very different perspective when it comes to the heart. Take Mosiah 5 for instance, where King Benjamin's people claimed that the Spirit "wrought a mighty *change* . . . in [their] hearts" (Mosiah 5:2; emphasis added). And in Ammon's account, the Anti-Nephi-Lehies said "their hearts had been *changed*; that they had no more desire to do evil" (Alma 19:33; emphasis added). Finally, in a stirring sermon to those in Zarahemla, Alma asked the Nephites, "Have ye experienced this mighty *change* in your hearts?" (Alma 5:14; emphasis added).

So if the Book of Mormon teaches that our heart needs to be changed, what does that say about its state *before* this mighty change? Didn't we just say our heart is our anchor? Isn't it the one thing we thought we could really trust? Why in the world do we need such a radical change of heart?

You might be shocked how one prophet answered those questions. In the pages of the Old Testament, Jeremiah dropped a bombshell when he declared, "The heart is deceitful, above all things, and desperately wicked" (Jeremiah 17:9). That's a pretty harsh statement if you ask me. In fact, I want you to carefully consider the language Jeremiah just used in that verse. Notice he didn't say that wicked and deceitful people possess these kinds of hearts. No, he said *the heart itself* is wicked and deceitful. The problem is, our hearts don't really feel that deceitful, and most of us don't see ourselves as wicked either. So why would Jeremiah use such negative language when referring to something as precious as the heart?

It may help to remember that each of us has urgent needs for life, joy, and love beating constantly within our hearts, and these ravenous desires are appetites longing to be fed. In the last chapter, we talked about how, through the beguiling voice of the adversary, "sin conceiveth in [our] hearts" (Moses 6:55), and we seek out forbidden fruit to satisfy our fervent desires. In other words, our heart actually *deceives us* at times into choosing wickedness rather than righteousness. Once our deceived heart leads us to sin, the Great Judge's gavel sounds and the "punishment which is affixed" (2 Nephi 2:10) descends upon us in full force. As much as our Heavenly Father loves His children, His justice cannot and will not be denied. Our heart falls, just as God said it would. We experience spiritual death. But what exactly *is* spiritual death? What happens to us when we die spiritually?

I think the idea we hear most often is that spiritual death involves a separation from God.[13] But if we take a closer look at the scriptures, the language is even more startling than that. Various verses reveal that when we died spiritually, we weren't just separated from our Father—we were actually "cast out" and "shut out from his presence," just like Adam and Eve (see Doctrine and Covenants 29:41; Moses 5:4; Moses 6:49). What's more, we were "cut off from the tree

13. See Gospel Topics, "Death, Spiritual," topics.ChurchofJesusChrist.org.

of life" (Alma 42:6), which Nephi says represents the "love of God" (1 Nephi 11:22). It was a complete separation from the One who was meant to be our light, our life, and our love. With this "cutting off" and "shutting out," we were isolated from His personal touch—from His tenderness, influence, nearness, and intimate care. The jarring reality of such a separation couldn't have been without some very serious consequences.

For instance, have you ever felt hopeless? Disconnected? Rejected? Abandoned? Or completely alone? These feelings are familiar to all of us, but have we ever really pinned down the root cause of our suffering? Yes, at times there have been earthly circumstances that contributed to our discontent, but could part of it also be our spirit mourning the loss of its true home? I believe we sense that loss deep in the hidden recesses of our heart, but we don't often realize where it's coming from. That's why it's so important to understand what happened to us when we died spiritually. In this state, we're not only "cut off from the presence of the Lord," but we're "*considered as dead*, both as to things temporal and to things spiritual" (Helaman 14:16; emphasis added). Even if we haven't fully grasped the effects of this type of death, there's no doubt it's a contributor to much of our personal misery.

But that's not all there is to our spiritual death.

Yes, it may mean having a few dark days or occasionally feeling hopeless and alone, but the fallout we experience in being separated from God is just the tip of the iceberg. The Book of Mormon also teaches us that something very serious happened to our inner man when we died spiritually.

In other words, something went wrong deep inside our heart.

I know that may be a little hard to process, but think for a minute about how much you've struggled to be the person you know that you should be. Like me, you've probably tried again and again to do what's right, but still you've continued to do things (and more importantly, *think* things) that cause you to feel sinful. Ashamed. Wicked. Rebellious. Unkind. Impatient. Guilty. Even out of control. The self-condemnation can be almost unbearable. Though we may try to push those feelings down or rationalize them away, the true question we need to ask ourselves is this: why do we continue to struggle so much with sin? After all, we know the commandments. We know how God wants us to live. Most of the time, we hate the sins we keep running back to. We want to be different. We want to stop. But we just keep getting sucked back in. Why can't we think and act like the person we know we were meant to become?

Returning to the scriptures, we'll learn exactly where this personal struggle comes from. When Alma taught that the Fall brought two kinds of death, he said this caused our inner man to become "*carnal, sensual, and devilish,* by nature" (Alma 42:9–10). The Doctrine and Covenants also unfolds the same doctrine: "But by the transgression of these holy laws man became *sensual and devilish,* and became fallen man" (Doctrine and Covenants 20:19–20; emphasis added). And Moses reveals that, as Satan "tempteth [us] to worship him, . . . [we] have become *carnal, sensual, and devilish,* and are shut out from the presence of God" (Moses 6:49; emphasis added). Last but not least, the brother of Jared sums up our spiritual death with this devastating statement: "Because of the fall our natures [meaning our inherent character or temperament[14]] have become *evil continually*" (Ether 3:2; emphasis added).

If this concept seems a little difficult to apply personally, I understand. I'll admit that I never paid much attention to verses that talk about our being carnal, sensual, and devilish. I thought those references applied to other people, not to me. "I go to church," I'd reason. "I have a temple recommend. I read my scriptures and say my prayers. I wouldn't label myself as carnal, sensual, or devilish at all." With that, I'd dismiss the concept without a second thought.

But there's a huge problem with that line of thinking. Abinadi clearly specifies that it's "*all* mankind" (Mosiah 16:3; emphasis added)—and not just the very wicked—that became "carnal, sensual, and devilish" as a result of the Fall. And the Book of Mormon shares four additional testimonies that "*all* mankind" are "lost" and "fallen" (see 1

---

14. *Dictionary.com*, s.v. "nature," accessed Apr. 1, 2023, https://www.dictionary.com/browse/nature.

Nephi 10:6; Mosiah 16:4; Alma 12:22; Alma 34:9). The truth presented in the scriptures is hard to deny. Through our spiritual death, every single one of us has developed a carnal, sensual, and devilish nature. King Benjamin simply labels this as our "natural man" (Mosiah 3:19).

To make this a little more relatable, let's take an in-depth look at the words *carnal* and *sensual* since our heart's desires may fit this terminology more than we'd care to admit.

First, let's consider the word *sensual* because it's probably the easier of the two to understand. A quick trip to an online dictionary says it means "pertaining to, inclined to, or preoccupied with the gratification of the senses or appetites."[15] Add to that the Apostle Paul's assertion that the natural man is "corrupt according to the deceitful lusts" (Ephesians 4:22). And remember, the "deceitful lusts" he's talking about aren't just sexual in nature. *Lust* is simply defined as "a passionate or overmastering desire or craving,"[16] which opens the door to many different cravings that can emanate from the depths of our natural man.

One way we can evaluate how sensually motivated our heart has become is to consider the activities we enjoy doing every day. Tell me: how much of your time is spent pursuing pleasure through the use of your senses? (In your thoughts too, not just your actions!) Really, how much? Driven by our sensual nature, our heart craves those things we can see, hear, touch, taste, read, play with, wear, drive, or buy. In short, we lust for all kinds of things that please the senses—things that deceive us into believing they're the only path to lasting happiness. Whenever we hear something funny, see something awesome, smell something alluring, taste something sumptuous, or feel something invigorating, the enjoyment our heart receives from the experience draws us back over and over again. But as our Eve craves more and more satisfaction from our senses—be it through a pan of brownies,

---

15. *Dictionary.com*, s.v. "sensual," accessed Apr. 1, 2023, https://www.dictionary.com/browse/sensual.

16. *Dictionary.com*, s.v. "lust," accessed Apr. 1, 2023, https://www.dictionary.com/browse/lust.

an online shopping spree, or an entire night in front of the TV—we have to admit how sensual our inner nature has become.

With that said, let's turn next to the word *carnal.* I think we often see it as a synonym for *sensual* since it also relates to our bodily senses and appetites. While that's certainly part of the definition, the scriptures offer us an even deeper meaning. To uncover it, we need to go to 1 Corinthians, the epistle Paul wrote to "the church of God which is at Corinth, to them that are . . . called to be saints" (1 Corinthians 1:2). In this epistle, Paul said that when he came to Corinth to preach, he "could not speak unto [them] as unto spiritual, but as unto carnal, even as unto babes in Christ" (1 Corinthians 3:1). A few verses later, he again declared that these Saints are "yet carnal" (verse 3). What exactly was he accusing the people of in this chapter?

The answer can be found by looking at the Greek word Paul used for *carnal.* Interestingly, it's *sarkikos,* which means not just "sensual" but also "worldly" and "sinful."[17] According to one Greek dictionary, a person who is *sarkikos* is "governed by human nature, instead of by the Spirit of God."[18] Can you see how this definition involves much more than just the gratification of our senses? By using this Greek word, Paul is implying that the Corinthians' nature—meaning the very core of who they are—is still worldly and sinful. In other words, they're led by a fallen Eve who wants to do her own will rather than heeding the voice of the Lord.

Surprisingly, Paul isn't the only one who used the word *carnal* in this broader sense. Several Book of Mormon writers did so as well. Alma revealed that because of the Fall, we're all subject to a "carnal mind" (Alma 30:53), and Abinadi begged his listeners to turn from their "carnal wills and desires" (Mosiah 16:12). Did you notice the emphasis in both verses on the thoughts of our mind and the desires of our heart? It just goes to show that our carnal nature includes much

---

17. James E. Strong, *The Strongest Strong's Exhaustive Concordance of the Bible* (Grand Rapids, MI: Zondervan, 2001), 1642.

18. W. E. Vine, *Vine's Complete Expository Dictionary of Old and New Testament Words* (Nashville, TN: Thomas Nelson, 1984), 89.

more than the cravings of our physical body. In the end, it really does involve our heart—the part of us that houses our internal thoughts, feelings, and desires.

I'll admit that once I better understood these scriptural concepts, I suddenly noticed my carnal nature popping up all the time in my everyday life. It even happened while sitting in the temple. I remember during one particular session, I suddenly realized that my thoughts had been drifting to a pair of shoes I'd been dying to buy. Then my mind jumped to the idea of going shopping for some new clothes . . . especially a top to go with that one skirt . . . then I thought about getting my hair cut like the lady in front of me . . . and on and on. I continued in this vein of thought for quite some time before I even realized I was doing it. I hate that I do that. But it was an undeniable reminder of how carnal my nature really is, even in the temple when my mind should be centered solely on God.

Has the same thing ever happened to you? During the sacrament, for instance, have you ever found your thoughts wandering to the movie you saw the night before or the football game coming on later, when you should be pondering the Lord's precious Atonement? Have you ever blown off your scriptures in favor of that best-selling novel or a favorite game on your phone? Have you ever ignored someone who needed assistance, judged someone based on their appearance, or held a grudge against someone in your heart? If so, it proves you have a carnal nature just like I do—that underneath the surface, your nature is prone to think and feel and do things that are ungodly, sinful, or even outright wicked.

We display our carnality in a million different ways. We show it when we know the latest headlines or the names of celebrities better than the doctrines in the scriptures. We show it when we have a hard time controlling our physical appetite, our spending habits, or our time on social media. We show it when we scroll through our phone while we're sitting in church, when we shout at another driver trying to merge into our lane, or when we reach for the remote rather than spending some much-needed time with our kids. So the question each of us needs to ask ourselves isn't whether or not we're carnal—the question is *how does carnality manifest itself in me*?

With that said, I have a personal confession to make.

As I began to process all the different concepts we've been talking about—especially the idea that my heart had become carnal, sensual, and devilish as a result of the Fall—I actually struggled to accept that those things were true. Yes, I knew I battled some sensual cravings and sinful passions from time to time, but deep down I still wanted to believe that the Lord saw my heart as trustworthy and good, not wicked and deceitful. For this reason, I dove into the scriptures and studied every single reference I could find on the heart.

And what I discovered rocked my world to the very core.

Yes, initially I found a few verses that talked about the joy, righteousness, and love that can live in my heart through the power of Jesus Christ. But apart from His influence, the picture of Eve that emerged was truly one of *fallenness* and *sinfulness*. Consider the following verses that summarize our heart's condition as a result of the Fall.

The writer of Proverbs declares, "He that trusteth in his own heart is a fool" (Proverbs 28:26). And Mormon claims, "How false, and [unsteady are] the hearts of the children of men" (Helaman 12:1). They say this because "out of the heart . . . proceed[s] evil thoughts, . . . covetousness, wickedness, deceit, . . . pride, [and] foolishness" (Mark 7:21–22). In our fallen state, we're capable of "think[ing] . . . evil in [our] heart" (Matthew 9:4) and "imagining up some vain thing in [our] hearts" (3 Nephi 2:2). And once our "hearts have waxed hard, . . . [our] ears [become] dull of hearing, and [our] eyes cannot see afar off" (Moses 6:27). Our fallen Eve also struggles with error (see Psalm 95:10) and blindness (see Ephesians 4:18), which "shut[s] . . . [our] hearts, that [we] cannot understand" (Isaiah 44:18) things as they really are.

As for the passions of the heart, the scriptures show that our Eve is subject to stubbornness (see Alma 32:16), willfulness (see Moroni 9:23), vanity (see Doctrine and Covenants 106:7), dissatisfaction (see Doctrine and Covenants 56:15), and faulty reasoning (see Mark 2:6–8). To add to that, our heart may also "swell with great pride, unto boasting, and unto great swelling, envying, strifes, malice, persecutions . . . and all manner of iniquities" (Helaman 13:22). When we become "polluted because of the pride of [our] hearts" (Mormon 8:36), it leads us to "[stir] up [our] hearts . . . to contend with anger, one with another" (3 Nephi 11:29). Once "[our] hearts are swallowed up in [our] pride, . . . [we] cry unto [God] with [our] mouths, while [we] are puffed up, even to greatness, with the vain things of the world" (Alma 31:27). For this reason, the prophet Jacob begs us not to let the "pride of [our] hearts destroy [our] souls" (Jacob 2:16).

If all that wasn't enough, our Eve is also very susceptible to the persuasion and influence of others. The seductive voices of the world may "put it into [our] heart" to sin (Ether 8:17) or "steal away [our] hearts" (Alma 39:4) from the Lord. In the Book of Mormon, for instance, the wicked Amalickiah "gained the hearts of the people" through his "fraud" (Alma 47:30; see also Mosiah 27:9). It just shows how the "precepts of men" and their influence on our Eve can lead us to "turn [our] hearts from [Jesus Christ]" (Doctrine and Covenants 45:29).

Finally, Satan seeks to flatter, "pacify," "lull," and "rage in the hearts of the children of men" (2 Nephi 28:20–22), hoping to "[take] away the word out of [our] hearts" (Luke 8:12). In fact, the adversary can so profoundly impact our hearts that our Eve may become "corrupt, and full of wickedness and abominations" (Doctrine and Covenants 10:21). When this happens, Satan begins to "reign" in our heart (see Doctrine and Covenants 86:3), and we take our "evil heart of unbelief" and "[depart] from the living God" (Hebrews 3:12).

So . . . this is the heart we've been trusting? No wonder it needs to be changed! Through this study, I finally began to understand what Jeremiah was talking about. The scriptures paint a picture of Eve that isn't stable or trustworthy *at all.* Our carnal, sensual nature really can deceive us into seeking out all kinds of forbidden fruit. Once we're beguiled, our heart's wayward desires will continue to influence our outward actions of our Adam again and again, often leading us to do things we may have never believed we'd ever choose to do.

I think the critical thing we need to remember is that something happened to our inner man or spirit when we fell. *It died.* As a result, not only do we inhabit a fallen physical body, but our fallen Eve also experiences her own difficult side effects—like vain imaginations and deceitful dispositions and unpleasant emotions and obsessive cravings. In short, our natural man can be impulsive, unmanageable, narrow-minded, immoral, or even corrupt. As we're influenced by our heart's sinful thoughts and desires—and we choose to act on them—it can leave us feeling depressed, guilty, ashamed, numb, or even dead inside. Sounds a lot like that emptiness we've been talking about all this time. Perhaps now we can see why we've struggled with these feelings for so long. Simply put, the reason we often feel like our inner flame has blown out is because *it has.*

That's what it feels like to be spiritually dead.

In fact, when Alma tried to capture what it's like to live in this "carnal state," he described it as "the gall of bitterness and . . . the bonds of iniquity" (Alma 41:11). When I saw that the word *gall* means "something bitter to endure,"[19] and *bitterness* means "distressful [or] hard to bear,"[20] it hit me that the reason life on earth is so bitter and hard to bear is in large part because of our spiritual death.

Think about it. All this time, we've been blaming our emptiness on our outward circumstances—on our kids or our spouse or our job or our meager finances or even the weather. While those things certainly aren't easy to deal with, the scriptures reveal that much of our suffering actually comes from the effects of our spiritual death. In short, we often struggle because we're viewing our lives through the lens of the gall of bitterness—a state chock-full of exasperating emotions and wayward desires that continue to plague us no matter how hard we try to leave them behind.

---

19. *Merriam-Webster.com Dictionary*, s.v. "gall," accessed Apr. 1, 2023, https://www.merriam-webster.com/dictionary/gall.

20. *Dictionary.com*, s.v. "bitterness," accessed Apr. 1, 2023, https://www.dictionary.com/browse/bitterness.

Are you beginning to realize the enormous consequences we're experiencing as a result of the Fall? It's almost more than our limited minds can comprehend.

For this reason, I think we need to pause and take a deep breath because that was an awful lot of information to take in. We may not have been emotionally prepared to look at our life—or our heart—through this troubling lens. So let's stop for a minute and regroup. I think it'll really help to put things into perspective. If our current path left you feeling confused, overwhelmed, or even a little depressed, I want to offer you a bit of encouragement.

As we continue to work through the many different side effects of the Fall, please don't forget that an incredible summit awaits us at the end of this trek. Believe me when I tell you that the reward you'll find when we get there will far outweigh any discomfort you may feel as we work our way through the various side effects of the Fall.

To that end, I want to share a little story that I hope will enlarge our vision and give us a little more clarity to help us on our journey. The adventure happened a few years ago when our family decided to try one of the most popular hikes in Grand Teton National Park. The locals call it Table Rock, and the prospect was quite daunting. We'd heard enough from others who hiked it that we knew what we were getting ourselves into. The climb was steep, intense, and stretched for more than ten miles round-trip, which meant we'd be on the mountain the entire day. With our kids at various ages and strength levels, we expected some challenging moments, but it sounded so cool that we all agreed to give it a go. So on a sunny summer day at the crack of dawn, the nine of us began our ascent.

The trail immediately put our muscles to the test, but there were vistas and wildflowers and lots of laughter to enjoy along the way. I'm sure we took more rests than my strong teenage sons would have liked, but we adapted our pace to those in the group (me!) who needed it. Occasionally, some of us grew frustrated when the trail seemed never-ending, but finally—after several grueling hours of nonstop climbing—the summit burst into view. And yet in our joy, we had no idea the toughest stretch was still to come. We found that the last quarter mile was a brutal section of trail with a lot of loose rock, and the high altitude made it even harder to breathe. I think if the peak wasn't already in sight, a few of us may have turned around and headed back home.

I'm so glad we didn't. The view when we reached the top was so spectacular that it made every single faltering step worth it. To say the sight was breathtaking doesn't even begin to capture it. The rugged beauty of the majestic Tetons felt close enough for us to reach out and touch. As we hugged each other and took celebratory pictures, a sense of accomplishment flooded us as we considered how far we'd come. The day felt unlike any other. As hard as it was, we all said it was worth the struggle just to experience those precious moments at the top.

I share this story because right now, we're having the very same experience. I know we've had to navigate some difficult paths so far on our quest. The things we've talked about can feel more discouraging than uplifting. And we've got additional trails ahead that may seem even more steep and rocky. At times, the journey may feel like it's never-ending, and you may even be tempted to turn and head down an easier path. But I'm asking you to please—*please*—stay with me for the rest of the climb.

Yes, the trail may be challenging, but it's the only way to reach what is truly an unbelievable summit. Trust me when I tell you that the peak we're pushing for has sights that will put even the jaw-dropping Tetons to shame. *I promise you with all my heart that it will be worth it.* Standing at the top, you'll see yourself, your life, your heart, and especially your Savior in a new and mind-blowing way. So keep those figurative hiking boots laced up tight. We'll continue to take it one small step at a time.

Readings & Reflections

Look again at both Jeremiah 17:9 and Ephesians 4:22. What does the word *deceitful* mean to you? Look it up in the dictionary if that helps. Can you come up with any examples in your past where you've trusted your heart only to have it deceive you?

Other Bible translations of Jeremiah 17:9 use different words to capture the original Greek in this verse. Some describe the heart as "desperately sick" (English Standard Version) or "extremely sick" (Amplified). Others use the phrase "beyond cure" (New International Version) or even "incurable" (Christian Standard Bible). As you've read through this chapter and evaluated the condition of your own heart, can you relate to any of these additional translations? Now read Jeremiah 17:14 and record any new thoughts and impressions that come.

Read the following scriptures and consider their different warnings regarding the heart:

- Deuteronomy 10:16
- Luke 21:34
- James 1:26
- 2 Nephi 9:33
- Doctrine and Covenants 112:2

How do the various insights in these verses add to our current discussion?

Consider Elder David A. Bednar's stark description of our fallen natural man, or as Jeremiah put it, our "wicked" and "deceitful" heart:

> To some degree, the natural man described by King Benjamin is alive and well in each of us (see Mosiah 3:19). The natural man or woman is unrepentant, is carnal and sensual (see Mosiah 16:5; Alma 42:10; Moses 5:13), is indulgent and excessive, and is prideful and selfish. As President Spencer W. Kimball taught, "The 'natural man' is the 'earthy man' who has allowed rude animal passions to overshadow his spiritual inclinations."[21]

Applying Elder Bednar's quote, when have you seen yourself act unrepentant, indulgent, excessive, prideful, or selfish? In what ways do you think that has contributed to your inner flame blowing out?

21. David A. Bednar, "We Believe in Being Chaste," *Ensign* or *Liahona*, May 2013, 42.

I know we talked about some difficult things in this chapter. Why do you think it's so critical to understand how your "natural man" manifests itself in your everyday life? What blessings could come from this painful yet important awareness?

Response

In what ways are you feeling prompted to respond to the concepts found in this chapter?

5

Those Unbreakable Chains

I'm guessing that for many of us, looking at the depths of our fallen heart wasn't that big of a surprise. In our weak and impetuous moments, we've seen ourselves bark at our family, ignore our scriptures, or covet our best friend's expensive new house. And King Benjamin's counsel hasn't been lost on us—we know we need to "put off" our natural man with all its corrupt appetites and passions (see Mosiah 3:19). So in order to tame our rebellious nature, we've tried focusing on one bad habit at a time, we've set new goals, or we've invented strategies to distract ourselves when we've started to misbehave. "Maybe," we thought, "with a lot of hard work and determination, I can finally overcome my sinful tendencies once and for all."

However, there's one aspect of our natural man that will quickly wash all those ambitious efforts right down the drain. But to uncover it, we need to dig a little deeper into the motivation of our enemy because the adversary sought an extremely sinister power in the Garden of Eden. For Satan, it wasn't enough merely to deceive Adam and Eve, and he wasn't content to watch them fall into temporal and spiritual death either. No, his greatest desire, according to Isaiah, was this: "I will ascend into heaven, I will exalt my throne above the stars of God: . . . *I will be like the most High*" (Isaiah 14:13–14; emphasis added). Lucifer again exposed his all-consuming hunger for power when he cried out to Moses, "I am the Only Begotten, worship me" (Moses 1:19). With the burning need to reign still driving him on, Satan now roams the earth, seeking to gain "dominion among men" (Moses 6:15) and make each of us "become [his] subjects" (Alma 5:20).

While we may think we'll never submit to the adversary as his obedient "subject," the scriptures reveal that there *is* a way Satan gains control over each and every one of us. Listen as Abinadi points it out: "He that persists in his own carnal nature . . . *remaineth in his fallen state* and *the devil hath all power over him*" (Mosiah 16:5; emphasis added). I want you to stop and read that verse one more time because it's absolutely crucial that we understand this important truth. Satan wants our obedience and worship all to himself, and he knows exactly how to get it. According to Abinadi, he does it through our fallen nature. Through the appetites and desires of our natural man, the adversary is able to "lead [us] captive at his will" (Moses 4:4).

Now, I know some may be thinking, "Wait just one minute. I may have some temptations that trouble me here and there, but that doesn't mean I've been taken *captive* by the adversary! Sure, I overeat or overspend or overreact when another driver cuts me off. But these minor weaknesses certainly don't qualify me as Satan's 'subject'! Shouldn't that label be reserved for people who are *really* wicked and sinful?"

If such thoughts sound familiar, let me ask you one simple question. What was your last New Year's resolution? You know . . . that goal you set to lose weight, get your budget under control, or stop yelling at your kids? Tell me, how long did you last before you failed completely? Be honest. How long until you found yourself right back at square one and thought, "Oh well, I'll try again next year"? Did you make it even one whole day? Or maybe, in a really valiant effort, one whole month? But then, crash. You fell. Right back to the very thing you promised yourself you wouldn't do or say.

Oh, how I can relate. I can count hundreds of times when I've told myself I'd never do this or that thing ever again, but eventually I blew it and went right back to that same undesirable behavior. It's a perfect example of the way Satan holds us captive. Through one appetite or another, one temptation or another, we're all the devil's subjects. No matter how hard we try, we continue to think and behave as a natural man. We're controlled by our corrupted appetites and deceitful passions. We can't seem to help ourselves, even if we set goal after goal after goal. It's like trying to hold a big beach ball under water. Sooner or later that ball pops right back up to the surface, no matter how hard we try to hold it down.

Remember, the brother of Jared taught that "because of the fall our natures have become evil continually" (Ether 3:2). I know most of us don't think of our behavior as *continually* evil, but doesn't that beach ball of misdeeds *continually* keep popping back up in our lives? Since our sinful behavior comes back again and again, King Benjamin labels each of us as "an enemy to God" (Mosiah 3:19), as one who *continually* acts, as Alma put it, in a way that is "contrary to the nature of God" (Alma 41:11).

I think it's intriguing that the Book of Mormon uses the imagery of chains to describe our inability to free ourselves from the influence of the adversary. Three different times in Alma 5, the prophet talks about the "bands of death, and the chains of hell" (Alma 5:7; see also verses 9–10). In 2 Nephi 9, Jacob tells us that "death" refers to the "death of [our] body," while "hell" is associated with "the death of [our] spirit" (2 Nephi 9:10). Put these scriptures together and we can see that our spiritual death is much more than just a fallen state—it's a state of confinement that locks us up in invisible chains. Again, each of us is held captive by the habits, desires, and behaviors of our fallen heart and our stubborn natural man.

Really, isn't that exactly how it feels—like we're chained to those behaviors we so desperately want to stop? And why can't we stop? It's because, like Alma said earlier, we're trapped in "the gall of bitterness and . . . the *bonds* of iniquity" (Alma 41:11; emphasis added). Even the Bible Dictionary mentions the spiritual bondage we experience while living in this sinful and fallen state. Under the heading "Atonement," we read: "By transgression man [lost] control over his own will and [became] the slave of sin." I'm sure that at one time or another, we've all felt like a "slave" to our sin, for no matter how hard we've tried to break free from our natural man's cravings, sins, or addictions, we haven't been able to do it. Perhaps now we can see why we never seem to make any progress. It's because, as Jacob put it, "the will of the flesh and the evil which is therein . . . giveth the spirit of the devil *power to captivate*" (2 Nephi 2:29; emphasis added).

An online search of the scriptures reveals even more evidence of this disturbing truth. In the Book of Mormon, there are thirty-two chapters that discuss the idea of "bondage" and forty-three chapters that mention "captivity." Why such an emphasis on this subject when most of us live in freedom today? Yes, the Nephites dealt with a great deal of bondage and captivity, but the Book of Mormon was written for *our* day. Why include so many chapters on this topic?

I believe it's because we're all captives, grasped firmly in the chains of our natural man. As Isaiah puts it, we're "tied to [our] sins like beasts to their burdens" (Isaiah 5:18, footnote *c*). To make this a little more personal, consider your own life for a minute. Can you think of any appetites or passions that have become your chains? Any obsessive thoughts that hold you captive? It could be something like anger, fear, impatience, worldliness, or a lack of self-control. It could be that your chains are made of something we haven't even mentioned yet, or you may feel bound by several different things as I've found to be true for me. No matter what our chains are made of, my guess is that each of us knows the form and shape of our bonds very well. After all, we've been lugging them around for a long time, since even our most noble efforts and heroic attempts have withered against the seemingly indestructible power of our natural man.

I can't tell you how many times my heart has cried out in anguish because I couldn't free myself from those exasperating bonds. Especially once I married and had children, certain stressful family moments brought out a side of me that wasn't pretty. Over and over, I'd try to control myself. Do better. Overcome my sins. Be more Christlike. But even as I'd sit in church listening to how I needed to be more like the Savior, fifteen minutes later I'd watch myself yell at fighting children in the car on the way home, and instinctually I knew—I couldn't be like Christ. Not even close. No matter how hard I tried. No matter how much I even *wanted* to.

Brought to my knees in my battle with my fallen, corrupted heart, my heart groaned in desperation: "I can't do it! I've tried and tried, but I'm just not strong enough. I'll *never* be able to overcome my sinful thoughts and behavior!" Has your Eve ever experienced the same hopelessness I felt? Having pulled, tugged, and strained against your natural man in an attempt to break free from its tyrannical grip, perhaps, like me, you've looked up to heaven and said, "I quit!"

Maybe it would help if I stated it loud and clear: the reason you haven't been able to overcome your fallen nature is because *you can't.* At least not on your own. It's true, you know. You can't simply *try harder.* Scripture after scripture has just shown us that the strength of Satan's chains will withstand our every effort. Haven't we suspected this all along? Haven't we learned it through every failed attempt to improve and every New Year's resolution gone wrong? Just like Adam and Eve, we "partook of the forbidden fruit," and as a result, we "became subject to the will of the devil, because [we] yielded to temptation" (Doctrine and Covenants 29:40). As a result, we're locked in a metaphorical prison cell that affects not only our Adam but also the thoughts, feelings, and desires of our fallen Eve. In the words of Elder Jeffrey R. Holland, as part of the "fallen human family," we're "mortal debtors, transgressors, and prisoners all. Every one of us is a debtor, and the verdict was imprisonment for every one of us."[22]

While it may be difficult to look at life through the eyes of a prisoner, at least our fight with unruly appetites and passions makes more sense. Our natural man is very real, and we're unable to break its chains on our own. The Book of Mormon even tells us that without someone to rescue us, we'll remain trapped in this awful prison for "an endless duration" (2 Nephi 9:7). In fact, as captives of an extremely evil adversary, our destiny is to "become devils, angels to a devil, to be shut out from the presence of our God, and to remain with the

---

22. Jeffrey R. Holland, "Be Ye Therefore Perfect—Eventually," *Ensign* or *Liahona,* Nov. 2017, 41.

father of lies, in misery" forever (2 Nephi 9:9). If you ask me, our situation here on earth couldn't possibly get any worse.

But don't lose hope because this is where the good news comes in—the news that our Father in Heaven has "[prepared] a way for our escape" (2 Nephi 9:10) from this awful prison. His plan involved sending a Redeemer and Deliverer, One who offers "liberty to the captives and the opening of the prison to them that were bound" (Isaiah 61:1). Even now our Savior holds the key to our freedom, with power to "loose the bands of death which bind his people" (Alma 7:12). This isn't just good news—it's the most awe-inspiring, joy-giving, wonder-bringing news ever to be preached on this earth! The prospect of a Rescuer—one who can truly release us from the chains of physical *and* spiritual death—should be music to our ears and exultation to our heart. In the jubilant words of the Prophet Joseph Smith:

> Let the dead speak forth anthems of eternal praise to the King Immanuel, who hath ordained, before the world was, *that which would enable us to redeem them out of their prison; for the prisoners shall go free.*
>
> Let the mountains shout for joy, and all ye valleys cry aloud; and all ye seas and dry lands tell the wonders of your Eternal King! And ye rivers, and brooks, and rills, flow down with gladness. Let the woods and all the trees of the field praise the Lord; and ye solid rocks weep for joy! And let the sun, moon, and the morning stars sing together, and let all the sons of God shout for joy! And let the eternal creations declare his name forever and ever! (Doctrine and Covenants 128:22–23; emphasis added)

Yes, we've struggled in our bonds, and yes, at times it's seemed like we could never escape the effects of our fallen, deceitful heart. But amazingly, *there IS a way to break those seemingly unbreakable chains.* Jesus Christ offers us freedom unlike anything we've ever experienced.

But in order to taste this life-giving rescue for ourselves, we've got some pathways left to travel. We haven't finished exploring our story quite yet. There's much more we need to learn about our heart that will help us understand how our Savior rescues, redeems, and revives our fallen Eve.

For instance, having examined that critical moment at the foot of the tree of knowledge of good and evil, and having discussed the consequences of Eve's choice to partake, it's now time to contemplate what she does *after* eating the forbidden fruit. What further choices does she make? And why would these choices even matter to us? The answer: because there are many more ripple effects to our spiritual death than we've yet discussed. The Fall left us in an incredibly difficult predicament, and we've responded to that situation in some really destructive ways, especially when it comes to the dynamics of our heart.

It's not just that we've *done* things—we've also *thought* things and *felt* things and *believed* things deep in our Eve that have had a staggering impact on our outward lives. (And we may not have even realized that it's happened.) We'll find a perfect example of this if we return to the story of Adam and Eve and explore a detail that's found only in the Doctrine and Covenants. In the middle of the discussion on Church organization found in section 20, there's a passage that talks about the Creation and the Fall, which gives us this essential information:

> There is a God in heaven, who is infinite and eternal, from everlasting to everlasting the same unchangeable God, the framer of heaven and earth, and all things which are in them;
>
> And . . . he created man, male and female, after his own image and in his own likeness, created he them;
>
> And gave unto them commandments that they should love and serve him, the only living and true God, and that he should be the only being whom they should worship. (Doctrine and Covenants 20:17–19)

Did you notice what commandment was given after the man and woman were created? It doesn't say anything about not eating the forbidden fruit. Instead, the instruction was three-fold: they were to "*love* and *serve* . . . the only living and true God, and . . . he should be the only being whom they should *worship*" (verse 19; emphasis added). After stating that directive, the Lord then reveals this unfortunate conclusion: that "by the transgression of these holy laws man became sensual and devilish, and became fallen man" (verse 20). Put those verses together and we learn that the main reason mankind fell wasn't just because of that fateful bite. It was because they offered their *love, service,* and *worship* to something or someone other than God.

Several years ago, the Lord asked me to take these verses personally. It was as if He said, "Jaci, I want you to evaluate how well you've kept these same 'holy laws.' Tell me, do you *love, serve,* and *worship* 'the only living and true God'?" Immediately, my mind answered, "Of course I do!" That verse about transgressing those laws didn't seem to fit me at all. To back up my claim, I thought of my long history of church and temple attendance, personal and family scripture study, and service in a variety of different callings. But rather than congratulating me, He brushed aside that long checklist and encouraged me to look deep inside: "Rather than focusing on your outward service, I'd like you to measure the love and worship living inside your heart."

His words took me by surprise. The more I thought about it, though, the more I could see that I really did use my outward service as the main measure of my love for Him. While that had always seemed like a reasonable standard, I could see some scenarios where it wouldn't work. Like the Pharisees in Jesus's day, I realized that it was possible to fill my life with service to God without ever loving or worshipping Him *at all.* In fact, those incredibly religious men had actually *rejected* Him and *denied* Him right in the middle of all their scripture-reading and commandment-keeping! So if I couldn't always use my outward works as an indication of my love and worship, how in the world was I supposed to measure it? What did it really mean to love and worship the Lord in my heart? How could I evaluate the true condition of my Eve?

To expand my perspective a little bit, I opened my thesaurus app and typed in the word *love.* There I found synonyms like affection, fondness, passion, tenderness, and friendship.[23] Then I typed in *worship* and found concepts like praise, admiration, awe, love, and

---

23. *Thesaurus.com*, s.v. "love," accessed Apr. 1, 2023, https://www.thesaurus.com/browse/love.

devotion.[24] As I sat there staring at those incredibly tender and emotional words, it hit me that I needed to dig a lot deeper into the depths of my heart. Yes, I had a schedule full of religious activities in my outward life, but how much passion, affection, fondness, and friendship did I really feel for my Savior? Was I like the Pharisees who were just outwardly putting on a show? Or did I truly love and worship the Lord "with all [my] heart, and with all [my] soul, and with all [my] mind" (Matthew 22:37)? I wasn't exactly sure how to answer those difficult questions.

I don't think it's a coincidence that around the same time, I came across the following quote from Christian author and pastor, Louie Giglio, that introduced me to an entirely different way of looking at worship. His explanation provided a whole new perspective on what was happening behind the scenes in my mind and heart:

> Think of it this way: Worship is simply about value. The simplest definition I can give is this: Worship is our response to what we value most.
>
> That's why worship is that thing we all do. It's what we're all about on any given day. Worship is about saying, "This person, this thing, this experience (this whatever) is what matters most to me . . . it's the thing of highest value in my life."
>
> That "thing" might be a relationship. A dream. A position. Status. Something you own. A name. A job. Some kind of pleasure. Whatever name you put on it, this "thing" is what you've concluded in your heart is worth most to you. And whatever is worth most to you is—you guessed it—what you worship. . . .
>
> So how do you know where and what you worship?
>
> It's easy. You simply follow the trail of your time, your affection, your energy, your money, and your allegiance. At the end of that trail you'll find a throne; and whatever, or whomever, is on that throne is what's of highest value to you. On that throne is what you worship.

24. *Thesaurus.com*, s.v. "worship," accessed Apr. 1, 2023, https://www.thesaurus.com/browse/worship.

> Sure, not too many of us walk around saying, "I worship my stuff. I worship my job. I worship this pleasure. I worship her. I worship my body. I worship me!"
>
> But the trail never lies. . . . In the end, our worship is more about what we do than what we say.[25]

The simplicity of Giglio's formula made a lot of sense to me. To find out what my heart truly loves and worships, all I had to do was follow the trail of my time, affection, energy, money, and allegiance. At first, I couldn't help but look again to my church activity as evidence of my Eve's high level of worship. But the Lord quickly pointed out several *other* things I devoted my time and energy to—things that consumed a great deal of the attention and affection of my heart. Suddenly, I began to wonder if my path led to a few thrones that the Lord wasn't sitting on. I had to ask myself, "Where does the trail of my time, affection, and energy actually lead? What is it I *love, serve,* and *worship* deep in my heart?"

On the next leg of our journey, we're going to explore those very questions. We need to uncover everything our spiritual death has led us to *think, feel,* and *believe* so we can better understand what's happened to our heart as a result of the Fall. As we pick up Adam and Eve's story where we left off, I think you'll marvel again at how well our footsteps align with their own.

Through each step on the paths ahead—paths that include some fig leaves and hiding places and even some bold-faced finger-pointing—I want you to pay close attention to how the details reveal not just the choices Adam and Eve made in the Garden of Eden but what's also taken place in our own individual hearts. We're about to see how much the second half of the story has to teach us about the complicated dynamics of our fallen Eve.

---

25. Louie Giglio, *The Air I Breathe: Worship as a Way of Life* (Sisters, OR: Multnomah, 2003), 10–11.

Readings & Reflections

Look up the hymn "I Believe in Christ" (*Hymns*, no. 134). Notice especially verse 3 where Elder Bruce R. McConkie (the lyricist) writes, "He ransoms me, from Satan's grasp he sets me free." What do these words mean to you after reading this chapter?

Let's build on that by studying these two eye-opening quotes from President Joseph F. Smith. Notice how he summarizes everything we've covered in the last two chapters about our spiritual death:

> I want to speak a word or two in relation to another death, which is a more terrible death than that of the body. When Adam, our first parent, partook of the forbidden fruit, transgressed the law of God, and became subject unto Satan, he was banished from the presence of God. . . . This was the first death. *Yet living, he was dead—dead to God, dead to light and truth, dead spiritually; cast out from the presence of God; communication between the Father and the Son cut off.* He was as absolutely thrust out from the presence of God as was Satan and the hosts that followed him. That was spiritual death.[26]

> I want to impress upon your minds—"wherein [Adam] became spiritually dead." Now what was his condition when he was placed in the Garden of Eden? He had access to the Father. He was in His presence. He walked and talked with Him face to face, as one man walks and talks with another. This was the condition of Adam and Eve when they were in the garden. But when they partook of

26. *Teachings of Presidents of the Church: Joseph F. Smith* (1998), 96; emphasis added.

> the forbidden fruit they were cast out and banished from the presence of God, . . . "Wherein they became spiritually dead, which is the first death." (See Doctrine and Covenants 29:41.) *And it was impossible for Adam in that condition to extricate himself from the position in which he had placed himself.* He was within the grasp of Satan. . . . He was "spiritually dead"—banished from the presence of God. And if there had not been a way of escape provided for him, his death would have been a perpetual, endless, eternal death, without any hope of redemption therefrom.[27]

While President Smith was talking specifically about Adam in this quote, how do his words help you better understand your own spiritual death? How does it change the way you understand your own personal need for redemption?

If we're truly in the grasp of Satan through our spiritual death, then we're in desperate need of a Redeemer, someone who can pay the ransom to set us free. Read Mosiah 14:5; Matthew 20:28; 1 Peter 1:18–19; and 1 Timothy 2:6. What was the cost Jesus willingly paid to release us from this captivity? For more from the Book of Mormon, study 2 Nephi 1:15 and 33:6; Mosiah 12:23 and 27:29; and Alma 33:22. Record your thoughts and impressions.

27. *Teachings of Presidents of the Church: Joseph F. Smith* (1998), 96; emphasis added.

Look up 2 Peter 2:19. One definition of the word *overcome* is "to overpower or overwhelm in body or mind.[28] Can you think of anything in your life that has overcome you to the point of bondage? Could it be something like shame? Loneliness? Or a sense of worthlessness? What is it that keeps you locked up in chains?

In the Topical Guide, find the entries for "Bondage, Spiritual" and "Man, Natural, Not Spiritually Reborn." Study any verses that stand out to you. In what way do these references add further clarification to the things we just discussed?

28. *Dictionary.com*, s.v. "overcome," accessed Apr. 1, 2023, https://www.dictionary.com/browse/overcome.

Next, carefully read Romans 6 (especially the second half of the chapter), keeping in mind the idea of captivity. Look specifically for what is given "dominion" or the power to "reign" over us in verses 12–14. Now answer the following questions.

What is it we "obey" in verse 12?

What are we "servants" of in verse 20?

What can we be "made free" from (through Christ) in verses 18 and 22?

How does this chapter build on the things we just discussed?

If you're wondering why we've spent so much time studying the Fall and its many consequences in our lives, consider this insight from President Ezra Taft Benson: "Just as a man does not really desire food until he is hungry, so he does not desire the salvation of Christ until he knows why he needs Christ. No one adequately and properly knows why he needs Christ until he understands and accepts the doctrine of the Fall and its effect upon all mankind."[29]

How does your heart respond to President Benson's words? Now that you've studied more about the Fall—especially the disturbing effects of your own spiritual death—how have your feelings for Jesus Christ changed? In what ways has it increased your own personal need for a Savior?

---

29. Ezra Taft Benson, *A Witness and a Warning: A Modern-Day Prophet Testifies of the Book of Mormon* (Salt Lake City, UT: Deseret Book, 1988), 33.

RESPONSE

In what ways are you feeling prompted to respond to the concepts found in this chapter?

Continuing in Eve's Footsteps

"Walked we not in the same steps?"

(2 Corinthians 12:18)

6

Fig Leaf Fashion

Have you ever had one of those dreams where you're out in public and suddenly you realize you're naked? To your horror, there you stand, completely exposed to the eyes of everyone around you. It's really more of a nightmare than a dream. As waves of shame wash over you, you scramble to find anything within reach that will cover you. When you're naked and desperate, any old thing will do, be it rags or a blanket or—in the case of our story—even a bunch of flimsy fig leaves.

You knew this part of the story was coming, right? Even so, I want you to try to see the details through a new and different lens. First, notice in Genesis 3:7 that the minute Adam and Eve eat the forbidden fruit, something immediately changes. The scriptures tell us their eyes are opened and they know that they're naked. For the first time, they're fully aware of the Father's all-seeing eyes, and the couple reacts just like we did in our dream. In a panic, they grab the closest thing they can find to cover themselves. It's something we can all relate to. We know all too well that nakedness—the state of being stripped of all covering—can cause enormous feelings of insecurity, anxiety, and vulnerability. We feel so exposed and unprotected that we'll do almost anything to cover ourselves up once again.

But remember, Adam and Eve have been naked from the very beginning, and they never even gave it a second thought. I think it's very telling that their feelings of insecurity didn't come until *after* they'd taken that bite. Up until that point, they'd lived in a completely innocent state, meaning they had nothing they needed to hide from God. There was no desperation, no panic, no need to cover or protect themselves. It was only after they'd eaten the fruit that they began scrambling for a covering to keep Him from seeing what they didn't want Him to see.

How can we apply this detail to our own hearts and lives? If you think about it, we also have ways we clothe ourselves in metaphorical fig leaves. Like the couple in the garden, our spiritual death opens our eyes to our nakedness, and there's suddenly an awful lot about ourselves that we feel the need to cover up. This seems to be an innate tendency in humans: whenever we sin and feel the resulting fear and shame wash over us, we do all we can to conceal it—to keep God (and others) from finding out what we've done. This instinct even shows up in children. We've all watched some sort of video where a child, with chocolate smeared all over their face, tells their mom that no, they *didn't* eat any of the cookies. The urge to cover up our stupid, sinful, or selfish choices is a very real part of human nature. So our personal fig leaves could represent the different ways we camouflage the shame of our sin and make ourselves look less guilty than we are. It's something we've all done at one time or another.

But I believe there's a lot more to our apron-making than that.

To take it a little deeper, let's consider the actual meaning of the word *fall.* You might be surprised to learn that one definition of the word is "to become less," or "to drop down suddenly to a lower position."[30] What if the effects of the Fall reach much further than just the guilt and shame of our personal sin? Could it be that, in a general sense, we really have *become less*—much less than we were in the premortal world? Could it be that we've dropped to a lower place, and

30. *Dictionary.com,* s.v. "fall," accessed Apr. 1, 2023, https://www.dictionary.com/browse/fall.

deep down, each of us can personally sense that—and we feel the need to cover it up?

It reminds me of a well-known verse the Lord revealed to the brother of Jared: "And if men come unto me I will show unto them their weakness. I give unto men weakness that they may be humble; and my grace is sufficient for all men that humble themselves before me; for if they humble themselves before me, and have faith in me, then will I make weak things become strong unto them" (Ether 12:27).

Notice that Christ didn't use the word *weaknesses* in this verse. The word is singular, as if He's describing a state or condition rather than a bunch of little faults and failures. What's more, He says *He's* the one who "gives" us this weakness. It's a startling thought—that He purposely designed mortality to be a state of weakness and powerlessness. A state where we're not always capable, where we can't always make things happen the way we want, and where we feel like we're not enough to handle everything we're asked to deal with. While that might be a difficult concept to accept, He tells us He's done it to keep us humble and dependent on Him as we move through everyday life.

While the Lord certainly had His reasons for giving us this weakness, I can't help but ask: doesn't that present a *huge* reason to want to cover ourselves up? Our God-given powerlessness really is an excruciating thing to have to live with. Chafing from our experience in this fallen, less-than, not-enough state, we do the same thing Adam and Eve did: we grab as many fig leaves as we can to hide our sense of inadequacy. It can feel incredibly vulnerable and humiliating and even naked to be that weak, so we cope with it by doing all we can to dress ourselves up. Authors Timothy Willard and Jason Locy capture our apron-making with these insightful words:

> Embarrassed by the scars of our humanity, we try to hide our brokenness. We use a veneer to cover over ourselves, hoping others will perceive us as having greater worth, as being more beautiful and perfect than we feel inside. Most of the time, we aren't aware that we're doing it; our culture is so glossed over with the sheen of fake perfection that we unknowingly comply.

> Some of us will go to any lengths to hide ourselves and create a false identity.[31]

If you're curious if you've gathered any of these "false identity" fig leaves, there's a simple way you can find out. Just picture yourself standing with a group of friends or loved ones. As you compare yourself with the rest, how do you hope the others will see you? Do you want to be known as the helpful one? The knowledgeable one? The strong one? The funny one? The nice one? The rich one? The attractive one? The busy one? The righteous one? Or even the rebellious one? Now ask yourself: do I hide behind any of these different veneers? As Willard and Locy pointed out, we often clothe ourselves in carefully chosen fig leaves that we hope will keep others from seeing the brokenness and weakness that exists inside us as a result of the Fall.

The problem with these kinds of aprons is that they require an awful lot of sewing to make them a success. After all, it takes great effort to make sure others only see what we want them to see. It may involve pretending we've got our act together or playing society's game to help us fit in. Or puffing up our strengths while at the same time tucking our weakness carefully out of sight. No matter how we choose to manage it, leaf by leaf, we construct our aprons in a way that we believe will help us—and others—forget about the Fall and what's really going on deep underneath the surface.

Personally, my false identity fig leaves were easy to recognize once I really began to look for them. From a very early age, I wrapped myself up tightly in the soothing warmth of a people-pleasing apron. It was a logical choice because my heart deeply craved the love and acceptance of others. This alluring apron promised to fill my emptiness and conceal all my personal struggles and self-doubt, so I subconsciously created a persona that I thought would bring me as much love and acceptance as humanly possible. I prided myself on being the one who was always agreeable, the one who never created any drama, and the one who was always looking out for others. My apron was so thick

31. Timothy D. Willard and Jason Locy, *Veneer: Living Deeply in a Surface Society* (Grand Rapids, MI: Zondervan, 2011), 24.

and familiar and comfortable that I really believed it was an innate part of my personality.

You may think, "What's so wrong with a little people-pleasing? Isn't it selfless to meet others' needs before your own?" While that might sound like a nice and even gospel-centered way to live, I'm here to tell you that being a people pleaser is anything but Christlike. Deep down, it isn't driven by a desire to serve but rather to control. Fueled by a paralyzing fear of conflict and confrontation, I make others happy so I can control how they treat me. I use my cheery, helpful smile to elicit others' praise and admiration. I'm the nicest person on earth—not because I'm filled with charity but so people won't get mad at me. In short, I'm using my service to others to meet my *own* needs, not theirs. While it's not a very emotionally stable apron, my Eve still donned it with all the zeal of a teen trying on her very first prom dress.

To make this apron a success, my Eve set certain ground rules as a foundation for her sewing. The most important rule was that everyone needed to love and accept me, but unfortunately, that wasn't always easy to accomplish. With life being what it is, friends and loved ones still got upset with me from time to time, and their anger left me floundering in such misery that I tried every possible strategy I could think of to regain their favor. This included burying my true feelings for the sake of what I called "keeping the peace." Sadly, I never realized that it wasn't the true "peace of God" (Alma 7:27) I was sacrificing for but a shallow and temporary substitute.

I'll admit that it drove my husband crazy to watch me repress my feelings to pacify those around me. Over and over, he'd try to persuade me to honestly express my opinion rather than hide it behind an artificial smile. But the thought of acting on his suggestion paralyzed my heart so completely that I wouldn't even consider it. My Eve remained convinced that I could only be happy if I kept my favorite fig leaves firmly in place.

Eventually, the Lord removed my blinders and showed me the reason for my stubborn paralysis. Just like Eve in the garden, my heart had been soundly and thoroughly deceived. Satan promised me that clothing myself with the approval and acceptance of others would cover my weakness and nakedness. It would spare me all conflict and confrontation. As irrational as his lies may sound, I wholeheartedly believed them. Repressing my true feelings seemed like a small price to pay to have everyone like me and think well of me. But behind all that outward approval, my people-pleasing was wreaking a great deal of havoc on my fallen heart.

When it came down to it, the biggest issue with this apron wasn't that it led me to repress my feelings. What plagued me the most was that my people-pleasing made me a slave to others' whims and wishes, often compelling me to do things I didn't want to do or refrain from saying things that really needed to be said. In addition, my Eve became so consumed with thoughts of "Does she like me?" "Will they approve?" or "Are they mad at me?" that it left my heart riddled with an enormous amount of fear and insecurity.

As the Lord continued to teach me about the consequences of my people-pleasing apron, I was surprised to learn that the implications were not only mental and emotional but spiritual as well. Because my heart was so focused on others' approval, I fit the scriptural profile of someone overtaken by the "fear of man" (Proverbs 29:25). It's a sin that's rebuked over and over in the pages of scripture (see 1 Samuel 15:24–25; Doctrine and Covenants 3:6–8). On an even deeper level, I discovered that my people-pleasing fig leaves found their roots in the sinful soil of *pride*. Listen to these stinging words from President Ezra Taft Benson:

> The proud stand more in fear of men's judgment than of God's judgment. (See Doctrine and Covenants 3:6–7; Doctrine and Covenants 30:1–2; Doctrine and Covenants 60:2). "What will men think of me?" weighs heavier than "What will God think of me?" . . .
>
> Fear of men's judgment manifests itself in competition for men's approval. The proud love "the praise of men more than the praise of God" (John 12:42–43). Our motives for the things we do are where the sin is manifest. Jesus said He did "always those things" that pleased God (John 8:29).[32]

---

32. Ezra Taft Benson, "Beware of Pride," *Ensign*, May 1989, 5.

Right there in black and white, the prophet summed up my entire apron—for my Eve *did* value "the praise of men more than the praise of God"; I *did* worry what other people would think of me; and I *did* compete for "men's approval." Finally, it hit me: whenever I tried to cover myself with this type of apron, what I was really doing was devoting my heart to a false belief system instead of my Savior. Yes, on the outside it seemed like a pretty decent way to cover my nakedness. But now I could see that this apron just created a complicated mess inside my Eve. I knew it was time to cast off these sinful fig leaves and return my heart to a way of living that was pleasing to the Lord. But I'd worn this apron for so long that I wasn't sure how to survive without it. I needed help to learn how to take apart the complicated little stitches one step at a time.

Now, I'll be the first to acknowledge that not everyone is wrapped up in a people-pleasing apron. But that's only one example of what this covering can look like. Because our aprons come in many different shapes and sizes—and some even masquerade as very attractive clothing—let's look at other kinds of false identity fig leaves our Eve may reach for to cover the nakedness and weakness we feel as a result of the Fall.

We may decide to drape ourselves in the apron of financial success, meaning we pursue the pseudo-security of a nice home, cars, toys, and possessions. Setting our heart on these things may make us feel like we've risen above our weakness and become someone important, but in the end, trusting in our possessions is just another type of fig leaf clothing. It's like the story of the rich man in Luke 12 who built up his personal holdings to the point where he said to his soul, "Soul, thou hast much goods laid up for many years; take thine ease, eat, drink, and be merry" (Luke 12:19). But his apron dissolved into nothing when the Lord said to him, "Thou fool, this night thy soul shall be required of thee: then whose shall those things be, which thou hast provided?" (verse 20).

Or we may decide that the fig leaves of busyness will cover our Eve with confidence, so we construct this apron with a nonstop list of tasks, errands, and responsibilities. We believe that checking off our to-do list proves our value and our worth. Though our jam-packed schedule seems to cover our nakedness and makes us feel like we're making a contribution, in the end, all it really does is keep us stressed out and distracted from the things that matter most.

Or we may cover ourselves in the fig leaves of comparison. As we look at others, we compare our spouses, children, talents, gifts, or accomplishments, hoping all the while to measure up to some made-up standard we see in them. When someone shows up with bigger and better fig leaves, Satan whispers to us that we're not good enough and we need to try harder to measure up. With his lies circling around in our head, we run back to our sewing in an effort to dress ourselves up all over again.

Can you see that the possibilities really are endless? Our aprons could be stitched together by the fig leaves of perfectionism. Or intellectual superiority. Or religious usefulness, or physical attractiveness, or gaining social media influencer status. There are as many fig leaf options as there are people in the world. So the question we need to ask ourselves isn't whether we're wearing any aprons, but what *kind* of fig leaves we've used to clothe ourselves over the years. I hope you can see that this part of our journey requires a little extra digging. If you're like me, it will take some prayer and pondering to figure out what types of false covering you've used to conceal your own personal weakness and vulnerability.

With that said, I want you to take a deep breath because we're about to push even further on this particular climb. On the next stretch of path, we're going to examine another fig leaf apron that our world loves to hand us when we're feeling inadequate. It's presented to us by teachers, speakers, therapists, authors, and experts. When we're feeling the not-enough and less-than feelings of the Fall, the world tells us to sew together the popular fig leaves of *self-esteem*. The voices handing us this apron are clear and loud: "If you're feeling bad about yourself, you need a more positive self-image. You can overcome all your inadequacy and insecurity by raising your self-esteem." At first glance, it feels like the perfect answer to address the many difficult effects of the Fall, so you may wonder why I'd call this a fig leaf apron.

Well, let's start by looking at where the concept of self-esteem actually came from.

Out of curiosity, I did a little investigating and found that the term *self-esteem* originated in the world of psychology. While the meaning of the word varied at first, definitions would eventually include "a favorable impression of oneself"[33] or "confidence and satisfaction in oneself."[34] Another theorist describes self-esteem as "a personal judgment of worthiness."[35] Put these together and the experts' message is clear: people who have healthy self-esteem believe in themselves. They believe they're worthy and capable of doing anything, being anything, and overcoming anything, no matter what obstacles stand in their way. It's certainly an appealing apron for those of us who struggle with inadequacy. In fact, those same experts offer all kinds of plans and programs that promise to increase our sense of self-esteem.

Now, I'll admit that over the years, I spent a lot of time sewing on this apron. My fig leaves took many different forms. I tried changing my self-talk, focusing on my strengths and talents, and setting more ambitious goals. I tried replacing negative thoughts with positive ones, forgiving myself for mistakes, and rewarding myself for achievements. But to be brutally honest, none of those things ever covered my insecurity completely. That's because every time I tried to raise my self-confidence, sooner or later something always happened to send that elevator crashing back down to the ground floor. Over and over, the cycle would repeat itself: build myself up, crash back down, build myself up, crash back down. I finally reached the point where I thought, "There's *got* to be an easier way!"

It was then that the questions began forming in my mind: What does the Lord think about our culture's focus on self-esteem? What do the scriptures have to say? Amazingly, the Spirit unveiled some very

33. *Dictionary.com*, s.v. "self-esteem," accessed Apr. 1, 2023, https://www.dictionary.com/browse/self-esteem.

34. *Merriam-Webster.com Dictionary*, s.v. "self-esteem," accessed Apr. 1, 2023, https://www.merriam-webster.com/dictionary/self-esteem.

35. Kim Lyon, "What Is Self-Esteem?," Explorable, Dec. 16, 2015, https://explorable.com/e/what-is-self-esteem.

powerful answers to those questions—answers that radically changed the way I look at this fig leaf apron.

To show you what I learned, we have to begin about as far from self-esteem as it's possible to get. For starters, read through the following verses and consider the theme that emerges:

- Alma 26:12—"Yea, I know that I am nothing."
- Helaman 12:7—"O how great is the nothingness of the children of men; yea, even they are less than the dust of the earth."
- Moses 1:10—"Now . . . I know that man is nothing, which thing I never had supposed."

We may wonder why these prophets would refer to themselves or humankind as "nothing." It seems like a pretty depressing view to take, especially coming from something as inspired as the scriptures. And lest we think this troubling idea is confined to these three verses alone, here are four more references that express a similar sentiment:

- Galatians 6:3—"For if a man think himself to be something, when he is nothing, he deceiveth himself."
- Mosiah 2:25—"Can ye say aught of yourselves? I answer you, Nay. Ye cannot say that ye are even as much as the dust of the earth."
- Mosiah 23:11—"I am unworthy to glory of myself."
- Ether 3:2—"Now behold, O Lord . . . we are unworthy before thee."

If we're looking for role models who display bold self-confidence or a sense of personal worthiness—if we're looking for scriptural evidence of strong self-esteem—we certainly won't find it in these verses. Both Alma and the brother of Jared just called themselves *un*worthy. Yet these are some of the greatest prophets who ever walked the earth! Why aren't they displaying the characteristics of healthy self-esteem? Don't they understand who they are? Don't they know the Lord declared that "the worth of souls is great in the sight of God" (Doctrine and Covenants 18:10)?

Thankfully, King Benjamin sheds some light on this dilemma in Mosiah 4, helping us to better understand the previous prophets' intent. There he introduces the very same concept, only he does so by asking his people this probing question: "[Has] the knowledge of the goodness of God at this time . . . awakened you to a sense of your nothingness, and your worthless and fallen state" (Mosiah 4:5)? In this verse, King Benjamin equates man's sense of "nothingness" not to his personal worth to God but to his "worthless and fallen *state.*" I believe this is the key to understanding all the verses that speak of the nothingness and worthlessness of the children of men.

Could this be the same state of "weakness" we discussed earlier in Ether 12:27? What if the concept of nothingness is just another way to describe what happened to us because of the Fall? It's tough to swallow but true nonetheless: even though we lived premortally with glorious heavenly parents, and even though we still retain our inherent worth as spirit children of deity, we now live in a fallen state, a state where we've literally become "less than the dust of the earth" (Mosiah 4:2). Note that the dust obeys God with perfect precision, but we don't. We're stuck with a natural man who "receiveth not the things of the Spirit" (1 Corinthians 2:14). So because each of us has "sinned, and come short of the glory of God" (Romans 3:23), it makes sense that the prophets describe both themselves and us as worthless and fallen—in a state of complete and utter nothingness.

There are actually many prophets in the scriptures who lament their own struggle with weakness and nothingness. For instance, Nephi exclaimed, "O wretched man that I am! . . . I am encompassed about, because of the temptations and the sins which do so easily beset me" (2 Nephi 4:17–18). Paul also cried out, "O wretched man that I am! who shall deliver me from the body of this death?" (Romans 7:24). Even Isaiah grieved, "Woe is me! for I am undone; because I am a man of unclean lips" (Isaiah 6:5.) Don't their cries sound just like we do on a low self-esteem day? As we're overtaken with feelings of inadequacy, failure, and weakness, we wonder if we'll ever measure up, if we'll ever do anything right, if our efforts will ever be worth anything to anyone.

To solve this problem, you'd think God would fill the scriptures with instructions on how to raise our self-esteem. But that's not the case at all. As former Brigham Young University professor M. Catherine Thomas points out, "The concept of self-esteem as a solution to man's most basic spiritual, emotional, and even physical needs *is not found in the scriptures.* One might be surprised to find that in the scriptures there are no positive references to self-esteem, self-confidence, or self-love. Not because God does not feel exquisite tenderness for human beings, but because he knows a better way for human flourishing than focusing on raising self-esteem."[36]

I know that may be tough to hear. Some may even think, "What about the verse that says, 'Love thy neighbor as thyself' (Matthew 22:39)? Isn't that proof that the scriptures encourage healthy self-esteem?" I entertained similar thoughts myself—until I looked at the actual reference. It didn't take long for me to see that nowhere in that verse—or in the other nine times the phrase appears in scripture[37]—are we actually commanded to focus on self-love. Christ seems to be referring instead to the need to show the same love and care for others that we tend to show for ourselves.

What's more, Jesus clearly taught in Matthew 22 that there are *two* great commandments: love God and love your neighbor. When we imply there's a *third* directive to build up our own self-image, all we're doing is putting words in the Savior's mouth. And the truth is, when it comes to the "self," Christ treats that subject very differently than the love of God or neighbor. For example, Jesus taught His disciples, "If any man will come after me, let him *deny himself,* and take up his cross daily, and follow me" (Luke 9:23; emphasis added). Never in over 2,400 pages of scripture does the Lord support the idea of building up or exalting or esteeming the self.

Now, please understand: I'm not saying there's nothing we can do about our weakness and inadequacy, and that we must accept our nothingness and leave it at that. Remember, Catherine Thomas told

---

36. M. Catherine Thomas, *Spiritual Lightening* (Salt Lake City, UT: Deseret Book, 1996), 18; emphasis added.

37. See Leviticus 19:18; Matthew 19:19; Mark 12:31; Luke 10:27; Romans 13:9; Galatians 5:14; James 2:8; Mosiah 23:15; Doctrine and Covenants 59:6.

us that "[God] knows *a better way* for human flourishing than focusing on raising self-esteem." But what could be better than believing in yourself? What could be better than a personal sense of confidence and worthiness? The answer may surprise you because it involves a doctrine most of us have heard all our lives. Believe it or not, this same doctrine is the very thing that addresses—and heals—all the weakness and nothingness we experience as a result of the Fall.

To introduce you to this "better way," let's quickly review the verse in Ether 12 that we quoted earlier: "And if men come unto me I will show unto them their weakness. I give unto men weakness that they may be humble; and *my grace is sufficient* for all men that humble themselves before me; for if they humble themselves before me, and have faith in *me*, then will *I* make weak things become strong unto them" (Ether 12:27; emphasis added).

In this scripture, how are we told to deal with our weakness? The instruction is clear: rather than putting our confidence in our own abilities, we're to exercise faith in Christ and His grace. The Book of Mormon continues this same theme in other chapters, reminding us that "since man had fallen he could not merit anything of himself" (Alma 22:14), and that the only solution for our worthless, weak, and fallen state is in "relying alone upon the merits of Christ" (Moroni 6:4) or in "relying wholly upon the merits of him who is mighty to save" (2 Nephi 31:19). Did you notice the repetition of the word *merit* in all these verses? The word is defined as "character or conduct deserving reward, honor, or *esteem*."[38] After all is said and done, isn't Jesus Christ the One who deserves all merit, honor, and reward? Isn't *He* the One we should be esteeming?

I love the powerful way that author Jennie Allen captures it:

> We are so often dragged along in the darkness, unable to save ourselves from our thoughts and from our shame and from our mistakes. We try to slap self-esteem tactics on our fears, but they don't stick because, well . . . it's true. We're not enough.

---

38. *Merriam-Webster.com Dictionary*, s.v. "merit," accessed Apr. 1, 2023, https://www.merriam-webster.com/dictionary/merit; emphasis added.

It would be a terribly depressing thought—if it weren't followed by the most freeing truth in all of eternity.

God knew we would never be enough. So He became enough for us. Jesus is our enough.[39]

Can you see how this beautiful truth has the potential to heal our entire struggle with low self-esteem? In fact, it's the very system the Lord outlines in the scriptures. To illustrate, let me show you four separate passages in the standard works where He has a one-on-one conversation with a prophet who is struggling. As you listen to the cries of God's servants, see if their words sound like we do on a low self-esteem day:

- Moses: "O my Lord, I am not eloquent . . . but I am slow of speech, and of a slow tongue" (Exodus 4:10).
- Gideon: "Oh my Lord, wherewith shall I save Israel? behold, my family is poor . . . and I am the least in my father's house" (Judges 6:15).
- Jeremiah: "Then said I, Ah, Lord God! behold, I cannot speak: for I am a child" (Jeremiah 1:6).
- Enoch: "[I] am but a lad, and all the people hate me; for I am slow of speech; wherefore am I thy servant?" (Moses 6:31)

Don't these men sound just like we do at times? We give the same excuses: "I'm terrible at this, I've failed at that. I'm just so weak!" Thankfully, these stories show us how Christ responded to these types of feelings. In each of the four accounts, did He pat His servant's head and reassure him with a "You're awesome—you can do it!" pep talk? Did He flatter His servant or build up his self-confidence? Did He outline the prophet's strengths and talents and attempt to raise his self-esteem? Not in even one of the four examples. Every single time, the Lord answered one way and one way only (and I'm paraphrasing all four accounts here): "Your strength and your ability will come through *My* strength and ability. Put your trust in *Me*. You'll

---

39. Jennie Allen, *Nothing to Prove: Why We Can Stop Trying So Hard* (Colorado Springs, CO: Waterbrook, 2017), 67; emphasis in original.

find success because *I* will be with you. Place all your esteem, child, in *Me*!"[40]

What it all boils down to is this: when we stop trying to dress ourselves up in a self-esteem apron and turn instead to the Lord, we're not sacrificing our personal needs—we're tapping into a source of strength and capacity far beyond our own, a supernatural power that will actually meet all our needs in a miraculous way. In addition, when we lay down this fig leaf apron and choose to rely on Christ alone, we're empowered to leave our nothingness and weakness behind and join ourselves to the most valuable, "esteem-able" force in the universe. As Catherine Thomas put it, "Being filled with the love of God [is] of far greater worth than any sense of self-confidence. If one grand objective of earth life is to gain access to the grace of Jesus Christ for our trials and divine development, we will immediately realize that *self-confidence is a puny substitute for God-confidence.*"[41]

I love that last phrase. Self-esteem really *is* a "puny substitute" for confidence in Christ. I want to rely on His merits, not my own. I want to rise above my weakness and become strong—not by building esteem in myself but by moving forward with faith in the power of His Atonement. Is there any chance you'd like to join me?

We do this by casting off the self-esteem apron our culture has talked us into wearing. It's not an easy task, for we may fear that as those fig leaves fall to the ground, our sense of personal significance and value will fall right along with them. I promise you, that's not going to happen. If you'll continue walking with me on the roads ahead, you'll learn how to free your mind from all obsessive thoughts of worthlessness and failure. It's quite an amazing transformation. As you undergo this mighty change, you'll obtain a sense of individual worth far greater than anything you've ever experienced. Trust

---

40. See Exodus 4:11–12; Judges 6:16; Jeremiah 1:7–10; Moses 6:32–34.

41. Thomas, *Spiritual Lightening*, 24; emphasis added. I highly recommend Sister Thomas's entire chapter entitled "Doer of Our Deeds." Her insights on self-esteem opened my eyes and blessed my life in more ways than I can ever express.

me—by the end of our journey, your Eve will find herself flying to higher heights than the pursuit of self-esteem ever dreamt of taking her.

So let's join Moses and Gideon and Jeremiah and Enoch and admit that on our own, we're not enough. Because of the Fall, we'll always feel weak and inadequate. But rather than trying to cover ourselves with a bunch of flimsy fig leaves, let's commit right here and now that we're going to place our faith in Christ. Really, I think it's a huge relief to quit acting like we have it all together and to acknowledge that we need His help. As we learn to trust Him, we really will find all the strength, adequacy, and worth we could possibly need.

Hopefully, as we've journeyed down this path, you've been able to uncover several of your personal fig leaf aprons. But because there are more possibilities than we've had time to explore, there's a chance you still need to dig a little deeper. So, before we travel any further, I'd like you to stop and really ponder this part of the story. Ask the Lord to show you all the metaphorical fig leaves you've used to cover your sin, shame, and weakness. Ask Him to help you see each and every one of your individual aprons. If you'll devote the time needed to work through this challenging task, it will not only open your eyes—it will prepare you for some life-changing discoveries waiting for us on the road ahead.

Readings & Reflections

Let's take a little more time to examine the complexities of our fig leaf aprons. Often we may construct them because others have convinced us it's in our best interest to believe what they're saying. To illustrate, study the following verses and note the disastrous effects of just one person's influence:

- Alma 31:1
- Alma 39:3–4
- Alma 48:1–3

Take a minute to review your life. Can you think of times when another person pressured your heart into making an apron (or adopting a belief system that seemed to cover your nakedness)? It may have been an author, leader, friend, family member, or even a social media influencer. How can you reject the pull of any deceptive voices that are trying to talk you into sewing an apron?

With that said, let's not forget Satan's influence in persuading us to make many different kinds of aprons. Read the following verses and ponder what you learn about how the adversary works:

- Luke 8:11–12
- 2 Nephi 28:20–23
- Helaman 6:21, 28–29
- 3 Nephi 1:22

With these verses in mind, can you identify any fig leaves that the adversary has quietly and deceptively "put . . . into [your] heart" (Helaman 6:29)?

Look up Isaiah 61:10. How does the Lord intend to clothe you in your nakedness? Also, turn to Ephesians 6:10–18 and Doctrine and Covenants 27:15–18 for another way He can cover and protect us in our weakness and vulnerability.

Let's return to the topic of self-esteem and explore this apron a little further. In our culture, the "raising" of one's self-worth is a fig leaf that's commonly offered to us. Surprisingly, one of the synonyms for *raise* is *exalt*. Look through the following scriptures on exalting ourselves: Daniel 11:36–37; Luke 14:7–11; Luke 18:9–14; 2 Nephi 12:17; Doctrine and Covenants 49:10; and Doctrine and Covenants 112:8, 15. What impressions are you left with?

The Apostle Paul offers some counsel that I believe applies perfectly to the pursuit of self-esteem. Read 2 Corinthians 10:12, 17–18 and ponder how his words could add to your understanding of this particular apron.

More insight from Paul can be found in 2 Timothy 3:2 where he describes what things will be like in the last days—in *our* day. Read this verse and decide what you think Paul could be referring to in the first phrase and how it could apply to the apron of self-esteem.

For a final explanation point from Paul, read 2 Corinthians 1:9, 3:5, and 4:5. What counsel does he give us about how we should see ourselves? Now look up Proverbs 3:7; Proverbs 20:6, 9; and 2 Nephi 15:21 and answer the same question.

As I've continued to research this topic, I've found many authors and teachers who join me in questioning our culture's preoccupation with self-esteem.

For instance, here's Jennie Allen again: "The world's message is simple: You are enough. All on your own, you are enough. But that mantra fails us either because we deep down know we aren't enough or because our self-esteem inflates and we charge through life independent of God and people. Either outcome leaves us lonely and disappointed. Self-esteem is not the answer."[42]

Or consider this unique view from John Piper:

> Love has been almost completely distorted in our world. For most people, to be loved is to be made much of. Almost everything in our Western culture serves this distortion of love. We are taught in a thousand ways that love means increasing one's self-esteem. Love is helping someone feel good about themselves. Love is giving someone a mirror and helping him like what he sees.
>
> This is not what the Bible means by the love of God. Love is doing what is best for someone. But making self the object of our highest affections is not best for us. It is, in fact, a lethal distraction. . . . To make [one] feel good about themselves when they were made to feel good about seeing God is like taking someone to the Alps and locking them in a room full of mirrors.[43]

I was also surprised to find that it's not just religiously inclined writers who are jumping on the bandwagon. Apparently, some in the secular world have their own reservations as well. In her aptly named book, *The Self-Esteem Trap: Raising Confident and Compassionate Kids in an Age of Self-Importance*, Polly Young-Eisendrath offers this insight:

> In the 1970s and 1980s teachers and parents began a campaign to cure low self-esteem in our young. Hoping to increase children's creativity and self-expression, this educational and parenting movement unwittingly promoted a self-esteem trap: unrealistic fantasies of achievement, wealth, power, and celebrity. When these expectations are not met in adult life—as inevitably they are not—the result is a negative evaluation of the self. And the trap of negative self-absorption cannot be eased or helped by more focus on the self. . . .
>
> [This is a] particularly threatening and perplexing problem. Obsessive self-focus, restless dissatisfaction, pressures to be exceptional, unreadiness to take on adult responsibilities, feelings of

---

42. Allen, *Nothing to Prove*, 213.

43. John Piper, *Don't Waste Your Life* (Wheaton, IL: Crossway, 2003), 33; emphasis added.

> superiority (or inferiority), and excessive fears of being humiliated are the pervasive symptoms of the self-esteem trap. . . .
>
> [This] trap, in its least troubling form, leads to unhappy adult children who feel defective because they are unable to have or be what they imagined for themselves. At its worst, unchecked over childhood and young adulthood, and reinforced by other social conditions, it can lead to chronic emotional disorders such as depression, narcissism, and addiction.[44]

After studying all these verses and quotes, what final thoughts do you have on self-esteem as a fig leaf apron?

If you'd like to study more on the fallacy of self-esteem, I recommend the following books:

- Jeffrey S. Reber and Steven P. Moody, *Are We Special? The Truth and the Lie about God's Chosen People* (Salt Lake City, UT: Deseret Book, 2013).
- Ester Rasband, *Confronting the Myth of Self-Esteem: Twelve Keys to Finding Peace* (Salt Lake City, UT: Deseret Book, 1998).
- Jennie Allen, *Nothing to Prove: Why We Can Stop Trying So Hard* (Colorado Springs, CO: Waterbrook, 2017).
- Jean M. Twenge, *Generation Me: Why Today's Young Americans Are More Confident, Assertive, Entitled—and More Miserable Than Ever Before* (New York: Free Press, 2006).

44. Polly Young-Eisendrath, *The Self-Esteem Trap: Raising Confident and Compassionate Kids in an Age of Self-Importance* (New York: Little, Brown Spark, 2008), 4, 21.

- Jay E. Adam, *The Biblical View of Self-Esteem, Self-Love, and Self-Image* (Eugene, Oregon: Harvest House Publishers, 1986).
- Paul Brownback, *The Danger of Self-Love* (Chicago: Moody Bible Institute, 1982).

Response

In what ways are you feeling prompted to respond to the concepts found in this chapter?

7

Hide and Seek

Ready to move on to the next detail in the story? We're going to take our time walking this road because there are some nuances that can be easy to miss. The Genesis account tells us that after making their aprons, Adam and Eve "heard the voice of the Lord God walking in the garden in the cool of the day," and they ran and "hid themselves" (Genesis 3:8) among the trees of the garden. When God later asks Adam why he ran, he answers, "I was afraid, *because I was naked*; and I hid myself" (Genesis 3:10; emphasis added).

Think carefully about his reply for just a minute. Weren't Adam and Eve both *wearing aprons* at this point in the story? Why in the world would Adam tell God he was naked? He'd worked hard to cover himself up, so why would he still experience feelings of fear? The answer for me came as a huge "aha" moment. It seems that despite all their efforts to sew fig leaf clothing, the moment they heard the voice of the Lord, that covering became completely useless. They felt as exposed as if they weren't wearing anything at all. Apparently, the leaves were enough to shield them when the two were alone in the garden, but they weren't enough to block out the all-seeing eye of the Almighty. It just goes to show that in the presence of the Lord, all our human attempts to clothe ourselves will wither into nothingness.

Our homemade wardrobe will never cover us the way we need to be covered.

Notice also that Adam and Eve weren't just playing a lighthearted game of hide and seek. The verse makes it clear they were trying to "[hide] themselves *from the presence of the Lord God*" (Genesis 3:8; emphasis added). To leave Him as fast as they possibly could. And they went into the trees, somewhere they thought would block out His presence even more. It appears to be yet another attempt to hide their nakedness from His piercing, penetrating vision.

It's such an odd part of the story because their running seems so fruitless. We may even picture Adam and Eve in our mind's eye and wonder, "Where in the world are you going?" But the most important question, of course, is this: in what ways do we do the same thing in our own lives? In what ways do we personally choose to run and hide from the presence of the Lord? I know our first thought may be, "I'm not running from God. I'm active in my religion. I read my scriptures and pray and go to church." But before we get too comfortable with that line of thinking, remember that we're not just looking at our Adam's outward activity on this quest. We're examining the motivation and intent that lives deep in the recesses of our Eve.

To help us do that, I'd like to shift the language just a little bit. What if instead of calling it *hiding,* we called it *escaping*? There's definitely a strong connection between those two words. Synonyms for *escape* include "sneak away," "cut and run," "disappear," "duck out," "flee," and "fly the coop."[45] However, my favorite definition of escape is "avoidance of reality."[46] I think that gives the concept a whole new perspective.

Looking at it through this lens, each of us could stop and ask ourselves: in what ways do I escape in an attempt to avoid reality? In what ways do I leave the presence of the Lord and run off somewhere

---

45. *Dictionary.com*, s.v. "escape," accessed Apr. 1, 2023, https://www.dictionary.com/browse/escape.

46. *Dictionary.com*, s.v. "escapism," accessed Apr. 1, 2023, https://www.dictionary.com/browse/escapism.

else? As we try to assess the different ways we do this, remember that we can escape by using either our Adam *or* our Eve . . . or even a combination of both. To show you what I mean, let's look at some of the most common hiding places we run to in our day and age. See if any of the behavior described hits home for either your Adam or your Eve.

Social media is a perfect example of a modern-day escape. One glance at our phone and our Adam is drawn in by the sight of all the funny, weird, or beautiful pictures parading across the screen. But those same images, words, and videos also transport our Eve to a new place mentally and emotionally. Whenever we're immersed in social media, we lose all conscious awareness of our present circumstances. For a time, it's almost as if we're living inside those platforms in our minds. We enter the realm through our Adam's eyes, but often stay there through its effects on our Eve's thoughts and feelings. Social media provides a way for us to avoid reality and live for a time in a different world—one that feels exciting, captivating, relaxing, entertaining, or even just distracting. It can be a very appealing place to run and hide, just like Adam and Eve did in the Garden of Eden.

Another common way we escape is by turning to food. Just one bite of that Krispy Kreme doughnut or that juicy flame-broiled steak and our Adam is instantly immersed in a state of blissful sensory pleasure. All our cares are forgotten as we lose ourselves in the tastes and textures rolling over our tongue. But again, this isn't just about our Adam's senses, for we all know that food can be an incredibly emotional experience. It's the reason the term *emotional eating* exists. Food can soothe, pacify, and numb our Eve whether we're stressed, bored, tired, frustrated, or overwhelmed. It's a hiding place we can run to several times a day through each and every snack—a mini escape that makes everything seem right in the world for a few delicious little moments.

Finally, think about our culture's affinity for binge watching TV and movies. You could also add video games or reading fiction to the list if you want. Talk about a hiding place that allows us to avoid reality! While this habit of watching, playing, or reading for hours certainly pleases our senses—meaning we love everything our Adam sees and hears—what it does for our Eve is even more powerful. Mentally and emotionally, we get to live vicariously through the characters on the screen. We become lost in their stories, completely absorbed in that fictional world to the point where we're experiencing *their* thoughts and feelings instead of our own. It's an incredibly tempting place to hide, especially if our own lives are filled with discouragement, difficulty, disappointment, or despair.

Having said that, I want to be clear that there's nothing inherently evil in any of the things I just described. All the apostles have social media accounts. The scriptures speak of food as a gift to "gladden the heart" and "enliven the soul" (see Doctrine and Covenants 59:16–20). And I've watched movies and read books that have had a profound impact on me. So the problem isn't the things themselves—*it's when we begin using them to escape.* When we run to them in an attempt to avoid reality. It may be that we're running to other things, like an obsession with sports or a favorite hobby or a daily dose of "retail therapy." No matter what our personal forest of trees looks like, what we really need to assess is how often these hiding places keep us separated from the presence of the Lord. Although we'd never say out loud that we love and worship our escapes more than our Savior, the amount of time we spend in these places spells out the truth in neon letters.

Why do we run to things like these? I believe one reason is that they make us forget. Like I keep saying, it's incredibly difficult to be fallen and spiritually dead. It's difficult to live with an awareness of our weakness and powerlessness. So when our fig leaves aren't enough to conceal that reality, our next option is to escape. We choose to run away, even if it's only through the thoughts of our mind. Our favorite hiding places feel so comforting and concealing that it's tempting to stay and live in these places—to make our hiding spots our home. After all, it's a lot easier to escape than to cope with all the unpleasant realities of the Fall. Especially the emptiness of our spiritual death. We've been taught that spiritual death is a separation from God, and we often assume that just happened when we left the premortal world and came to live on earth. But what if the separation is actually exacerbated by our personal choice to turn our hearts from the Lord and run off into hiding? It's a startling reality to begin to contemplate.

I think the most troubling thing about our hiding places is that they don't just make us forget about our fallenness—they also make us forget about the Lord. There are consequences that come from spending so much time separated from His presence. Author A. W. Tozer explains it well: "So the life of man upon the earth is a life away from the Presence, wrenched loose from that 'blissful center' which is our right and proper dwelling place . . . *the loss of which is the cause of our unceasing restlessness*."[47]

Think about all the restlessness and emptiness and emotional pain we experience throughout our lives. We talked earlier about how we tend to blame it on our circumstances—on our stress or financial problems or that fight we had with a loved one. But what if we're missing the whole point of Adam and Eve's story? What if our escaping—our leaving the "blissful center" of the Lord's presence—is the very thing that's causing all our misery? What if all we really need to do to soothe our restlessness is to run back to Him? What would happen if we simply chose to come out of hiding for good?

As simple as that concept may seem, leaving our escapes isn't always as easy as turning off the TV or doing a social media fast. Like we learned with our fig leaves, the dynamics of the heart are a lot more complicated than that. So in order to confront *all* our escapes, we need to spend some time looking at other ways we hide—ways that may be a lot harder to see than the obvious examples we just mentioned.

For instance, as I continued to think outside the box, it hit me one day that it's possible to hide ourselves in plain sight—right in the minutia of our everyday lives—and not even realize that we're doing it. Consider this: if we spend the majority of our day never thinking of the Lord, never asking Him to be with us, never including Him in the stresses and strains of our daily routine, what else is to be concluded

---

47. A. W. Tozer, *The Pursuit of God* (Sunnyvale, CA: Loki's Publishing, 2017), 22; emphasis added.

but that—just like Adam and Eve—we're keeping ourselves separated from His presence?

Yes, I know most of us draw near when we're doing something "spiritual" like reading our scriptures or going to church, but what about the rest of the day? Do we ever seek His help to get through traffic without losing it, or to deal with a screaming toddler, or to know what to cook for dinner when we're completely out of options? Forgetting His promise that "I am with the faithful always" (Doctrine and Covenants 62:9), how often do we spend the majority of our day without giving Him a second thought? Anytime we live without the blessing of His presence, we're essentially choosing to leave Him behind and run off into our own personal forest. We're trying to do life on our own. But thankfully, He's always there, calling us to come out of hiding.

As we continue to ponder this tendency we have to run from the Lord, I actually want to go even deeper and explore another escape that is specific to our Eve—one we've all experienced at one time or another. When we're unwilling to face the reality of our fallenness, our minds can be tempted to sneak off to this quiet little place and make it our home. How do we do it? By living in *denial*. Denial about what? Really, the options are endless.

We may be living in denial about our sin or our deep-seated weakness or our need to repent. Or we may deny that our coping mechanisms are getting in the way of our healing, or that our personal worship is attached to something other than the Lord. No matter what form it takes, this hiding place exists deep inside our subconscious mind and promises to shield our heart from all feelings of shame, weakness, and insecurity. In the words of therapist and professor Dan Allender, "All denial of what is true is ultimately a commitment to create a world that is more in accord with our wishes. Denial is not just a flight from the truth, it is a *reconstruction of the truth*."[48] This

---

48. Dan B. Allender and Cathy Loerzel, *Redeeming Heartache: How Past Suffering Reveals Our True Calling* (Grand Rapids, MI: Zondervan, 2021), 109, Kindle edition; emphasis added.

escape works for one very powerful reason: when our heart is hidden away in denial, there's no Fall and no sin and no reason to feel naked or ashamed. In short, denial allows us to continue in our sins without feeling the stinging effects of our negative choices.

You may be surprised to learn that denial is a recurring theme found throughout the scriptures. In the book of Jeremiah, for instance, the Jews were living in such deep denial of their sin that Jehovah sounded almost incredulous as He rebuked them through the words of His prophet: "How canst thou say, I am not polluted, I have not gone after Baalim? see thy way in the valley, know what thou hast done: . . . Yet thou sayest, Because I am innocent, surely his anger shall turn from me. Behold, I will plead with thee, because thou sayest, I have not sinned" (Jeremiah 2:23, 35).

Is there a chance we ever do the same thing?

We'll find another example of this in the Book of Mormon where the wicked priests of King Noah exhibit the same stubborn, unyielding spirit as the Israelites. Even after Abinadi boldly testified of their sin, the men still wouldn't own up to their fallen nature. I bet it shocked Abinadi to hear the priests' deep denial of their sinful lifestyle:

> And now, O king, what great evil hast thou done, or what great sins have thy people committed, that we should be condemned of God or judged of this man?
>
> And now, O king, behold, we are guiltless, and thou, O king, hast not sinned; therefore, [Abinadi] has lied concerning you, and he has prophesied in vain.
>
> And behold, we are strong, we shall not come into bondage, or be taken captive by our enemies; yea, and thou hast prospered in the land, and thou shalt also prosper. (Mosiah 12:13–15)

Let's face it: sinfulness can be an extremely difficult thing to admit. Again, our heart often chooses to hide away in denial because it offers us a temporary form of comfort—a short-term escape from the consequences of the Fall. But whether we choose to face it or not, the truth is firmly established in the scriptures. Each of us is fallen and spiritually dead. The longer we try to run and hide from our fallen nature, the longer we remain captive to its passions and appetites. I believe Satan counts it a great success when our hearts remain hidden away in denial of our sin. But rather than give him that victory, we can pray for the courage to face our fallen condition. In the words of Elder Neal A. Maxwell, "Whether by provocation, introspection, or wrenching remembrance, *denial must be dissolved.*"[49]

Before we move on, though, I want to add a quick clarifier. The scriptural stories I just used were both examples of really wicked people living in denial of their sin, and they may not seem to apply to those of us who have the religious checklist all checked off. It's that same list we talked about earlier: We go to church—check. We pay our tithing—check. We read our scriptures, say our prayers, and serve other people—check, check, check. Because of all our industrious efforts, we may not think we could ever be accused of living in denial. It may be that you're a Relief Society president or a bishopric member or a really dedicated Nursery leader. Perhaps you've spent hours doing family history work or serving in the temple or ministering to the people in your ward. With all that sacrifice and dedication under your belt, you may feel pretty confident that, spiritually speaking, your heart hasn't run off into hiding.

But I'm here to tell you that even if you're the most active person in your ward, and even if you can quote the entire Book of Mormon backward and forward, you could *still* be living in denial. At least that's what the Lord taught me as I continued walking the paths of my own personal journey.

To show you what I learned, let's turn first to the book of Luke where Jesus reveals this short but enlightening little story:

> Two men went up into the temple to pray; the one a Pharisee, and the other a publican.
>
> The Pharisee stood and prayed thus with himself, God, I thank thee, that I am not as other men are, extortioners, unjust, adulterers, or even as this publican.
>
> I fast twice in the week, I give tithes of all that I possess.

---

49. Neal A. Maxwell, "Repentance," *Ensign*, Nov. 1991, 30; emphasis added.

> And the publican, standing afar off, would not lift up so much as his eyes unto heaven, but smote upon his breast, saying, God be merciful to me a sinner.
>
> I tell you, this man went down to his house justified rather than the other: for every one that exalteth himself shall be abased; and he that humbleth himself shall be exalted. (Luke 18:10–14)

Can't you just picture the Pharisee holding up his long, impressive checklist to God? Can't you hear him saying, "I fast twice a week, I give tithes of all I possess—check, check, check"? Yes, on the outside he seemed like a very righteous man. In fact, the Jews viewed the Pharisees as the most spiritual men on the planet. If we measured this man by his outward works, he doesn't appear to be hiding at all—he seems very active and involved in the worship of his God.

But the Lord judged the Pharisees differently than most. "This people draweth nigh unto me with their mouth, and honoureth me with their lips," Jesus said, "*but their heart is far from me*" (Matthew 15:8; emphasis added). Notice the true location of the Pharisees' Eve. Even though their Adam was going through all the right motions on the outside, inwardly these Israelites had run away into hiding, meaning the so-called spiritual leaders had "removed their hearts far from [Jesus Christ]" (2 Nephi 27:25).

Do we ever do the same thing when it comes to our good works? While we may not pray the same prayer as the Pharisee, don't we often think the same thoughts? Deep down, don't we see ourselves as more righteous than others because we have a long list of righteous works and they don't? What we tend to forget is that even though our works look impressive on the outside, on the inside our Eve may still be living in hiding. It's another perfect example of hiding in plain sight—hiding, in fact, *right in the middle of our busy involvement in Church culture.* To everyone else, we look like a devoted servant of God, but deep inside, our hearts may be far away from Jesus Christ.

Personally, I'll admit that I didn't like the thought of comparing my life with those arrogant, prideful Pharisees. I didn't see myself acting like those puffed up, self-righteous men at all. (More of that denial going on.) But finally, the Lord began to open my eyes and show me times when I drew near to Him on the outside while my heart had run off into hiding. Let me share a few scenarios from my religious life, and you'll quickly see how easily my Eve disappeared into the trees. You may want to ask yourself if your heart has ever sought out similar internal hideouts.

- Even though my Adam was diligently studying the scriptures, inwardly my Eve's mind was a million miles away, so I'd read the verse again . . . then again . . . and I'd still have no idea what I just read.
- Even though my Adam faithfully attended a temple session, inwardly my Eve spent the entire time distracted with thoughts that had absolutely nothing to do with God.
- Even though my Adam dutifully knelt to participate in family prayer, inwardly my Eve missed every word that was said because she was mulling over the day's to-do list.
- Even though I sat through that talk or lesson in church, my Eve was bored, disconnected, and unable to hear anything I might have otherwise been taught by the Spirit.

Notice how in each of these examples, my Adam was doing the "right" thing on the outside, but inwardly my Eve displayed all the symptoms of having removed herself from Jesus Christ. Subtly but clearly, she'd run off into hiding.

Moments like these forced me to acknowledge that underneath all my outward religious activity, my heart often felt apathetic, preoccupied, disconnected, or annoyed. In these times, my Eve wasn't drawing close to Christ at all—she was leaving Him in favor of more intriguing interests. It seems that even though I loved the Lord and wanted very much to keep my covenants, my Eve didn't always want to come along for the ride. Off she would run, leaving my Adam to try to function on his own. I knew that this frustrating characteristic of my natural man needed to be overcome, but how was I going to get my heart to quit playing hide and seek? Controlling my Adam's outward actions seemed much easier than filling my Eve with the right intentions. Yet just as it was with the Pharisees, the Lord's main concern wasn't my outward works but my disengaged, disappearing heart.

If you think about it, religious hiding is actually one of the most dangerous forms of hiding because it doesn't look like we're playing hide and seek at all. While we're throwing ourselves into hours of outward service and devotion, inwardly we may be just like that Pharisee praying in the temple: *in complete denial that we're just as much a sinner as the lowly "publicans" we look down on*. What's worse, this kind of self-righteous denial keeps us from coming to Jesus's feet in desperation; from seeking His glorious, life-giving redemption; and from begging for His mercy like the humble and repentant publican. There's no sense of awe or wonder or worship for our Savior because our Eve has focused her attention elsewhere, confident that her Adam has her religious life completely under control.

To explore this idea a little further, let's look at one familiar story that shows how easy it is to get pulled away into hiding while trying to serve the Lord. It's the familiar tale of Mary and Martha in Luke 10. If you remember, on this important night, the two sisters had the privilege of hosting Christ (and probably several of His disciples) for a meal and some personal instruction. With Mary sitting at Jesus's feet, Martha "was cumbered about much serving," so she turned to Him and said, "Lord, dost thou not care that my sister hath left me to serve alone? bid her therefore that she help me" (verse 40).

I can just imagine Christ's eyes locking on to Martha's in this tense and emotional scene. With His voice laced with love and concern, I can hear Him telling His friend, "Martha, Martha, thou art careful and troubled about many things: But one thing is needful: and Mary hath chosen that good part, which shall not be taken away from her" (Luke 10:41–42).

Before we judge Martha too harshly, let me first say I don't believe the Lord had an issue with her making dinner for the group. After all, that's a responsibility that's been given to women through the ages. Even in today's world, the sisters are called on again and again to feed the masses, whether it be in our own homes, church functions, or even holiday parties. For this reason, I don't think Martha's cooking was the problem at all. I believe it had more to do with the state of her heart. (For further evidence, note that in John 12:1–3, Martha was again preparing the meal, but this time the Lord didn't correct her in any way.)

So what was Martha struggling with in this instance? We know the verse says she felt "cumbered about" while laboring away in the kitchen. Since the English word *cumber* means "to overload or burden,"[50] we often conclude that Martha had taken too much on herself—that she was buckling under the strain of all the responsibility on her shoulders. But the Greek word that's translated as *cumbered* in this verse is *perispao*—and it doesn't mean to overload or weigh down. It means "to draw away" or "distract."[51] In fact, my Greek dictionary points out that it's used "in the sense of being *over-occupied* about a thing,"[52] not overburdened.

I believe *perispao* paints a perfect picture of Martha's heart being pulled away into hiding. Rather than rejoicing in the gift of having the Lord in her home, she was lost in her service and completely separated from His life-giving presence. The scriptures even tell us she was "careful and troubled about many things" (Luke 10:41). If you check the footnote for this verse, you'll see that *careful* means "worried." And note that Martha was worried and troubled about *many* things. I'm sure most of us have been there at one time or another. These are the moments when our stress level is approaching full meltdown status. As I heard a friend say once, these are the moments when we're about to have a "come apart."

First and foremost, we need to remember that feelings of stress, worry, and fear aren't coming from the Spirit of the Lord. Paul tells us that "the fruit of the Spirit is love, joy, peace, longsuffering, gentleness, goodness, [and] faith" (Galatians 5:22). So why did Martha lose all

50. *Dictionary.com*, s.v. "cumber," accessed Apr. 1, 2023, https://www.dictionary.com/browse/cumber.

51. James E. Strong, *The Strongest Strong's Exhaustive Concordance of the Bible* (Grand Rapids, MI: Zondervan, 2001), 1636.

52. W. E. Vine, *Vine's Complete Expository Dictionary of Old and New Testament Words* (Nashville, TN: Thomas Nelson, 1984), 140; emphasis added.

sense of peace in this instance? Because she allowed her heart to be distracted and drawn away into hiding. (To give Martha a little credit, after Lazarus's death, it was she who ran to Jesus while Mary "sat still in the house" [John 11:20]. In that instance, Mary was the one whose heart needed to be called out of hiding.)

What I love most about this story is that Jesus immediately recognized what the issue was and tried to draw Martha back to what was "needful" for her weary soul—*Him*. It wasn't necessarily that she needed to stop cooking. What she needed was to turn her heart to the "light and life of the world" (Mosiah 16:9) so He could calm her stress, empower her service, and clarify her perspective. Only Christ could put the brakes on the crazy roller coaster of her heart. And the same thing holds true for each of us. Only the Lord can give us *His* peace (see John 14:27)—a peace that will sustain us whether we're doing something Martha-ish like attending a work meeting or something Mary-ish like worshipping in the temple. Only He can pull our heart out of hiding and show us how to live every day bathed in His calming and stress-relieving light.

As I've thought about this little encounter and how often I've been "careful and troubled about many things," I've found myself wondering why we get so stressed out in the first place. I mean, Christ never functioned that way, but many of us lose our cool on a regular basis. So what is it that brings out these feelings of frustration, irritability, or resentment? What keeps our hearts distracted and separated from our precious Lord? I believe we can find some answers if we read between the lines of Martha's story. While we'll never know exactly what was going on in this sweet woman's head, I don't think it would hurt if we threw out a few possible scenarios.

It could be that Martha liked being in control, and she was having a hard time convincing others to do things her way. Perhaps she had a picture in her head of exactly how she wanted the evening to go, but the harder she worked, the more her plan seemed to unravel. I've definitely seen the need for control cause some stressful moments in my everyday life. Yet I've learned that whenever I "exercise control or dominion or compulsion" (Doctrine and Covenants 121:37) on my family members or others, all it does is distract me and draw my heart away from the Lord and further into hiding.

It could be that Martha felt overcome by what some like to call the "Martyr Syndrome." After pouring ourselves into serving others, the thoughts quietly creep into our head: "No one appreciates everything I do around here. They all take me for granted. I'm tired of being the responsible one. But if I don't take care of things, no one will!" Personally, this has been one of my heart's favorite places to hide. As a mother of a large family, it's been an easy spot to run to when I felt like no one is paying attention and no one really cares.

Or it could be that Martha did something we've all probably done at some point—she dove into service without stopping to ask Jesus what *He* wanted her to do on that particular evening. Maybe she thought she had to make an extravagant meal when Christ would have been satisfied with a little bread and cheese. Maybe, if she'd asked, He would have simplified her task so she could have joined Mary and sat for a while at His feet. That's the tricky part about trying to serve the Lord: even if something seems worthwhile and beneficial to us, it's entirely possible that Christ has something different in mind . . . but we simply forget to ask.

In his beloved book *My Utmost for His Highest*, Oswald Chambers pinpointed the problem with throwing ourselves into service without first asking for the Lord's guidance and direction:

> So much Christian work today . . . simply come[s] into being by impulse! In our Lord's life every project was disciplined to the will of His Father. There was never the slightest tendency to follow the impulse of His own will. . . . Then compare this with what we do—*we take every thought and project that comes to us by impulse and jump into action immediately, instead of . . . disciplining ourselves to obey Christ. . . .*
>
> It is inconceivable, but true nonetheless, that saints . . . are simply doing work for God *that has been instigated by their own human nature.*[53]

---

53. Oswald Chambers, *My Utmost for His Highest* (Grand Rapids, MI: Discovery House, 1992), entry for September 9; emphasis added.

It's quite a startling thought—that we may be serving God in a way that isn't inspired at all but simply "instigated by [our] own human nature." Since many of us spend a great deal of time doing what Chambers calls "work for God," perhaps it's time to stop and evaluate *why* we're doing all these busy things we're doing. Where is our motivation coming from? Is it because we love the Lord and we're seeking to draw closer to Him? Or could there be other, less-than-noble reasons hiding quietly in the depths of our Eve?

For instance:

- Could we be serving others because we're stuck in the throes of people-pleasing and we've never learned the healthy habit of saying no?
- Could we be planning that church activity because we saw it online and thought it was cute, but we never asked the Lord for His guidance and direction?
- Could we be posting spiritual thoughts on social media because we like being seen as a good person and we love all the flattering comments that come as a result?
- Could we be calling it service when we're actually enabling someone's sinful behavior and the Lord would rather have us set some firm but loving boundaries?
- Could we be using our "righteous" efforts to subtly control or manipulate our friends, loved ones, or ward members to bend to our will?

The possibilities go on and on. I know it can be difficult to find these less-than-admirable motives hiding quietly behind the scenes in our heart. But it's vital that we shake off all remnants of denial and admit that as honorable as our intentions may seem, the inner motivation driving our gospel service isn't always as pure and inspired as we'd like to think. In fact, the reason we may be so "careful and troubled about many things" is because our heart is distracted by these false motivations, which keeps our Eve separated from the Lord and tucked away in hiding.

I believe this kind of religious life—the one where our Adam is busily serving while our Eve has run off into hiding—is the effort described by Isaiah as the "labour . . . which satisfieth not" (Isaiah 55:2). This type of gospel service certainly didn't cut it for the Pharisees, and it even kept Martha from experiencing her Master's life-transforming peace. So whether our Eve is far removed from Christ like the Jewish leaders, or only a step away in the next room as Martha was, somehow we need to coax her out of hiding. But how do we get ourselves to quit running off and instead "cleave unto [the Lord] with all [our] heart" (Doctrine and Covenants 11:19)?

Thankfully, this journey will answer that question for each of us. But to get the answers we need, it's critical that we pause and do the same thing we did with our fig leaf aprons—to take some time for introspection. Because we didn't have a chance to explore every type of hiding spot in this chapter, I want you to set up camp here as long as needed to understand each of your personal escapes. Ask the Lord to show you the places that you've run to. Ask for help to see how you've been tempted to avoid reality—whether it's been with your Adam, your Eve, or both. Pray for help to see your own individual hiding places and why you've chosen to take cover there. I know that can be a difficult thing to see in yourself, but it's an important step that will help you prepare for upcoming paths on our journey.

I promise that if you'll continue to press forward with me down the roads ahead, the things you'll learn and the sights you'll see will help convince your Eve to abandon her secret hideouts for good. As she flees with joy to her Savior's side, you'll hear your heart echo the beautiful words found in the book of Psalms: "Thou art my hiding place" (Psalm 32:7). In the end, there's no better escape in the world for our fallen Eve.

Readings & Reflections

For more on the subject of denial, read through the following scriptures and notice how these people didn't deny their fallen condition but actually acknowledged their sinful state and turned to Christ for redemption:

- Mosiah 4:1–2

- Alma 36:6–21
- Ether 3:1–5

How could these verses apply to the inner workings of your own heart?

For further evidence of this, look at the reaction of some people to Samuel's message in Helaman 16:1. What was it the people *didn't* do?

President Spencer W. Kimball clearly outlined the danger of living in denial:

> Repentance can never come until one has bared his soul and admitted his actions without excuses or rationalizations. He must admit to himself that he has sinned, without the slightest minimization of the offense or rationalizing of its seriousness, or without soft-pedaling its gravity. He must admit that his sin is as big as it really is and not call a pound an ounce. . . .
>
> *But when we attempt to excuse our actions by saying, "This is the way I wish to live" or "I am different" or "God made me this way" or*

"My parents or society are responsible," then we have arrived at a tragic state in our relationship with ourselves and with God.[54]

What personal application can you glean from President Kimball's words?

In Moroni 7:5–9, the prophet specifically outlines what happens when our Adam is busy working while our Eve remains in hiding. Read these verses and consider how it could apply to your personal life.

Let's return to the list of misguided motivations that may be fueling our service. I'll reprint it again here to use as a reference:

- Could we be serving others because we're stuck in the throes of people-pleasing and we've never learned the healthy habit of saying no?

54. Spencer W. Kimball, "The Gospel of Repentance," *Ensign*, Oct. 1982; emphasis added.

- Could we be planning that church activity because we saw it online and thought it was cute, but we never asked the Lord for His guidance and direction?
- Could we be posting spiritual thoughts on social media because we like being seen as a good person and we love all the flattering comments that come as a result?
- Could we be calling it service when we're actually enabling someone's sinful behavior and the Lord would rather have us set some firm but loving boundaries?
- Could we be using our "righteous" efforts to subtly control or manipulate our friends, loved ones, or ward members to bend to our will?

Because these kinds of motivations can live very deep under the surface, I want you to take some time to ponder and pray about what's going on in your own heart. Ask the Lord if there are any false motivations driving your efforts to serve. Like He did with Martha, how do you think Christ could pull your heart out of hiding?

As we conclude our look at both our fig leaf aprons and our hiding places, the following quote from author Colleen Harrison offers us some powerful insight: "Miserable as we like to pretend life makes us, the truth is that it feels pretty comfortable the way it is. All our worries and distractions, our compulsions and obsessions, feel like old friends who seem more familiar than trusting in God."[55]

55. Colleen G. Harrison, *He Did Deliver Me From Bondage* (Hyrum, UT: Windhaven, 2002), 36.

When it comes to your favorite aprons and escapes, would you say they feel more like old friends than undesirable coping mechanisms? Have they become "comfortable" and "familiar" to you? Do you feel like you could never survive without them? If so, why do you think that is?

Response

In what ways are you feeling prompted to respond to the concepts found in this chapter?

8

Our Pointing Finger

We've covered quite a bit of ground over the last few miles. I hope you haven't minded the trip. What's more, I hope you can see how important each of these trails has been for us to explore. I'm praying that your eyes are being opened to new vistas and unique perspectives that have left a lasting impression on your mind and heart. Without this kind of deeply personal exploration, we could never reach the heights waiting for us on this journey. If you'll hang in there just a little longer, I promise that our first glimpse of the summit will soon burst into view.

Let's quickly review the details we've studied so far in our story. We know that after eating the fruit, Adam and Eve tried to clothe themselves with fig leaves, but that didn't work. Then they tried hiding in deeper cover, but the Father knew where they were all along. So at this point in our story, the time of reckoning has finally come. God is ready to put an end to the couple's fruitless games of cover-up and hide and seek.

In Genesis 3:9, we'll hear Him call Adam out of his hiding place. He interviews both the man and the woman, asking if they've eaten the forbidden fruit. Here's how the couple chooses to respond:

Adam: "The woman whom thou gavest to be with me, she gave me of the tree, and I did eat" (Genesis 3:12).

Eve: "The serpent beguiled me, and I did eat" (Genesis 3:13).

Did you notice the similarity in their answers? Adam and Eve both pointed the finger of blame at someone else. It was *her* fault. It was *the serpent's* fault. When coming face to face with the consequences of our actions, do we ever make similar claims?

I'll admit that this very thing happened to me as the Lord continued to unveil the fig leaves and hiding places that were cluttering my fallen heart. I began to point my finger of blame not only at people in my past but also those in my present. Here's a generic look at what I was thinking: "You know, if ________ would just change ________, then I wouldn't be forced to act the way I do. And what about when ________did ________? Most of my aprons and escapes come as a direct result of coping with *their* actions. *They* are the reason I'm like this!"

Before we start talking about how this kind of finger-pointing could fit your own life and your own relationships with others, I want to pause for a minute because this part of our journey stirs up some really sensitive issues. Mortal life on earth is hard, and it's not just because we're dealing with the misery of our own fallen hearts. We also have imperfect family members and friends, and as we live in such close contact with others who are fallen, the consequences of *their* actions at times inflicts a great deal of pain on *us*. I'm talking about heartbreaking trials like abandonment, rejection, humiliation, offense, divorce, betrayal, and abuse. Did you experience any of these things growing up—or perhaps even more recently?

One perceptive writer calls these trials the "arrows" of life. He notes that they pierce us all at one time or another, whether we like it or not. See if author Brent Curtis's insight reaches into the deepest places of your heart as it did into mine:

> At some point we all face the same decision—what will we do with the Arrows we've known? Maybe a better way to say it is, what have they tempted us to do? However they come to us, whether through a loss we experience as abandonment or some deep violation we feel

> as abuse, their message is always the same: Kill your heart. Divorce it, neglect it, run from it, or indulge it with some anesthetic (our various addictions). Think of how you've handled the affliction that has pierced your own heart. How did the Arrows come to you? Where did they land? Are they still there? What have you done as a result?
>
> To say we all face a decision when we're pierced by an Arrow is misleading. It makes the process sound so rational, as though we have the option of coolly assessing the situation and choosing a logical response. Life isn't like that—the heart cannot be managed in a detached sort of way (certainly not when we are young, when some of the most defining Arrows strike). It feels more like an ambush and our response is at a gut level. We may never put words to it. Our deepest convictions are formed without conscious effort, but the effect is a shift deep in our soul. Commitments form never to be in that position again, never to know that sort of pain again. The result is an approach to life that we often call our personality. If you'll listen carefully to your life, you may begin to see how it has been shaped by the unique Arrows you've known and the particular convictions you've embraced as a result.[56]

Oh, the suffering these horrible arrows have caused. As we've found ourselves let down or rejected, abandoned or abused, disappointed or mistreated, is it any wonder that we end up blaming? Because others' actions have at times left our hearts deeply injured and scarred, it's easy to point our finger at those who either created our suffering or turned a blind eye to it. But regardless of our feelings, the damage is done and our Eve is left with a badly mangled, bruised, or broken heart.

Now, this is where Satan isn't just deceitful and cunning—he's downright mean. As he sees us lying there, wounded and bleeding, he walks to the cupboard, takes out the salt, and proceeds to rub it into each and every mark the arrows hit. "This is all your fault," he whispers. Then, depending on the type of arrow that has struck, he molds additional lies to fit each situation: "If you were good enough or

---

56. Brent Curtis and John Eldredge, *The Sacred Romance: Drawing Closer to the Heart of God* (Nashville, TN: Thomas Nelson, 2001), 27–28.

had tried hard enough, this never would have happened." "Others will always hurt you and leave you and let you down." "You'll never find the love your heart has been searching for." Over and over he taunts us, and in our weakened, traumatized state, we often take it all in.

The minute we accept and embrace the adversary's lies—even if we do it subconsciously—they sink deep into our belief system and we vow never to trust again. Once this happens, our Eve quietly begins to sew a new apron, one she believes will protect her from further pain and vulnerability. Elder Gerald N. Lund describes these fig leaves well:

> Early in our lives, we learn to guard our hearts. It is like we erect a fence around our hearts with a gate in it. No one can enter that gate unless we allow him or her to. . . . [Some] hearts have been so hurt or so deadened by sin that they have an eight-foot chain-link fence topped with razor wire around them. The gate is padlocked and has a large No Trespassing sign on it.[57]

Left unchecked, this chain-link fence not only blocks our hearts from others and from the Lord—it also traps us in feelings of bitterness and resentment. Consumed with animosity toward those who have caused our painful wounds, we wrap ourselves tightly in the apron of unforgiveness. And Satan works very hard to keep us draped in those burdensome fig leaves. He knows that will keep us from receiving Christ's powerful healing.

So in order to counteract the enemy's strategies, the Lord commands us to forgive. There are no exceptions: we're to forgive everyone . . . for everything (see Matthew 18:21–22; Mosiah 26:31; Doctrine and Covenants 64:10). While it may not be too hard to forgive the little blunders, irritations, and mistakes of others, what about devastating, undeserved, life-altering arrows? The ones that hurt so bad we carry the pain of it for years? How can God ask us to forgive when these kinds of arrows ravaged our very souls and left us broken, bleeding, and horribly scarred? Why would a loving Father even ask such a thing?

---

57. Gerald N. Lund, "Opening Our Hearts," *Ensign* or *Liahona*, May 2008, 33.

Without discounting the damage these brutal arrows cause, the truth is that forgiveness is mainly for *us*. The Lord is asking us to release our anger, hurt, and bitterness because He knows that if our hearts remain focused on our own finger-pointing, He can never ignite our spiritually dead Eve. In the words of President Thomas S. Monson, "Blame keeps wounds open. Only forgiveness heals."[58]

However, forgiving doesn't mean we have to say the archer's behavior was okay, or pretend he or she didn't shoot the arrows. Those arrows were real and our Savior knows it. He acknowledges every single wound, no matter how small or hidden, and He promises to make up for all the pain, anguish, and injustice we've experienced throughout our lives. But for now, the only way He can "restore health unto [us], and . . . heal [us] of [our] wounds" (Jeremiah 30:17) is if we choose to forgive. As Catherine Marshall keenly observes, "[Christ] cannot give us that gift [of healing] so long as bitterness and resentment have slammed shut the door of the heart and unforgiveness stands sentinel at the door lest love open and enter. *Forgiveness is the precondition of love.*"[59]

As I reviewed the handful of people my Eve was pointing her finger at, I knew releasing that resentment was a good place for me to begin. But then I was prompted to pray that my eyes would be opened to *all* unkind feelings hiding in the depths of my fallen heart. As I pondered and prayed over the issue for several days, I was shocked as the Spirit uncovered more than twenty different names. I was doing way more finger-pointing than I even realized! What surprised me the most about this new list was the fact that I didn't hold any outright animosity for most of these people. If truth be told, I'd simply judged them unfairly or labeled each of them according to my own limited perception. Unfortunately, those labels pushed their way to center stage every time I encountered them—and I never even thought twice about it.

---

58. Thomas S. Monson, "The Peril of Hidden Wedges," *Ensign*, July 2007, 6.

59. Catherine Marshall, *Something More: In Search of a Deeper Faith* (New York: McGraw Hill, 1974), 39; emphasis added.

I'm sure most of us have experienced the same thing at one time or another. Without even realizing it, we label this person as "strange" and that person as "difficult to deal with." We think a certain ward member is weird and the guy down the street is annoying. We judge our extended family, our coworkers, and the people in the grocery store based on what we think they're doing wrong or on some flaw we see in their character (without even considering our own personal flaws and weaknesses). Unfortunately, these feelings grow stronger and stronger inside our heart and limit our ability to live in peace and love with those around us.

President Dieter F. Uchtdorf offers this insight about the labels we tend to place on other people:

> We can so clearly and easily see the harmful results that come when others judge and hold grudges. And we certainly don't like it when people judge us. But when it comes to our own prejudices and grievances, we too often justify our anger as righteous and our judgment as reliable and only appropriate. Though we cannot look into another's heart, we assume that we know a bad motive or even a bad person when we see one. We make exceptions when it comes to our own bitterness because we feel that, in our case, we have all the information we need to hold someone else in contempt.[60]

Surprisingly, that's the very thing Jesus's disciples did while traveling with their beloved Master. Here's how the Lord describes it in the Doctrine and Covenants:

> My disciples, in days of old, sought occasion against one another and forgave not one another in their hearts; and for this evil they were afflicted and sorely chastened.
>
> Wherefore, I say unto you, that ye ought to forgive one another; for he that forgiveth not his brother his trespasses standeth condemned before the Lord; for there remaineth in him the greater sin.
>
> I, the Lord, will forgive whom I will forgive, but of you it is required to forgive all men.

---

60. Dieter F. Uchtdorf, "The Merciful Obtain Mercy," *Ensign* or *Liahona*, May 2012, 70.

> And ye ought to say in your hearts—let God judge between me and thee, and reward thee according to thy deeds. (Doctrine and Covenants 64:8–11)

The bottom line is this: even if someone else really is strange or obnoxious or difficult to deal with, we still shouldn't hold these kinds of negative feelings in our hearts. As former patriarch of the Church, Eldred G. Smith explained, "When you have ill feelings toward anyone, you have an uneasiness in [their] presence. You will go out of your way to avoid [them]. *You become, to a degree, mentally ill.*"[61] So the only way "the peace of God" can "keep [our] hearts and minds through Christ Jesus" (Philippians 4:7) is to let go of *all* unkind feelings we have for others, no matter how inconsequential, trivial, or justified those feelings may be.

Of course, I'll be the first to admit that letting go isn't easy, especially if our wounds are many and deep. Thankfully, the latter part of our journey will teach us how to cast off the fig leaves of unforgiveness, prejudice, and judgment with the help of our Savior. But for now, our objective is simply to uncover all resentment and hostility still living in our hearts and acknowledge that we can't be healed as long as these feelings remain.

With that said, our path is about to ascend to even higher ground. You see, as I continued to work through my tendency to point my finger in blame, the Lord awakened me to an entirely new perspective—one I'd never even considered before. It seems I had a way of blaming that had nothing to do with those who'd wounded, offended, or even annoyed me. Instead, my accusations at times turned to my greatest supporters and companions. But why would I accuse the ones I treasured most? It was to charge them with not doing enough to heal the emotional pain I felt as a result of the Fall. Let me give you an example of what I mean.

One discouraging evening many years ago, I felt like my heart was sinking fast into a pit of frustration and despair. While it's obvious to me now that the cause of my misery was a fallen, wounded, and

---

61. Eldred G. Smith, in Conference Report, Apr. 1961, 68–69; emphasis added.

spiritually dead heart, at the time I didn't see it that way. All I knew was that I felt unhappy and depressed, and I needed help. But rather than me turning to the One "with healing in his wings" (3 Nephi 25:2), the enemy crept in and persuaded me to blame my suffering on someone I dearly loved: my poor, unsuspecting husband. By stirring up the blame and accusation inside of me, Satan convinced me that my husband, Greg, held the medicine my wounded heart needed and that he was being negligent in applying it. Out my pointing finger finally came.

This kind of scenario usually led me to sit Greg down for "the talk." I'm sure other wives know the kind of conversation I mean. It's the one where I'd tell my husband all the things he needed to change to make me happy. Where I'd lay out step by step exactly how he could heal my suffering heart, only I'd do so by wrapping it up in the language of my "needs." It's clear to me now that this kind of discussion doesn't fit the kind of love described in Moroni 7:45—the "charity [that] suffereth long, and is kind, and envieth not, and is not puffed up, seeketh not her own, [and] is not easily provoked." But in that moment, none of that mattered. I'd been blinded by the influence of the adversary, and I felt completely justified in laying my wounded heart's demands at my husband's feet.

Only this time, before I had a chance to launch into my carefully prepared speech, an overwhelming prompting came with great force into my mind. It was as if the Lord took me by the shoulders, looked me squarely in the eyes, and said quite boldly, "Jaci, you will not say one word to Greg. Period."

I didn't like that direction at all, and I quickly began arguing right back in my head. You know all that stuff about how you should talk things out in marriage and never go to bed upset? I had issues I wanted to address! I felt like I would explode if I didn't vent! But the impression continued: "Not this time. I will not allow you to place such a heavy burden on your husband."

Sadly, that was not what I wanted to hear. I wanted to blame Greg. I wanted it to be his responsibility to give my Eve the love she needed. After all, wasn't that his job as my husband? Wasn't he supposed to make me feel better and heal my hurting heart? But regardless of my unruly feelings, the Lord was unyielding in His rebuke.

As I began to calm down and pray for greater understanding, He quietly reminded me that once again I was looking for healing somewhere other than Him. At that moment, I felt His gentle whisper: "Jaci, I know your heart is suffering. I know how desperate you are to be filled and renewed. But Greg isn't your Deliverer. I'm the only One who can truly rescue you from all the difficult effects of the Fall."

With that thought, some favorite words from Isaiah came to mind: "Fear thou not; for I am with thee: be not dismayed; for I am thy God: I will strengthen thee; yea, I will help thee; yea, I will uphold thee with the right hand of my righteousness" (Isaiah 41:10).

His promises were all right there in black and white. Yet in my pain, I'd reached instead for a very sweet but very human, mortal person as my savior. And it was causing me to worship the wrong source for help and relief. It was an eye-opening revelation that I've never forgotten to this day.

As I spent more time studying this concept, I was surprised to find that the Lord taught this same principle during His earthly ministry. Listen, for instance, to the following verse from the gospel of Luke, paying close attention to the language Christ used as He introduced this doctrine to His would-be disciples: "If any man come to me, and hate not his father, and mother, and wife, and children, and brethren, and sisters, yea, and his own life also, he cannot be my disciple" (Luke 14:26).

It might come as a relief to know that Joseph Smith retranslated this verse for us. Seeing the way the scripture is phrased, you'd think Joseph would replace the word *hate* since it seems so opposite from the strong family focus in the Church today. Jesus wouldn't really use the word *hate* when referring to such close family members, would He? To find out, look up Luke 14:26 and check out the footnote. Not only does the word *hate* stay put, but Joseph went to the trouble to add *husband* to the list of family members we must "hate" in order to be the Lord's disciples. Why was such an addition important? What in the world is up with this scripture?

Here's what Elder James E. Talmage had to say about this particular reference: "Literal hatred toward one's family was not specified as a condition of discipleship; indeed a man who indulges hatred or any other evil passion is a subject for repentance and reformation."[62]

So how do we interpret this perplexing little verse? I think footnote *a* is an incredibly helpful cross-reference. In Matthew 10:37, it says, "He that loveth father or mother *more than me* is not worthy of me: and he that loveth son or daughter *more than me* is not worthy of me" (emphasis added). Here we see that in commanding us to "hate" all others (especially our closest loved ones), we're not being asked to literally hate our family. Instead, we're simply being invited to focus all our worship on the Lord Jesus Christ, for He alone can heal us and deliver us from the Fall. He alone can break down that gate around our hearts and rescue us from our "state of endless misery and woe" (Alma 9:11). His love is the incomparable balm that will make us happy.

There is no other Deliverer for us. Not even the sweet love of a spouse, parent, child, or friend. In the words of King Benjamin, "I say unto you, that there shall be *no other name given* . . . whereby salvation can come unto the children of men, only in and through the name of Christ, the Lord Omnipotent" (Mosiah 3:17; emphasis added). That even includes the names of our closest and most precious loved ones.

I believe that's the very thing Christ was trying to teach the woman at the well in John 4. Remember, this woman had gone through five husbands and was now living with a sixth man (see verse 18). Could it be that her heart had been wounded? And yet where was she looking for healing? It seems that in her desperate search for happiness, no man could give enough, so she continued to move on, continually searching for one who could make her fallen heart whole. As the Lord sat before the woman, amazingly He didn't rebuke her for her actions, and He didn't tell her to get her act together either. What Jesus did, which is so characteristic of how He works, was to acknowledge her need—her fallen heart's misery and pain. He simply said, "Come.

---

62. James E. Talmage, *Jesus the Christ* (1916), 421.

You're looking for living water in the wrong place. I can give you all you'll ever need! Come!" (my own paraphrasing from John 4:5–26).

Amazingly, this same offer is extended to each of us, for no matter what our hearts are aching for—no matter how we've been offended, betrayed, or injured, and no matter how many arrows have pierced our fallen hearts—Jesus has the perfect medicine. But the only way we can receive His ministering is to surrender our Eve's tendency to judge, accuse, and blame. Whether we're pointing in anger at those who have irritated or wounded us, or we're pointing at our loved ones for not doing enough to help, the only way we can move forward is by surrendering our tendency to condemn and blame. Only by laying all accusation and judgment at His feet can we learn how to deal with those feelings in a way that will finally bring true restoration and healing.

As we spend some time pondering how this detail in Adam and Eve's story can apply to our personal lives, I want you to consider one final way we can blame—and it can be a pretty tough one to contemplate. What if, like Job, your most painful arrows seem to have come not from others but from *God Himself* (perhaps through the death of a spouse or a debilitating illness)? What if the place your finger really wants to point in blame is up toward heaven?

Just like we talked about earlier with the arrows, life brings many kinds of pain and suffering, and it's often hard to understand why the Lord allows us to go through such difficult trials. We may harbor resentment toward Him because, in our minds, He could have changed our circumstances. He could have made that disease go away. He could have kept that loved one alive, or stopped that financial crisis from happening, or prevented that child from making such tragic, life-altering choices. If He truly loves us, we wonder, why doesn't He always act like it? Why are His ways so confusing and hard to understand?

The longer we shake our fist toward heaven, though, the longer we'll stay wrapped up in the fig leaves of accusation and resentment. Part of our forgiveness, then, may also involve working through any negative feelings we have for the Lord—especially if those feelings have been quietly brewing underneath the surface and we haven't even acknowledged that they're there. I know these are complicated issues, and they're generally not resolved quickly or easily, but our goal is to open our eyes to every type of bitterness that exists deep in our soul. Our Savior really can soothe our hurts and help us forgive, even if some of those feelings have been directed at Him.

With that said, I have some great news for you. After hiking several steep and rocky sections, we're now just steps away from an entirely new and life-changing view. If you remember, we started this part of our journey by asking ourselves, "Where does my trail lead?" The goal was to look beyond our Adam's outward busyness and focus instead on the *love, service,* and *worship* of our Eve. By now, I hope it's evident that each of us has at times turned our heart from Jesus Christ in an attempt to manage the effects of the Fall on our own. Considering all the aprons we've created, the hiding places we've run to, and the people we've blamed, we can see how often our hearts have led us in the wrong direction. Just like Adam and Eve in the garden, our trail has at times taken us far away from the Lord. Of our own volition, we've left Him and developed our own coping mechanisms, not only through our Adam but also through our Eve.

But rather than feeling hopeless about that or flooding ourselves with waves of guilt and shame, let's stop and take a deep breath because our quest is about to take a whole new turn. While it was important for us to explore Adam and Eve's story and its personal application to our lives—especially the complicated dynamics of our heart that have come because of the Fall—we've now arrived at a whole new point in our journey. Put simply, we're about to feast our eyes on one of the most spectacular landscapes we've ever encountered. It's a transcendent view that will change the entire course of our journey. So make sure to finish working through any self-evaluation that's still needed on this path, then lift your eyes heavenward—because the panorama we're about to encounter will make all that difficult trekking completely worth it.

Readings & Reflections

I think it's important to work through all the different arrows you've experienced throughout your life. Take some time to write about how others have hurt you, insulted you, abused you, rejected you, or taken advantage of you, and evaluate how you've coped with each of those painful wounds. Now read Doctrine and Covenants 64:8–11 again, only this time make it personal. In light of your wounds, how does your heart respond to the Lord's counsel in these verses?

The dictionary says that to *resent* someone is "to feel or show displeasure or indignation . . . from a sense of injury or insult,"[63] and to *forgive* means "to cease to feel resentment against."[64] How do you think you can release all your displeasure, indignation, and resentment toward those who have wounded you and actually begin to love them instead?

63. *Dictionary.com*, s.v. "resent," accessed Apr. 1, 2023, https://www.dictionary.com/browse/resent.

64. See also *Dictionary.com*, s.v. "forgive," accessed Apr. 1, 2023, https://www.dictionary.com/browse/forgive.

Listen to this powerful perspective on forgiveness from President Dieter F. Uchtdorf:

> "Yes," you might say, "I would be willing to love my enemies—if only they were willing to do the same."
>
> But that doesn't really matter, does it? We are responsible for our own discipleship, and it has little—if anything—to do with the way others treat us. We obviously hope that they will be understanding and charitable in return, but our love for them is independent of their feelings toward us.
>
> Perhaps our effort to love our enemies will soften their hearts and influence them for good. Perhaps it will not. But that does not change our commitment to follow Jesus Christ.
>
> So, as members of the Church of Jesus Christ, we will love our enemies.
>
> We will overcome anger or hate.
>
> We will fill our hearts with love for all of God's children.
>
> We will reach out to bless others and minister to them—even those who might "despitefully use [us] and persecute [us]."[65]

How does your heart respond to this quote? If you're struggling with his words, why do you think that is?

65. Dieter F. Uchtdorf, "Three Sisters," *Ensign* or *Liahona*, Nov. 2017, 18.

Next, consider this perspective from Elder David E. Sorenson:

> President Brigham Young once compared being offended to a poisonous snakebite. He said that "there are two courses of action to follow when one is bitten by a rattlesnake. One may, in anger, fear, or vengefulness, pursue the creature and kill it. Or he may make full haste to get the venom out of his system." He said, "If we pursue the latter course we will likely survive, but if we attempt to follow the former, we may not be around long enough to finish it."[66]

In what ways could we have the venom of unforgiveness flowing through our system? Assess how those feelings of "anger, fear, or vengefulness" have harmed you deep in your heart.

____

____

____

____

____

____

____

____

Joseph Smith once said, "If you will throw a cloak of charity over my sins, I will over yours—for charity covereth a multitude of sins."[67] To go along with that, study the following scriptures on forgiveness and note your impressions:

- Matthew 18:23–35
- Mark 11:25–26
- Doctrine and Covenants 82:1–3

Now ask yourself: who is it that I need to forgive? Allow the Spirit to help you make your own personal list. Perhaps you too will be surprised at some of the names that turn up.

---

66. David E. Sorenson, "Forgiveness Will Change Bitterness to Love," *Ensign* or *Liahona*, May 2003, 11.

67. *Teachings of the Prophet Joseph Smith*, sel. Joseph Fielding Smith (1976), 193.

For further study, I highly recommend President James E. Faust's powerful talk from the April 2007 general conference called "The Healing Power of Forgiveness." (I wanted to include a quote here, but I couldn't choose just one!)

Response

In what ways are you feeling prompted to respond to the concepts found in this chapter?

The Secret of Our Heartlight

"He is the light and the life of the world; yea, a light that is endless, that can never be darkened; yea, and also a life which is endless, that there can be no more death."

(Mosiah 16:9)

9

If You Only Knew

Earlier, we touched briefly on the Savior's encounter with the woman at the well. It's a story most of us are familiar with. Yet as simple as this passage may seem, the truth is that it actually contains a mystery—one so great that it will open up a vision unlike anything we've ever experienced. If you're willing, I'd like to return to this insightful little tale and uncover this mystery so its jaw-dropping beauty will begin to unfold before our view.

The story is unusual right from the start. For one thing, Jewish men never spoke to Samaritans—especially the women—since they believed the people to be lowly apostates who'd intermarried with Gentiles and corrupted the true form of worship. So imagine this woman's surprise when the Lord not only singled her out but went so far as to ask her for a drink of water. With what I'm guessing were raised eyebrows, she warily replied, "How is it that thou, being a Jew, askest drink of me, which am a woman of Samaria? for the Jews have no dealings with the Samaritans" (John 4:9).

I love how her candor didn't ruffle Jesus for a second. I can just picture Him leaning forward with a twinkle in His eye and offering a statement that's absolutely loaded with meaning and significance: "If thou knewest the gift of God, and who it is that saith to thee, Give me to drink; thou wouldest have asked of him, and he would have given thee living water" (verse 10). Then, to make things even more interesting, He topped it off with this little beauty: "But whosoever drinketh of the water that I shall give him shall never thirst; but the water that I shall give him shall be in him a well of water springing up into everlasting life" (verse 14).

If you're wondering what's so mysterious about Christ's words to the woman, we could point to phrases like "the gift of God" and "everlasting life"—phrases that we'll eventually learn to see in a whole new light. But for now, I want to latch on to the three little words that came out of Jesus's mouth right from the start. "If thou knewest," He said. *If you only knew.* It's as if Jesus was telling the woman, "If you only knew who I was and what I am offering you, you wouldn't be raising your eyebrows at me or questioning me . . . you'd be *asking* me. Perhaps even *begging* me. And I would happily give you absolutely everything you ask."

If she only knew.

I'll admit that in earlier years, I read this story almost with an attitude of overconfidence. I was positive that unlike the woman, *I* knew what Jesus was talking about. To me, it seemed like He was trying to teach her the gospel. The exchange appeared quite straightforward—nothing miraculous or unusual, just an invitation from the Master to learn basic truths I thought I already understood. I never dreamed there might be more packed into this little dialogue than I'd ever thought possible, truths that would rock my world in ways I can hardly find words to describe.

If I only knew.

My light bulb moment finally came several years ago while I was serving as the Sunday school teacher for the sixteen- to eighteen-year-old class. It was then that I made a discovery that completely altered not just my view of the woman at the well but my entire understanding of Jesus Christ and what He came to offer us. We were studying the New Testament that year, so I was spending a great deal of time immersed in the Gospels. And for some reason, the more I learned about John, the more I felt drawn to his writings. As I returned again and again to the Apostle's words, I noticed a theme running like a thread through his entire book.

Curious, I grabbed a green marking pen, and starting in chapter one, I slowly worked my way through the book of John, highlighting only those verses that included this one theme. By the time I was finished, I had green markings in almost every chapter. The idea seemed to be integrated into nearly everything the Apostle wrote.

Let me show you a few verses and you'll easily pick up the theme:

- "He that believeth on the Son hath everlasting life" (John 3:36).
- "He that heareth my word, and believeth on him that sent me, hath everlasting life" (John 5:24).
- "And ye will not come to me, that ye might have life" (John 5:40).
- "And Jesus said unto them, I am the bread of life" (John 6:35).
- "He that believeth on me hath everlasting life" (John 6:47).
- "I am come that they might have life" (John 10:10).
- "My sheep hear my voice . . . and I give unto them eternal life" (John 10:27–28).
- "I am the resurrection, and the life" (John 11:25).

I'll stop there, but you get the idea. The beloved Apostle's message is clear: eternal, everlasting life is found in Jesus Christ. But as obvious as that may seem, I was only just beginning to understand what John was trying to say.

One morning, green marking pen still in hand, I sensed something different from the Lord than I'd ever felt before. He almost seemed *excited* to teach me that day. And with that, He immediately had my undivided attention. As I opened my New Testament, I was led to another of John's verses on eternal life, only this time the Apostle approached the subject in a completely different way. Directing his words to those filled with hatred, John declared, "Whosoever hateth his brother is a murderer: and ye know that no murderer hath *eternal life abiding in him*" (1 John 3:15; emphasis added).

"Eternal life abiding in him." The phrase definitely caught my eye. Understanding the "abiding" part came easy because Elder Jeffrey R. Holland had already taught me that "to abide" means "to remain [or] stay," with the idea of permanence also being implied: to "stay—but stay forever."[68] But what intrigued me most was the "in him" part of the verse. That's because I'd never thought of eternal life as something *in* me. Instead, I viewed it as the kind of life I would live with God after my resurrection, as the reward waiting in the celestial kingdom if I proved faithful here on earth. However, after looking again through John's chapters, I discovered that the Savior Himself also spoke of this life as something "in you" (John 6:53).

As I continued to check out different footnotes and cross-references, I noticed that John also used an interesting verb tense when he spoke of eternal life. Four different times the Apostle claimed, "He that believeth on the Son *hath* everlasting life" (John 3:36; see also John 5:24; 6:47, 54). Instead of saying that believers "will have" eternal life someday after they die, John used the present tense of the verb—a Greek word that literally means to have, hold, or possess.[69] I even checked other translations and they all reflected that same present tense. In these verses, John seemed to be implying that everlasting life is something we can possess right here and now—long before our future resurrection.

At that point, I decided to look up some synonyms for *eternal.* As I read words like perpetual, ceaseless, endless, and enduring,[70] I began to wonder if eternal life was something that could exist inside me in a way that was unceasing or endless. With that new thought stirring around my head, I came across Doctrine and Covenants 19. There the Lord talks about punishment for the wicked, but He also unveils

---

68. Jeffrey R. Holland, "Abide in Me," *Ensign* or *Liahona*, May 2004, 32.

69. "2192. echó," BibleHub, accessed Apr. 1, 2023, https://biblehub.com/greek/2192.htm.

70. *Dictionary.com*, s.v. "eternal," accessed Apr. 1, 2023, https://www.dictionary.com/browse/eternal.

a secret about the words *endless* and *eternal* that went like a lightning bolt straight through my heart:

> Nevertheless, it is not written that there shall be no end to this torment, but it is written endless torment. . . .
>
> Wherefore, I will explain unto you this mystery, for it is meet unto you to know even as mine apostles. . . .
>
> For, behold, the mystery of godliness, how great is it! For, behold, *I am endless*, and the punishment which is given from my hand is endless punishment, for *Endless is my name*. Wherefore—
>
> Eternal punishment is God's punishment.
>
> Endless punishment is God's punishment. (Doctrine and Covenants 19:6, 8, 10–12; emphasis added)

These verses shifted my entire mental paradigm. If the words *endless* and *eternal* are just another way of describing who Christ is—if these concepts can actually represent *His name*—then that means eternal life isn't just perpetual or ceaseless—it's a way of describing *Jesus's* life. *The very life He possesses deep within.* Suddenly eternal life became much more than just a future state—much more than my limited mind had even begun to comprehend. And I finally began to understand what John was trying to say.

Throughout his entire Gospel, the beloved Apostle seemed to be testifying that Jesus Christ holds the power—while we still live in mortality—*to bring our fallen, captive, spiritually dead hearts back to life*!

Stop and take it in for a minute. Over and over, John describes eternal life not only as a reward for our *future* but also as a gift for our *present*; not only as exaltation in the life to come but also as an enduring sense of life that can live *inside us* here and now. I could hardly process the enormity of this life-changing truth. In essence, John was saying that *Jesus can fill us with the same kind of life that He possesses*—a perpetual, light-filled life that will completely eradicate all traces of our spiritual death. I was truly blown away by the possibilities of such a glorious doctrine. It was as if a whole new room opened up in my gospel understanding, and it was a space I desperately wanted to explore.

In the weeks following my discovery, I spent as much time as I could in the scriptures. I wanted to see if I could find this concept anywhere else in the standard works. While many references did refer to eternal life as exaltation in the celestial kingdom, with the Lord's urging, I continued to search with greater intensity. To my delight, I discovered John's message in several different places in the Book of Mormon.

The first example is found in Alma 22. There Aaron introduced the gospel to the Lamanite king, and one of the first things he did was explain "the fall of man" and our resulting "carnal state," as well as the "plan of redemption, which was prepared from the foundation of the world, through Christ" (verse 13). This piqued the King's interest, and he asked Aaron in verse 15, "What shall I do that I may have this *eternal life* of which thou hast spoken?" (emphasis added). But he didn't then say, "That I may live forever with God after I die." Listen to the way he clarified what he was asking for: "Yea, what shall I do that I may be *born of God*, having this *wicked spirit rooted out of my breast,* and *receive his Spirit*, that I may be *filled with joy?"* (verse 15; emphasis added).

I think it's intriguing that what the king wanted was to have the "wicked spirit rooted out of [his] breast." He was hoping that once that happened, his heart would not only be "filled with joy" but also with "eternal life." Through such a request, the Lamanite leader seemed to be hungering for the same thing John portrayed—for a new, abiding sense of life to ignite his spiritually dead heart, causing him to inwardly become "born of God."

As I continued to study, I learned that Aaron wasn't the only one of Mosiah's sons who understood this view of eternal life. To my surprise, I also found the same idea woven into Ammon's teachings. Only this time, the account spelled out John's message with a clarity and richness that took my breath away.

If you're familiar with Ammon's missionary story, you'll remember that after he shared the gospel message with Lamoni, the young Lamanite king cried out to God for mercy (see Alma 18:41). Immediately following his plea, he fell unconscious. We're then given a beautiful description of what happened to Lamoni's heart during this pivotal experience:

> For . . . king Lamoni was under the power of God; . . . the dark veil of unbelief was being cast away from his mind, and the light which did light up his mind, which was the light of the glory of God, which was a marvelous light of his goodness—yea, this light had infused such joy into his soul, the cloud of darkness having been dispelled, and that *the light of everlasting life was lit up in his soul*, yea, . . . this had overcome his natural frame, and he was carried away in God. (Alma 19:6; emphasis added)

I think this is one of the most mind-blowing verses ever recorded in the pages of scripture. Note that everlasting life wasn't reserved for after Lamoni died. Amazingly, it was "lit up in his soul" right that very minute! In fact, it "infused such joy" into Lamoni that it "[overcame] his natural frame, and he was carried away in God."

Just imagine what happened to the king during this life-altering experience. As the flame of everlasting life struck his spiritually dead heart, it ignited the depths of his soul with heavenly light and life. In that moment, eternal life finally lived *in* Lamoni, just like John promised in the New Testament. He was born again. No longer spiritually dead, his soul was infused with a perpetual sense of life springing up deep within him. I believe this is the most awe-inspiring gift we could ever be offered through the power of our Savior's Atonement.

With all these examples to support John's message of eternal life in us, I have to add one more that almost made me jump out of my chair in Relief Society the day I saw it. It came as we were discussing the teachings of Joseph Smith. As I scanned the quotes included in the lesson, one simple prayer from Joseph suddenly lit up the page almost as if in neon: "O Thou, who seest and knowest the hearts of all men . . . look down upon Thy servant Joseph at this time; . . . and *let the lamp of eternal life be lit up in his heart, never to be taken away.*"[71] I could hardly believe it. In this short, one-sentence prayer,

---

71. *Teachings of Presidents of the Church: Joseph Smith* (2007), 131; emphasis added.

Joseph Smith described eternal life the same way John and the sons of Mosiah did—as an internal flame that can be "lit up in his heart." He was pleading for eternal life to abide *in* him, "never to be taken away."

To me, this compelling evidence from both the scriptures and a modern-day prophet reveals that there's an inner flame that's only possible through Jesus Christ. It's a spiritual awakening that can happen right now in our everyday experience. As the Lord ignites the lamp of everlasting life in our heart, He will revive our spiritually dead Eve. And with that, we'll truly be born again through the power of our Savior. Like Lamoni, we too will have "the cloud of darkness . . . dispelled" and experience "the light of the glory of God," an incredible heartlight that nothing in this world can ever dim.

In fact, I believe this inner heartlight is exactly what Jesus was offering to the woman at the well. If you remember, He told her (speaking of one who follows Him), "The water that I shall give him shall be *in him* a well of water springing up into *everlasting life*" (John 4:14; emphasis added). I'd read that verse countless times over the years, but I'd never noticed that the "everlasting life" He offered would be springing up *in me.* Again, not after I die but *inside my heart* right now in my mortal experience. It's a whole new way to view the conversation between Christ and the woman—one that should ignite our desire to receive the very same gift He was holding out to her.

The most amazing thing about this heartlight is that it's exactly what our Eve has been searching for all along. In a desperate attempt to escape our fallenness, we've tried making fig leaf aprons and we've run to all kinds of different hiding places to make ourselves feel better. But we've forgotten that the Lord knows all about our fallen condition, and He's ready and waiting to cover our nakedness. As we're told in Genesis 3:21, "Unto Adam also and to his wife did the Lord God make coats of skins, and clothed them." How does He do this? While there may be many ways to answer that, I love the way Paul describes it: "For we that are in this tabernacle do groan, being burdened: not for that we would be unclothed, but *clothed upon*, that mortality might be swallowed up *of life*" (2 Corinthians 5:4; emphasis added).

In our spiritual deadness, what we need most is life. Perpetual, continual, everlasting, never-ending life. And we don't just need it after we die. We need eternal life *inside us* right here and now. To fill our emptiness. To make our fallen hearts whole. To ignite our inner flame with more fire than we ever thought possible. In fact, this gift is the entire focus of our journey—the summit we've been pushing so hard for this entire time. In the beautiful words of President Dieter F. Uchtdorf, "It is our quest to seek the Lord *until His light of everlasting life burns brightly within us*."[72]

If you're wondering like I did what it feels like to experience this glorious heartlight, I found that the scriptures actually go to great lengths to describe it. To illustrate, let's look at a wonderful little metaphor that shows up in both the Book of Mormon and the Doctrine and Covenants. I believe this metaphor reveals exactly what it's like to be spiritually reborn and lit up with the light of everlasting life. In order to grasp the imagery, we're going look at some verses that describe the lives of little children. As you read each reference, I want you to try to see the words differently—to again think outside the box. By reading between the lines, we'll discover how these verses apply not only to our little ones but also to our own individual hearts:

- "And little children also have eternal life" (Mosiah 15:25).
- "Little children are whole . . . and partakers of salvation" (Moroni 8:8, 17).
- "Little children are alive in Christ, . . . for they are all alive in him because of his mercy" (Moroni 8:12, 19).
- "Little children are redeemed . . . through mine Only Begotten" (Doctrine and Covenants 29:46).
- "Little children are holy, being sanctified through the atonement of Jesus Christ" (Doctrine and Covenants 74:7).

First, consider the way each reference is phrased. Moroni tells us that little children *are* whole and they *are* alive in Christ, not that they *will be* these things someday. We know children are assured exaltation

72. Dieter F. Uchtdorf, "Bearers of Heavenly Light," *Ensign* or *Liahona*, Nov. 2017, 81; emphasis added.

if they pass away in childhood,[73] but that's not what's being taught here. To me, the language used in these verses doesn't refer to the future state of little children but to their present condition while in mortality. When Mosiah says they *have* eternal life, he seems to be joining John, Aaron, and Ammon in talking about an internal kind of life that can be possessed right here and now.

If we take these scriptures as they're written, we learn that through the Atonement of Jesus Christ, young children enjoy hearts that are sanctified, holy, redeemed, and whole—or in other words, filled to the brim with everlasting life. In short, the little ones scampering happily under our feet provide a walking, talking picture of an ignited heart, of what it looks like and feels like to be "alive in Christ" through the amazing power of His redemption.

Just spend a few minutes with a small child and this truth will quickly reveal itself. You'll soon see that a child's heart is vibrantly alive—alive with laughter, alive with hope, alive with faith, alive with enthusiasm, and alive with love. Rather than exhibiting signs of depression, cynicism, or stress, young children live unencumbered by life's demands and unhindered by the heavy mantle of anxiety we adults so often bear. Wrapped in a sense of wonder, they find delight in simple things like a bug, a flower, or the feel of the breeze. With the dawning of each new day, they eagerly throw themselves into the magic of childhood discovery and live each day to its absolute fullest. When was the last time your life could be described that way?

Now, I know little children aren't perfect and they sometimes display a nature that is more selfish or disobedient than sanctified, redeemed, and holy. But Jesus gives us this explanation in the Book of Mormon: "Listen to the words of Christ, your Redeemer, your Lord and your God. Behold . . . little children are whole, for they are not capable of committing sin; wherefore *the curse of Adam is taken from them in me, that it hath no power over them*" (Moroni 8:8; emphasis added).

---

73. This is a doctrine that's been firmly established in modern-day scripture. For example, see Moroni 8:4–26 and Doctrine and Covenants 137:10.

King Benjamin also explained, "And even if it were possible that little children could sin they could not be saved; but I say unto you they are blessed; for behold, *as in Adam, or by nature, they fall, even so the blood of Christ atoneth for their sins*" (Mosiah 3:16; emphasis added).

So even though small children are subject to the Fall (and the natural man) just like the rest of us, the scriptures tell us that they're automatically redeemed through the Atonement of Jesus Christ. As a result, they don't have to live with the effects of spiritual death, which leaves their hearts filled to overflowing with everlasting life. And the same thing can happen to each of us. Once we've been spiritually reborn through the Lord's atoning power, the "curse of Adam" (Moroni 8:8) will be removed from our fallen hearts, and just like the happy little children in our midst, we too will finally be "alive in Christ" (Moroni 8:12). We too will be alive with laughter, alive with hope, alive with faith, alive with enthusiasm, and alive with love. It's a gift available to all through the Lord Jesus Christ. Through Him, we really can live with a heart as vibrant, full, and alive as that of a child.

It's difficult to put into words how much this beautiful doctrine means to me. For many years, my heart has battled feelings of burnout, restlessness, stress, frustration, and unhappiness. During one particularly challenging season, I remember writing in my journal that no matter how hard I tried, it felt like I couldn't get my inner pilot light relit. While it helped to learn that my emptiness came as a result of my spiritual death, still, I didn't think there was much I could do but continue to endure it. Then John came, blazing a trail of eternal life that filtered into the farthest reaches of my mind and heart. Suddenly, an intense desire to obtain the lamp of everlasting life began to stir within me. If a spiritually dead heart could be brought back to life—if Lamoni, Lamoni's father, John, and Joseph Smith had all experienced it—then it was possible for me too. Any chance you're feeling the same way?

If so, you need to know that we've reached a critical point in our journey. With such an extraordinary landscape in view, we must carefully consider what to do next because eternal life doesn't come automatically. There are still several pathways left to travel before we can experience this magnificent heartlight for ourselves. If it's okay with you, I'd like to pick up the pace because there's so much still waiting to be discovered.

READINGS & REFLECTIONS

Read and study the following verses and see if they take on new meaning if we define eternal life not only as our ultimate reward in the celestial kingdom but also as a lamp of everlasting life that can ignite our hearts right here and now:

- John 10:10
- 2 Nephi 9:39
- Jacob 6:11
- Alma 5:28, 34 (notice the word *hath* in verse 28)
- Helaman 8:15
- Doctrine and Covenants 11:7 (*hath* is used in this verse as well)
- Doctrine and Covenants 18:8
- Doctrine and Covenants 42:61
- Moses 5:11

What impressions came as you read those verses through this new lens?

____

____

____

____

____

____

____

____

In my personal study, I discovered that John also uses another word to describe a heart being lit up with everlasting life. He calls it being "quickened." First, look up John 5:21 and check footnote *b*.

What does the word *quickened* mean in the original Greek? For the same idea, see Colossians 2:13, footnote *a*. What kind of death and rebirth (or coming to life) is this verse referring to?

To relate the concept of quickening to a heart brought back to life, read the following:

- John 6:63
- Romans 8:4–13
- Ephesians 2:1–7
- Doctrine and Covenants 88:49–50

How do you think these scriptures illustrate the inner heartlight that's possible through Jesus Christ?

Look up Moses 6:65. In this verse, we learn that Adam is "quickened in the inner man" long before his death. After further study, I found that Paul and Alma call this process being "illuminated" (see Hebrews 10:32; Alma 5:7), while Mormon uses the term "enlightened"

(Helaman 15:10). How do you think these ideas tie in with the light that was ignited in Lamoni's heart in Alma 19:6?

Read John 5:24 and 1 John 3:14. In both scriptures, the Apostle talks about someone having "passed from death unto life." But if you take a closer look at the language in these verses, it appears that yet again, John isn't referring to our experiencing physical death followed by a resurrection but to our being *spiritually* reborn—passing from spiritual death into everlasting life. In the second reference, what's one way we'll know that this process has been accomplished in our personal lives?

For more evidence that the Lord can bring our fallen heart back to life, check out these additional verses:

- Psalm 22:26
- Proverbs 8:35
- Isaiah 55:3
- Alma 37:46–47

Finally, read Alma 32 and 33. In Alma 33:22–23, we're taught that the word we must plant in our heart is that the Son will "redeem his people." What does verse 23 promise as a result of this planting? Where exactly will the tree of everlasting life spring up? "*In you.*" Now compare that to John 4:14. Echoes of John's message are everywhere! With these beautiful truths in mind, what thoughts are you having at this point in our journey?

RESPONSE

In what ways are you feeling prompted to respond to the concepts found in this chapter?

10

Christ in Us

Eternal life. It's not just exaltation in the celestial kingdom. It's also a glorious heartlight that can ignite our spiritually dead Eve. Once we're born again through Christ, this flame will not only light up our mind and infuse our soul with joy (see Alma 19:6), but it will completely fill all our emptiness and hunger. For me, the possibilities of such a concept left my mind whirling with questions. More than anything, I wanted to know what I needed to do to experience the lamp of everlasting life for myself.

So let's tackle that question right off the bat: what *do* we have to do? Do we have to work harder at making sure our religious checklist is all checked off? If we never miss a Sunday at church, if we read an hour of scriptures every day, if we fast, pray, and attend the temple, then can we have this lamp blazing brightly within us? Surprisingly, that's not the answer I found in the scriptures. In fact, the more I studied this concept, the more I could see that it didn't matter what reference I turned to on eternal life—I never found a checklist of religious duties I could use to ignite the depths of my fallen heart. Instead, I discovered a very different idea emerging. And one of the best places I found it was (yep, you guessed it) right back in the life-changing Gospel of John. Chapter 17 to be exact.

The setting was just hours before Christ's excruciating experience in Gethsemane. After finishing their Passover supper, Jesus washed His disciples' feet and shared some final teachings with His beloved friends. Then He finished the evening by offering what has come to be known as the great Intercessory Prayer. And the first words out of the Lord's mouth were these: "Father, the hour is come; glorify thy Son, that thy Son also may glorify thee: As thou hast given him power over all flesh, that he should give *eternal life* to as many as thou hast given him" (John 17:1–2; emphasis added). He then uttered this simple two-sentence statement that not only answers our question but sets us on a whole new path on our journey: "And *this is life eternal*, that they might *know thee* the only true God, and Jesus Christ, whom thou hast sent" (John 17:3, emphasis added; see also Doctrine and Covenants 132:24).

In these verses, did Jesus outline a long checklist of works that will ignite our Eve with everlasting life? Not at all. Instead, He said that this beautiful, inner life can be found one way and one way only: by coming to know Him and His Father. In other words, the lamp of everlasting life is lit within us not by checking off a list of religious exercises but by pursuing a personal relationship with Jesus Christ—and then through Him, knowing the Father. (See the Lord's teachings on this in John 8:19 and John 14:8–11.)

To keep things simple, then, we're going to focus specifically on knowing Christ because that's what opens the door to the lamp of everlasting life. The Apostle John captures this beautifully: "And we know that the Son of God is come, and hath given us an understanding, that we may *know him* that is true, and we are *in him* that is true, even in his Son Jesus Christ. This is the true God, *and eternal life*" (1 John 5:20; emphasis added).

While the concept may seem easy enough to grasp, the truth is that we still have a lot to learn about what it means to really come to know our Savior. At this point, we at least understand that it involves building some sort of relationship with Him. That's something our leaders have talked about a lot over the years. Here are just a few of my favorites:

- Elder M. Russell Ballard: "I would like to encourage you with all the strength of my soul to learn to build a real relationship with the Savior of the world."[74]
- President Lorenzo Snow: "The Lord wishes to establish a closer and more intimate relationship between Himself and us."[75]
- Elder F. Enzio Busche: "[The] real treasure . . . [is to] develop a close relationship with Christ, the Savior, the Redeemer, the Messiah, Jehovah, the Only Begotten of Elohim, and let him and his Spirit take possession of our lives. . . . I am speaking about the treasure of having found Christ, of being able to know him—not merely to know all about him, but really to know him."[76]
- President Brigham Young: "The greatest and most important of all requirements of our Father in heaven and of his Son Jesus Christ, is . . . to believe in Jesus Christ, confess him, seek him, cling to him, make friends with him. Take a course to open and to keep open communication with your Elder Brother or file-leader—our Savior."[77]
- President James E. Faust: "Is not the greatest need in all the world for every person to have a personal, ongoing, daily, continuing relationship with the Savior? . . . We should earnestly seek not just to know about the Master, but . . . to be one with Him."[78]

Did you notice how these brethren said our relationship with Christ should be *real, close, intimate, ongoing, personal, daily*, and *continuing*? In fact, Brigham Young spoke not just of seeking Him but of clinging to Him, making friends with Him, and even talking to Him. And President Faust said our ultimate goal is to become one with our Savior. But how do we do that? And how is our personal relationship

---

74. M. Russell Ballard, "You—The Leaders in 1988," *Ensign*, Mar. 1979, 69–73.

75. Lorenzo Snow, in *Journal of Discourses*, 23:193.

76. F. Enzio Busche, "The Only Real Treasure," *New Era*, Dec. 1979.

77. Brigham Young, in *Journal of Discourses*, 8:339.

78. James E. Faust, "A Personal Relationship with the Savior," *Ensign*, Nov. 1976, 58.

with the Lord connected to the beautiful inner lamp of everlasting life? Thankfully, the scriptures will unfold all the answers we need to help us in our quest.

Believe it or not, one of my favorite passages on this subject hides quietly at the end of Ephesians 5. I say "hides" because there are two inconspicuous verses there that no one really seems to notice. But we can't miss them today because in these short little verses, Paul gives us a whole new way to look at our relationship with Jesus Christ. Here's the analogy he uses: "For this cause shall a man leave his father and mother, and shall be joined unto his wife, and they two shall be one flesh. *This is a great mystery: but I speak concerning Christ and the church*" (Ephesians 5:31–32; emphasis added).

I want you to read those lines a few more times until the words start to sink in. First, Paul zeroes in on the close, personal relationship between a husband and wife, especially how they join together to become "one flesh." Then he makes the astonishing conclusion that this—the most intimate of all relationships—is a symbol for what should happen between Christ and the Church—*between Jesus and each one of us.* For Paul, there's no greater metaphor for knowing the Lord than the joining of two people in marriage. The beautiful image of a husband and wife coming together physically, mentally, emotionally, and spiritually is a perfect representation of how we become one with our beloved Savior.

It's a helpful analogy because we're all familiar with the dynamics of marriage, so we already know what it takes to establish this kind of intimate bond. We could ask ourselves: how do a man and a woman who start out as strangers eventually unite so fully that they become "one flesh"? The answer is simple. They do so by establishing a relationship of *love.* Yes, the two begin by knowing *about* one another, but if things don't move past that point, the relationship is dead in the water. To truly become one, the couple must intertwine their lives in a very profound and personal way.

Put simply, they must invest the time needed to share their hopes and dreams and feelings with each other. They must be willing to be vulnerable and authentic and let down all their emotional walls and barriers. They must freely open themselves to a deep and weighty kind of love, a love they'll share with no one else on the planet. This whole-souled joining of hearts, minds, and bodies is what will eventually make them one in every sense of the word. And thanks to Paul, we now know that the same holds true in our relationship with Jesus Christ.

The truth is, when the Lord said "the great commandment" is to love Him with all our heart, soul, and mind (see Matthew 22:37), what He was really doing was defining the kind of relationship He hopes to have with us. Notice that He didn't just want a servant or a follower or a worker bee. What He really wants is for us to intermingle our lives with His in a very real and intimate way—to love Him as deeply and fully as we'd love a spouse. To know Christ, then, is to love and adore Him with everything we are and open our hearts to His love in return.

I believe that's the very thing He was trying to teach Peter in John 21. Their conversation is familiar to many of us:

> So when they had dined, Jesus saith to Simon Peter, Simon, son of Jonas, lovest thou me more than these? He saith unto him, Yea, Lord; thou knowest that I love thee. . . .
>
> He saith to him again the second time, Simon, son of Jonas, lovest thou me? He saith unto him, Yea, Lord; thou knowest that I love thee. . . .
>
> He saith unto him the third time, Simon, son of Jonas, lovest thou me? Peter was grieved because he said unto him the third time, Lovest thou me? And he said unto him, Lord, thou knowest all things; thou knowest that I love thee. (John 21:15–17)

At first glance, the dialogue seems a little odd or even awkward. Why would Jesus repeat the same question to Peter three different times? Thankfully, we can better understand His intent if we look at the original Greek. You see, in ancient Greek there were several different verbs that could be translated as *love.* One of those verbs is *phileo,* which refers to "affection and regard of a very high order."[79] On

79. James E. Strong, *The Strongest Strong's Exhaustive Concordance of the Bible* (Grand Rapids, MI: Zondervan, 2001), 1652.

an even deeper level is the word *agapao* (or *agape*), which is charity or the pure love of God.[80] My Greek dictionary points out that there's a "distinction between the two verbs" in that "they are never used indiscriminately in the same passage; if each is used with reference to the same objects, . . . each word retains its distinctive and essential character."[81]

With these definitions in mind, let's return to the exchange between the Lord and Peter, only this time I'll add the Greek words the men actually used when they spoke of love:

> So when they had dined, Jesus saith to Simon Peter, Simon, son of Jonas, ***agape*** thou me more than these? He saith unto him, Yea, Lord; thou knowest that I ***phileo*** thee . . .
>
> He saith to him again the second time, Simon, son of Jonas, ***agape*** thou me? He saith unto him, Yea, Lord; thou knowest that I ***phileo*** thee. . .
>
> He saith unto him the third time, Simon, son of Jonas, ***phileo*** thou me? Peter was grieved because he said unto him the third time, ***Phileo*** thou me? And he said unto him, Lord, thou knowest all things; thou knowest that I ***phileo*** thee. (John 21:15–17)

We all know Peter loved the Lord. In this passage, he seemed to be trying very hard to communicate his *phileo* or "affection and regard" for his beloved Master. But it appears that Peter didn't yet understand the kind of love Jesus was asking for. As deep as Peter's affection may have been, the truth is that it wasn't enough. Jesus wanted Peter to love Him with an *agape* type of love—the love that "suffereth long," and "beareth" and "believeth" and "endureth" anything Peter would be asked to face for sake of the Lord's kingdom (see Moroni 7:45). And it's the same love Christ is asking for from each of us.[82]

---

80. Strong, *The Strongest Strong's Exhaustive Concordance of the Bible*, 1587.

81. W. E. Vine, *Vine's Complete Expository Dictionary of Old and New Testament Words* (Nashville, TN: Thomas Nelson, 1984), 382.

82. I'm sure you already know how Peter's story ends. Yes, he eventually developed true *agape* for the Lord. We know this because in 1 Peter 1:8, he used the Greek word *agape* rather than *phileo* when he spoke of his love for his precious Master. (See *The Strongest Strong's Exhaustive Concordance of the Bible* for evidence of this and also for the usage of *agape* and *phileo* in John 21:15–17.)

Hannah Whitall Smith, a Christian activist who lived in the nineteenth century, paints a beautiful picture of *agape* with these stirring words:

> Continually at every heart He is knocking, and asking to be taken in as the supreme object of love. "Wilt thou have me," He says to the believer, "to be thy Beloved? Wilt thou follow me into suffering and loneliness, and endure hardness for my sake, and ask for no reward but my smile of approval, and my word of praise? Wilt thou throw thyself with utter abandonment into my will? Wilt thou give up to me the absolute control of thyself and all that thou art? Wilt thou be content with pleasing me and me only? May I have my way with thee in all things? Wilt thou come into so close a union with me as to make a separation from the world necessary? Wilt thou accept me for thy only Lord, and leave all others, to cleave only unto Me?"[83]

Can you see the depth of commitment Jesus is looking for? To truly know our Savior, we must make Him our "Beloved," or the "supreme object of [our] love."

As inspiring as this idea may seem, we still have more ground to cover. That's because there's an even more personal way of knowing Christ than just learning to love Him with an *agape* kind of love. If you remember, in Ephesians 5, Paul specifically chose the analogy of a man and woman becoming "one flesh" to illustrate our relationship with our Savior. The connection he made reminds me of the scripture in Genesis that says, "Adam *knew* his wife; and she conceived, and bare [a son]" (Genesis 4:1). It shows that knowing someone in the scriptural sense refers to joining with them in the most intimate way possible.

So how can we unite so fully with our Savior that we become "one flesh"? Jesus actually explained this in a powerful sermon recorded in the Gospel of John. There He provided a metaphor that illustrates how deep our oneness with Him needs to go.

---

83. Hannah Whitall Smith, *The Christian's Secret of a Happy Life* (Peabody, MA: Hendrickson, 2004), 151.

In John 6:24, we find a crowd of thousands clamoring after Jesus. He'd fed them by turning five loaves and two fishes into a humongous feast, so the next morning they sought him again in the hopes of getting another free meal. Frustrated by their lack of vision, Christ suddenly got very serious about His ministry—about why He'd come and how He had much more to offer than just food for their stomachs. Passionately, He pleaded, "Labour not for the meat which perisheth, but for that meat which endureth unto *everlasting life,* which the Son of man shall give unto you" (John 6:27; emphasis added). And what kind of feast would give them this "everlasting life"? His answer was unmistakable: "*I am the bread of life*: he that cometh to me shall *never hunger*; and he that believeth on me shall *never thirst*" (verse 35; emphasis added).

Hopefully, we've come far enough on our journey that we can see the gift He was offering the people. It was *His life*—a kind of life so perpetual and vibrant that it could live continually inside them and fill all their soul's hunger and thirst. It's the very lamp of everlasting life that we've been talking about. But that's not the only thing Jesus wanted this crowd to understand. It was also important that they knew how to *partake* of this soul-filling bread. And this is the metaphor He chose in order to illustrate it:

> I am the living bread which came down from heaven: if any man eat of this bread, he shall live for ever: and the bread that I will give is my flesh, which I will give for the life of the world.
>
> The Jews therefore strove among themselves, saying, How can this man give us his flesh to eat?
>
> Then Jesus said unto them, Verily, verily, I say unto you, *Except ye eat the flesh of the Son of man, and drink his blood, ye have no life in you.*
>
> *Whoso eateth my flesh, and drinketh my blood, hath eternal life*; and I will raise him up at the last day.
>
> For my flesh is meat indeed, and my blood is drink indeed. (John 6:51–55)

Again, Christ's teachings may seem a little unorthodox here. The most unsettling part may be His statement that the only way we can have life *in* us is if we eat His flesh and drink His blood. Note that He said all who do so "*hath* eternal life." While we understand more now about how eternal life can be lit up inside us, we may struggle to see how that inner lamp is connected to the idea of eating His flesh and drinking His blood.

To make things even more complicated, we need to remember that the Law of Moses forbade the drinking of blood, which means the Lord chose a metaphor with the potential not only to offend the Jews' sensitivity but to cause them (and possibly us) to turn away in revulsion. In fact, if we read ahead a few verses, we'll see that's exactly what happened in the end (see verse 66). So why would Jesus choose such a graphic analogy if He knew it was going to cause a stir? Why not tell His followers to serve Him or follow Him or obey Him or even just love Him? What's so important about the idea of eating His flesh and drinking His blood that He would risk losing followers in order to use it?

Some may say it's because He's alluding to the sacrament (see John 6:54, footnote *a*). That idea certainly puts us on the right track because the sacrament would eventually come to symbolize the doctrine the Lord was teaching here (see 3 Nephi 20:8). But Christ gave this sermon long before He introduced that important ordinance to His disciples. Plus, most of us already participate in the sacrament every Sunday, and our souls have still been haunted by a recurring sense of hunger and thirst. For this reason, we need to dig a little deeper and look at what the sacrament actually represents. What was Jesus's intent when He encouraged the Jews—and us—to eat His flesh and drink His blood?

Perhaps it would help if we pictured what happens every time we eat or drink something. The food or beverage literally becomes *part of us*, doesn't it? It's synthesized into the marrow of our bones and enters into the fleshy chambers of our beating heart. It's no longer outside us—we literally become *one* with that particular substance. The food or drink is now *in us* rather than somewhere near us or beside us.

I believe Jesus used this analogy so He could show us that the same thing needs to happen in our personal relationship with Him.

To find the kind of soul satisfaction where we no longer hunger or thirst, it's not enough just to obey Him or serve Him or listen to Him or follow Him. To gain everlasting life and be spiritually reborn through Him, Jesus Christ must become *part of us* the same way food or drink does whenever we partake of it. In the words of Elder D. Todd Christofferson, "To eat His flesh and drink His blood is a striking way of expressing how completely we must bring the Savior into our life—*into our very being*—that we may be one."[84]

Believe it or not, that's exactly how Jesus summed up His metaphor in John 6. He said, "He that eateth my flesh, and drinketh my blood, *dwelleth in me, and I in him*" (John 6:56; emphasis added). I love the way Elder David A. Bednar captured this beautiful inner union: "It is one thing to know that Jesus Christ came to earth to die for us—that is fundamental and foundational to the doctrine of Christ. But we also need to appreciate that the Lord desires, through His Atonement and by the power of the Holy Ghost, to *live in us*—not only to direct us but also to empower us."[85]

Have you ever considered the possibility that Christ can *live in you*? It's quite a remarkable concept. What's even more remarkable is that once our eyes are opened to see it, we'll find it sprinkled all throughout the standard works. For instance, in John 15—one of the final teachings Jesus would offer while in the flesh—the Lord described this very same union, only He called it *abiding in Him*. Listen to His poignant invitation: "Abide in me and I in you. As the branch cannot bear fruit of itself, except it abide in the vine; no more can ye, except ye abide in me. I am the vine, ye are the branches: He that abideth in me, and I in him, the same bringeth forth much fruit: for without me, ye can do nothing" (John 15:4–5).[86]

---

84. D. Todd Christofferson, "The Living Bread Which Came Down From Heaven," *Ensign* or *Liahona*, Nov. 2017, 36; emphasis added.

85. David A. Bednar, "The Atonement and the Journey of Mortality," *Ensign* or *Liahona*, May 2012, 42; emphasis added.

86. See also David A. Bednar, "Abide in Me, and I in You; Therefore Walk with Me," *Liahona*, May 2023.

To make these verses jump off the page a little more, let's create two mental images to help us visualize what the Lord is teaching in this passage. First, think of a green branch that's absolutely bursting with fresh, juicy fruit. In your mind, feel the heaviness of the fruit weighing down the strong, vibrant limb. Imagine the lushness and abundance of the crop exploding all over that healthy branch. Now use that image to represent what it looks like when we're alive in Christ—when our soul hunger is completely and totally satisfied. As we're joined fully and completely to the vine, our branch (or our life) will have all the nourishment necessary to satisfy our many inner needs.

Next, picture what would happen if I took a saw and cut that branch away from the tree. Within hours, the leaves would begin to fall off and all the juicy fruit would wither away. Before long, the branch would be completely bare and lifeless. Dead and empty of all signs of life. This is what it looks like to be spiritually dead. Christ is teaching here that the only way to restore life to that branch is by reconnecting it to the life-giving power of the vine. Put another way, *connectedness to the vine is the key to everlasting life.* As a branch, we must be completely united with Jesus Christ to have the continual nourishment our soul so desperately needs. And what's the most powerful way we can do that? By abiding in Him. By dwelling in Him and He in us. By letting Christ *live in us* and truly becoming one with Him in the most personal way we possibly can.

Really, this doctrine shouldn't be that surprising since Jesus enjoyed a similar relationship with His Father during His earthly ministry. When Philip asked him, "Lord, shew us the Father," Christ replied, "Believest thou not that *I am in the Father, and the Father in me*? the words that I speak unto you I speak not of myself: but *the Father that dwelleth in me, he doeth the works*" (John 14:8–10, emphasis added; see also Doctrine and Covenants 93:3). Imagine that: through the power of the Spirit, God the Father was actually able to dwell *in* God the Son to strengthen, direct, and empower Him.

But here's the most amazing part: Jesus also told Philip that after His Resurrection, He would share the *very same union* with His own followers. Notice how, in verses 16–18, He promised that the "Spirit of truth" would dwell with them and be in them. But before we assume He's talking about the Holy Ghost, remember that in Doctrine and Covenants 93, Christ says *He* is the Spirit of truth (see verses 9, 11, and 26). I believe that's the reason He told Philip, "I will not leave you comfortless: *I will come to you*" (John 14:18; emphasis added). Jesus then concluded with these insightful words: "Yet a little while, and the world seeth me no more; but ye see me*: because I live, ye shall live also.* At that day ye shall know that *I am in my Father, and ye in me, and I in you*" (verses 19–20; emphasis added).

In those verses, did you notice how He tied the idea of *life* or *coming alive* to His ability to dwell in us? It shows us exactly how the lamp of eternal life is lit up in our hearts. It comes *as a direct result of our inner union with the Lord.* Through this union, we'll become one with our beloved Savior in the most intimate way possible. And once He lives in us through the power of the Spirit, our hearts will be not only spiritually reborn but filled to overflowing with perpetual, unending, everlasting life.

Can you picture what it would be like to have Christ living continually inside your heart? Can you imagine what it would feel like to have Him ignite your inner flame so that it shimmers and dances continually throughout each day? It really is possible, you know. Once we learn to abide in Him—meaning He dwells in us and we in Him—we'll finally experience the beautiful inner heartlight we've been searching for. At last, our fallen and spiritually dead hearts will be ignited with everlasting life, and with this inner light will come greater blessings than any we've ever known.

For one thing, having Christ in us means His life will be our life, His joy will be our joy, His strength will be our strength, His patience will be our patience, and His love will be our love. It means we'll never again want to wrap ourselves in fig leaves, run to our hiding places, or point our finger in blame. Why would we want to pursue any of that when we have our Savior living inside us to fill us and strengthen us and make our fallen hearts whole? Just like the scriptures promise, "If any man be *in Christ*, he is a new creature: old things are passed away; behold, all things are become new" (2 Corinthians 5:17; emphasis added).

Put simply, having Christ in us will give us access to all of the Lord's amazing strengths, qualities, and attributes. As a result, our lives will be transformed in a miraculous and mind-blowing way. On the outside, we'll still do the same dishes, drive the same carpool, and clock in at the same time at work. We'll still deal with the same fighting children, tackle the same mountain of laundry, and check off the same to-do list. But the difference is that we'll no longer be handling any of those challenges on our own. With Christ in us, we'll conduct our meetings more efficiently, cope with our difficulties more successfully, and handle our conversations more compassionately. We'll deal with our children more effectively, finish our errands more rapidly, and carry out our assignments more creatively, for the Lord can "give unto [us] strength such as is not known among men" (Doctrine and Covenants 24:12). As He joins us in each of our responsibilities, meshing His life, love, and joy with our own, we'll find the results of this partnership so spectacular that we'll wonder how we ever accomplished anything without Him.

Having Christ in us truly is the answer for every problem that plagues us, every weakness that taunts us, and every frustration that follows us. It's the way we are spiritually reborn through Him. It's the path not only to becoming the person we've always wanted to be but to having an incredibly precious relationship with our beloved Savior.

Now that we've set eyes on this beautiful, awe-inspiring vista, I'm curious: are you longing for the Lord to dwell inside you and ignite the depths of your heart with the lamp of everlasting life? Are you hungering to experience this one-of-a-kind relationship with Him? Are you craving for the infusion of internal light that only He can give? If so, all I ask is that you continue with me on the next leg of our journey, for nothing will change your life more than coming to know your Savior in this very intimate and personal way.

READINGS & REFLECTIONS

Turn to Luke 10:25–28. What does this passage teach us about how we gain eternal life? Now read 1 John 5:11–12 and Doctrine and Covenants 132:22–24 and answer the same question.

For further evidence of the importance of coming to know Christ, read Mosiah 26:24–27 and 3 Nephi 14:21–23. After everything we've discussed, has your understanding of what it means to "know" Him changed? How so?

To learn more about Jesus Christ as the light that illuminates and quickens our fallen heart, read through the following references:

- Psalm 18:28
- Isaiah 60:19
- 2 Corinthians 4:6
- Revelation 22:5
- Alma 28:14
- Doctrine and Covenants 93:2, 9

What insights stand out to you in these verses?

For some additional verses that talk about Christ living in us, look up Mosiah 2:37, Alma 34:36, and 3 Nephi 19:23, 29. How do these references relate to the concept of abiding in Him and He in us? Now turn to Colossians 1:26–27 and answer the same question.

Next, look up Doctrine and Covenants 97:3. Why is the Lord pleased with Parley P. Pratt in this scripture? Do you think He could say the same about you? Why or why not? (See also Moses 6:34.)

Of all the scriptural writers, John is undoubtedly the most vocal proponent of Christ dwelling inside our heart. If you search his first epistle, you'll find some version of "in him" or "in you" over *thirty-five times*. For instance, look up 1 John 2:5–6; 3:24; 4:4, 13–16. How do you think John felt about this particular doctrine?

Before we move on, we need to deal with one tricky verse written by Joseph Smith in the Doctrine and Covenants. Regarding John 14:23, the prophet writes, "The appearing of the Father and the Son, in that verse, is a personal appearance; and the idea that the Father and the Son dwell in a man's heart is an old sectarian notion, and is false" (Doctrine and Covenants 130:3).

I'll admit that when I compared this verse to the countless others that talk about Christ living in our heart, it left me perplexed. But as I continued to study this seeming contradiction, additional understanding finally began to come.

First, it hit me that Joseph was trying to teach in this section that the Father and Son have actual physical bodies, which was a radically new concept at the time (see verse 22). Looking at it through that lens, having the Lord *literally* or *physically* dwell inside our heart really is impossible, which means the idea would be false just like Joseph said.

But thankfully, we have Elder Bednar's teachings (and the many other quotes and verses we just studied) that show us *it can be done spiritually* through the power of the Spirit.

I also found another quote from President Spencer W. Kimball that I believe adds a layer of clarity. Speaking of Doctrine and Covenants 130:3, he said, "The Prophet Joseph Smith explained [that] this means that the coming of the Father and the Son to a person is a reality—a personal appearance—and not *merely* dwelling in his heart."[87]

If you put all this evidence together, I believe it unfolds an amazing progression. First, as the scriptures teach us again and again, Christ can live in our heart—not literally but spiritually through the power of the Spirit. In doing this, He can teach us and guide us and take us through the sanctification process (for example, see verse 3 of "Testimony," *Hymns*, no. 137).

Then, as Joseph Smith so beautifully taught us, there's a deeper level we can attain in our relationship with the Lord. Here's how he explained it:

> After a person has faith in Christ, repents of his sins, and is baptized for the remission of his sins and receives the Holy Ghost (by the laying on of hands), which is the first Comforter, then let him continue to humble himself before God, hungering and thirsting after righteousness, and living by every word of God, and the Lord will soon say unto him, Son, thou shalt be exalted. When the Lord has thoroughly proved him, and finds that the man is determined to serve Him at all hazards, then the man will find his calling and his election made sure, then it will be his privilege to receive *the other Comforter*, which the Lord hath promised the Saints, as is recorded in the testimony of St. John, in the 14th chapter, from the 12th to the 27th verses. . . .
>
> Now what is this other Comforter? *It is no more nor less than the Lord Jesus Christ Himself*; . . . when any man obtains this last Comforter, *he will have the personage of Jesus Christ to attend him, or appear unto him from time to time, and even He will manifest the Father unto him, and they will take up their abode with him*, and the visions of the heavens will be opened unto him, and *the Lord will*

87. Spencer W. Kimball, in Conference Report, Nov. 1968, 129; emphasis added.

> *teach him face to face*, and he may have a perfect knowledge of the mysteries of the Kingdom of God.[88]

This same blessing is also captured in the Doctrine and Covenants:

> And again, verily I say unto you that it is your privilege, and a promise I give unto you that have been ordained unto this ministry, that inasmuch as you strip yourselves from jealousies and fears, and humble yourselves before me, for ye are not sufficiently humble, the veil shall be rent and *you shall see me and know that I am*—not with the carnal neither natural mind, but with the spiritual. (Doctrine and Covenants 67:10; emphasis added)
>
> Therefore, sanctify yourselves that your minds become single to God, and the days will come *that you shall see him*; *for he will unveil his face unto you*, and it shall be in his own time, and in his own way, and according to his own will (Doctrine and Covenants 88:68, emphasis added; see also Doctrine and Covenants 93:1; 2 Nephi 32:6).

The thought of such an experience takes my breath away! How incredible to know that this "other Comforter" (meaning the presence of Jesus Christ Himself) isn't just reserved for prophets like Joseph Smith, Nephi, or the brother of Jared (see 2 Nephi 11:2 and Ether 3:13). Instead, it's something each of us can attain if we truly hunger and thirst to find the Lord. We begin by seeking His presence within our hearts, and then if we're faithful and continue to nurture our relationship with Him, we're promised that someday we can actually see Him in person. I believe nothing should motivate us more to continue this priceless journey if we know it can reach such an extraordinary end.

---

88. *Teachings of the Prophet Joseph Smith*, sel. Joseph Fielding Smith (1976), 150–51; emphasis added.

Response

In what ways are you feeling prompted to respond to the concepts found in this chapter?

11

Prone to Wander

If you're truly longing for a deeper relationship with Christ, and you're truly longing for the lamp of everlasting life to flicker and dance inside you with a vibrancy that never burns out, what we need to do now is make sure we're on the path that leads to this spiritual rebirth. Thankfully, our journey has already taught us that we'll never get there by checking off a list of religious duties and obligations. Instead, we need to build a relationship of love with the Lord that echoes that of a man and woman becoming one flesh.

It reminds me of the Old Testament story of the prophet Hosea and his wife Gomer. Even though Gomer married Hosea and had three children with him—meaning she went through the motions of "becoming one" with him—she never gave the prophet her full love and devotion. Instead, she continued to "follow after her lovers" (Hosea 2:7), which caused Hosea to lament, "She is not my wife, neither am I her husband" (Hosea 2:2). Though the two were legally united in matrimony, they were never truly united in an intimate relationship of love.

I know most of us probably cringe at the details of this story, but we're actually going to use it to do a little soul-searching of our own. You see, Hosea and Gomer teach us an incredibly important lesson that we need very much at this point in our quest. It's that there comes a time in every relationship when the only way it can progress to the next level is if the two partners sacrifice every other competing love and devote themselves entirely to their significant other. It's the very thing Gomer *didn't* do, and it kept her from experiencing the wonderfully satisfying bond she could have had with her husband.

This story brings up some difficult questions that we need to tackle on this leg of our journey. The first one is this: as much as we may detest the choices Gomer made, could it be that we resemble her more than we initially thought? Could it be that we too have other "lovers" that we're more devoted to than the Lord? I'm talking about metaphorical lovers, or the aprons and escapes that have reached out and stolen our heart. While we've spent a great deal of time exploring each of these things, we may not have realized how much they were distracting us and keeping us focused on anything and everything but our personal relationship with our Savior.

Recently, I saw this portrayed online in a very powerful way, and I want to recreate it here to help illustrate my point. Pretend for a minute that I've planned a fancy dinner with my husband, Greg, to celebrate our upcoming anniversary. After making reservations at our favorite restaurant, I suggest we dress up and make it a special occasion. Once we arrive and our host takes us to our table, Greg notices it's been set for five people, not two. I squeeze his hand and tell him not to worry but to just look over the menu and decide what he wants to order.

A few minutes later, a visitor arrives at our table. It's one of the guys I used to date in college. I greet him with a kiss and invite him to sit at the place on my other side. Before Greg has a chance to protest, an old high school flame shows up next, and I offer him a welcome hug and another invitation to join us. Finally, a male colleague I know from work rushes in, pecks my cheek, and says, "Sorry I'm late." He takes the final seat at the table.

Obviously, at this point, Greg isn't just angry—he's feeling incredibly hurt and betrayed. With a pained expression, he asks, "Jaci, how could you do this to me?" I grab his hand again, stroke it, and whisper in his ear, "Hon, don't worry, I spend the majority of my time with you. I even *married* you. You'll always be my favorite. I just want to spend a little time with these other guys too, that's all." Then I turn back to my visitors and try to smooth over the tension with a coy little laugh and a smile.

Now tell me this: is there any chance my husband would sit quietly at the table and endure this awful arrangement? Any chance he'd accept my explanation and wait patiently while I fuss over my other visitors? Not in a million years. None of us would. The thought is almost ludicrous to contemplate. And yet we can be guilty of that same behavior when it comes to our relationship with Jesus Christ.

Just like any loving "Bridegroom" (Doctrine and Covenants 133:10), Christ wants all our heart—not just part of it. Think about how He refers to the Church as His "bride," thus revealing the kind of exclusive relationship He hopes to have with His people (see Isaiah 62:5; Revelation 21:2, 9; Doctrine and Covenants 109:73–74). Think about how His gospel includes the making of covenants—just like in a marriage—where we promise all we have and are to our King (see Mosiah 5:1–8; Alma 46:21; Doctrine and Covenants 97:8). Think about how He's told us that He's a "jealous god" (see Exodus 20:5; Deuteronomy 4:24; Joshua 24:19; Mosiah 13:13), meaning He isn't willing to share our worship with anything or anyone else. Think about how we're asked to "offer [our] *whole souls* as an offering unto him" (Omni 1:26; emphasis added) and to "render to him *all* that [we] have and are" (Mosiah 2:34; emphasis added). Maybe now we can understand why, if we cling to other loves like in the dinner analogy, the Lord actually labels it as a type of spiritual infidelity, like "a wife that committeth adultery, which taketh strangers instead of her husband" (Ezekiel 16:32).

Again and again, our Savior has asked us to love Him "with all [our] heart, and with all [our] soul, and with all [our] strength, and with all [our] mind" (Luke 10:27; see also Deuteronomy 6:5; Matthew 22:37; Mark 12:30; Doctrine and Covenants 59:5). Yet for some reason, we convince ourselves that we can give our passion and attention to all sorts of other things and He won't mind at all. But the truth is, just like my husband in the story, the Lord isn't going to sit idly by while we dress ourselves up in our favorite aprons or run off into hiding. When we reject Him like that, He feels the same kind of anger, hurt, and betrayal my husband would have felt, only we're often too blind to see what we're doing.

Perhaps it's time for us to view our fig leaves and hiding places for what they really are—not just distractions or diversions but *other lovers.* I say that because we've run to these things in an attempt to soothe our pain, to gain validation, and to find a little happiness in this complicated world. Isn't that what lovers do for our heart? Just like seductive suitors, our aprons and escapes have offered us a temporary rush that has helped us forget our spiritual deadness for a little while. Being with them—or participating in them—has made us feel better. They've been our bliss, our happy place, or our pick-me-up when we have felt low. Like Gomer, we too could admit that "these are my rewards that my lovers have given me" (Hosea 2:12).

Though we may wish things were different, the sad reality is that we've been Gomer every time we've clothed ourselves in a fig leaf apron, every time we've run off into hiding, and every time we've pointed our finger in blame. Just like Gomer's restless heart, our Eve has clung to these strategies in the hopes of finding the love, life, and joy she's been longing for.

This tendency to turn to other things for fulfillment is actually found all throughout the scriptures, not just in the book of Hosea. Consider Isaiah's lament: "All we like sheep have gone astray; we have turned every one to his own way" (Isaiah 53:6). Paul also reminds us that "we all [walked] . . . in times past in the lusts of our flesh, fulfilling the desires of the flesh and of the mind" (Ephesians 2:3). Finally, Nephi quotes this bombshell from Isaiah, thus making the prophet's words applicable to our day and not just his own:

> O house of Jacob, . . . ye have all gone astray, every one to his wicked ways. . . .
>
> Because [ye have] replenished from the east, and hearken[ed] unto soothsayers . . . and . . . please[d] [your]selves in the children of strangers.

> [Your] land also is full of silver and gold, neither is there any end of [your] treasures; . . .
>
> [Your] land is also full of idols; [and you] worship the work of [your] own hands, that which [your] own fingers have made. (2 Nephi 12:5–8)

Note that these verses don't just say *some* of us have strayed but that *all* of us have. This inclination to depart from the Lord is one of the defining characteristics of fallen humanity. We really are "prone to wander" just like the popular song says.[89]

One way to see how we do this is by considering Jesus's request that we look to Him "in every thought" (Doctrine and Covenants 6:36). Alma echoed the same idea when he said, "let *all* thy thoughts be directed unto the Lord; yea, *let the affections of thy heart be placed upon the Lord forever*" (Alma 37:36; emphasis added). If we really love and worship our Savior as much as we say we do, this commandment should be an easy one to keep.

But if we take an honest look at where our thoughts and affections have been focused throughout the day—meaning how often we *haven't* been thinking of Christ but enthralled with all sorts of other things—we can see how many times we've rejected Him. How often have we snuck in a few minutes (or even hours) to spend in our favorite escapes? How often have we continued to indulge in our guilty pleasures? It just goes to show that, like Gomer, our lovers are never very far from our minds. Though we may claim to treasure the Lord more than anything else, the thoughts and feelings of our Eve have continued to prove otherwise.

Another reason we may struggle to see ourselves as Gomer is that many of our aprons and escapes have a very justifiable place in our lives. Often, they're just seemingly harmless things like a little too much busyness or social media or binge-watching TV. And that makes them a whole lot easier to rationalize. We tell ourselves that everyone

89. "Come Thou Fount of Every Blessing," The Church of Jesus Christ of Latter-day Saints, accessed Apr. 1, 2023, https://www.churchofjesuschrist.org/music/text/other/come-thou-fount-of-every-blessing.

eats a quart of ice cream when they've had a bad day. Or a little "retail therapy" is good for our mental health. We believe we can participate in our escapes and still get a temple recommend, so how could they be counterfeit lovers? But in the end, we need to face the reality of our choices. No matter what kind of lovers we've turned to, we've relied on these things to fill our emptiness. And that's a form of spiritual infidelity that's kept us from giving our whole heart to the Lord.

The problem is, we've often been so mired in denial that we couldn't see what we were doing. Because many of our lovers didn't fit the typical profile of adulterous suitors, it made it even easier for us to be deceived. Take my attachment to people-pleasing for instance, or illusory lovers like perfectionism or pharisaical righteousness. Whenever we've embraced coping mechanisms like these, it gave us the appearance of having Christlike habits and actions, so we assumed we were on the right track. But underneath the surface, these aprons quietly ruled our lives with an iron fist, forcing us to align ourselves with a false belief system that controlled us more fully than an abusive lover ever could. This type of suitor convinced us that it had our best interests in mind, but deep down we were caught in a dysfunctional dynamic that dominated not just our thoughts and feelings but our outward behavior as well.

It may even be that we turned church work itself into one of our counterfeit lovers. Earlier we talked about the less-than-noble motivations that can hide behind our Christian good works. Like the super-religious Pharisees, we may have spent years performing a huge amount of service and sacrifice, but under the surface, all we were really doing was feeding our empty soul on all the validation and praise that came from being the ward superhero. It's a tricky trap—one that looks great on the outside but, like Gomer, still keeps our hearts separated and distanced from Jesus Christ.

It all boils down to something the Lord said in 3 Nephi 11 when He visited the Nephites. Before He showed Himself to the people, He called out to the "more righteous," or those who had avoided destruction because they "received the prophets and stoned them not" (3 Nephi 10:12). What did He say to these busy, active, church-going people? His haunting words should give us pause: *"Will ye not now return unto me, and repent of your sins, and be converted, that I may heal you?"* (3 Nephi 9:13). If you ask me, that sounds a lot like Hosea calling out to his long-lost wife. Surprisingly, even the "more righteous" people still needed to return, repent, and be healed. Why? Because despite all their religious efforts, their hearts were still fallen, wounded, and spiritually dead. And the same thing applies to each of us. In our own way, *each of us* has acted like Gomer. And that means *each of us* desperately needs to *return, repent,* and *be healed.*

So this is the point where we need to get really honest about what's going on deep inside our hearts. To do that, I'd like you to think back through all the roads we've traversed and reexamine all the baggage you've uncovered throughout our journey. Look again at each of your aprons and escapes. Ponder all the times you relied on these things for happiness, security, or a sense of identity. Reflect on all the passions, obsessions, and distractions you've turned to in an attempt to find fulfillment. Contemplate how much time and energy you've devoted to embracing them and making sure they remained close by.

Now tell me: didn't these things call out to you like attractive suitors, offering your Eve the life, love, and joy that she's been longing for? Didn't they seduce you and woo you into believing they could solve all your problems and make you endlessly happy and content? Didn't your credit card or that bestselling novel or all the social media "likes" light up your heart for a time—almost as if you were head over heels in love? Even when your Eve was consumed with feelings of lust, anger, or greed, didn't those passions have their own way of making you feel very alive, if only for a little while? Truly, our hearts have been pulled in a thousand directions by all kinds of counterfeit lovers who have promised us perpetual bliss and never-ending fulfillment.

But perhaps the most important question we need to ask ourselves is this: in all that time we spent seeking happiness in other lovers—in all that playing and grasping and chasing and reaching and craving and coveting—did we ever find the eternal happiness and overflowing love our heart was longing for? Did those other lovers ignite our soul with everlasting light or infuse us with more joy than we ever thought possible? Were they able to fill our heart so full that we never hungered or thirsted ever again?

Not even close.

The truth is, things actually turned out far different. Yes, at times our heart's suitors made us feel very alive and happy, but other times they failed us miserably. Like the time our vacation was rained out. Or we got the credit card bill in the mail. Or we binged on chocolate chip cookie dough until we were sick. Or when our hours of church service went unnoticed. Or we couldn't force our plan to work out the way we wanted it to. Unfortunately, we've learned the hard way that these kinds of suitors can be extremely erratic and unpredictable.

A similar thing happened when we turned the people in our lives into counterfeit lovers. It could be that we relied on the world of romance to fill our Eve's empty cup, or maybe we fed on the attention of friends and family members to soothe our inner void. But eventually we found that even our most precious loved ones couldn't truly fulfill us. Instead, there were days we didn't get along *at all.* Days when we drove each other nuts. Days when our significant other couldn't meet our needs because they were too consumed with their own personal burdens.

In the end, there hasn't been a single person in our lives who could bring our spiritually dead hearts back to life, no matter how much they loved us or how well-intentioned they may have been. Author Beth Moore puts it this way: "We're meant to have the closest of loves and relationships with other people, but we can become so tightly wound up in them that the life force of Christ is reduced to an occasional random drip. The irony is that the relationships we've prioritized over Christ have been cut off from the very force that's capable of making them flourish."[90]

Put simply, our heart's needs are just too high and wide and deep for any mortal person to satisfy. As much as we like to think our

---

90. Beth Moore, *Chasing Vines: Finding Your Way to an Immensely Fruitful Life* (Carol Stream, IL: Tyndale Momentum, 2020), 143–144.

human relationships can save us, there's only One who can truly bring our fallen hearts back to life.

Really, haven't we experienced the same outcome with every single apron or escape? Even if we obtained all the career success we've ever wanted, even if we lost all that unwanted weight and kept it off, even if we published that book or became a social media influencer or finally found the money to build our dream house, didn't the restlessness and emptiness *always* come back in the end? Of course, we probably continued to cling to these deceptive lovers, but they never filled our void the way we hoped they would. That's because nothing on this earth can fix a fallen heart, no matter how much we want to believe otherwise. Author Lysa TerKeurst captures the irony of the situation perfectly:

> How dangerous it is when our souls are grasping for God but we're too distracted flirting with the world to notice. Flirting will give you brief surges of fun feelings but will never really pull you in and hold you close. Indeed, the world entices your flesh but never embraces your soul. All the while, the only love caring enough to embrace us and complete enough to fill us, waits.
>
> He waits every day with every answer we need, every comfort we crave, every affection we're desperate for, while we look everywhere else but at Him. . . .
>
> How it must break His heart when we walk around so desperate for a love He waits to give us each and every day.[91]

You know, I think if we were completely honest with ourselves, we'd admit that, deep down, we've always sensed the futility of chasing other lovers. We've probably also sensed that we needed to give them up eventually. But knowing that and doing it are two very different things. Even though we knew what we "should" do, most of the time we've ignored those nagging feelings and reached for a little more instant gratification. The scenarios are all too familiar: we knew we didn't need another pair of shoes, but we whipped out our credit card anyway. We knew we weren't eating because we were hungry, but we

91. Lysa Terkeurst, *Uninvited: Living Loved When You Feel Less Than, Left Out, and Lonely* (Nashville, TN: Thomas Nelson, 2016), 35–36.

downed that package of Oreos anyway. We knew we shouldn't continue to hold that grudge, but we reveled in our secret hatred anyway. We knew we needed to turn to the Lord, but our Eve continued to cling to her favorite things, completely oblivious to the depths of her spiritual infidelity.

Isn't it strange how the fallen heart works? Even though we suspected that our lovers weren't really working for us, our Eve continued to cling to them with a vengeance that almost seemed insatiable. We knew we shouldn't want them, but want them we did—and with a desperation that almost seemed scary. As a result, these things became more than our obsessions . . . they became our addictions. Now, I know *addiction* may seem like a strong word to use at this point, but there's a simple test to see if it fits. Just try to give them up. Try turning your back on your favorite things and walking away. It's not that easy, is it? In the end, we're more attached than we want to believe.

Perhaps, like me, you've even hit rock bottom and decided you really wanted to be free from all that baggage. In a big rush of effort, you rounded up all the willpower and good intentions you could possibly muster. You promised yourself that from that moment on, things were finally going to be different. But despite all your best-laid plans, your desire for your lovers continued to haunt you. Even if you were tired of all the yelling, binging, spending, fantasizing, controlling, obsessing, or people-pleasing, your Eve simply refused to cooperate. You tried quitting cold turkey, but she went through withdrawals. You tried setting more goals, but she craved and pined and pleaded with you to give in. You tried repressing your longings, but she reminded you how dismal and lifeless you felt without them. Eventually, you buckled under the pressure, and like Gomer, you ran back for more of the "rewards" your lovers continued to promise you.

In the end, isn't that the sign of a true addict? To want very much to give something up and not be able to do it? I know the word may make us uncomfortable, but it's crucial that we understand the depths to which our deceitful heart has sunk in the hopes of finding the love, life, and joy we were created for. Consider this profound gospel perspective on addiction from Dr. Gerald G. May:

> Spiritually, addiction is a deep-seated form of idolatry. The objects of our addictions become our false gods. *These are what we worship, what we attend to, where we give our time and energy, instead of love.* Addiction, then, *displaces and supplants God's love as the source and object of our deepest true desire.* . . . Because of our addictions, we will always be storing up treasures somewhere other than heaven, and these treasures will kidnap our hearts and souls and strength.[92]

In the end, we've got to realize that Jeremiah was right: our heart really is "deceitful above all things, and desperately wicked" (Jeremiah 17:9). Simply put, our Eve hasn't always desired those things that are best for us. Instead, she's often craved the very things that ended up hurting, distracting, misleading, or even enslaving us. In other words, our heart has been seduced again and again by Satan's lies, and we haven't even thought twice about it.

It could be our Eve was convinced that a bigger house, nicer car, or better wardrobe was all we needed to be happy. Or that the hours we spent immersed in mindless entertainment had no effect on our relationship with the Lord. Or that the busier we were, the more righteous we were in the eyes of our Father in Heaven. No matter how you spin it, the desires of our heart have led us astray time and time again. Beth Moore sums up the deceptiveness of our fallen heart with these insightful words:

> The long and short of it is, our wants can be really messed up. And if they are, our lives will be really messed up because we humans, except in matters of survival, are driven most by what we desire. We can want things desperately, clawing and clamoring, that we know have the capacity to destroy us. The gratification of desire is so strong that we, with our eyes wide open, are willing to satisfy it today even if we dearly pay for ten thousand tomorrows.[93]

So why are the desires of our Eve so "messed up"? Why do we often want things that are all wrong for us and may even end up

---

92. Gerald G. May, *Addiction and Grace: Love and Spirituality in the Healing of Addictions* (New York: HarperOne, 1988), 14, 16; emphasis added.

93. Beth Moore, *Audacious* (Nashville, TN: B&H Books, 2015), 108.

ruining our lives? Why are we so addicted to the instant gratification and temporary fulfillment of our counterfeit lovers?

Perhaps we think our core desires themselves are the problem, and what we really need to do is repress those persistent longings. But that will never work because our Eve was *created* to need love, life, and joy. Those inner longings were given to us by God (for example, see 2 Nephi 2:25). They're woven inextricably into the deepest thoughts of our minds and the most poignant feelings of our heart. Saying we can live without them is like saying we can hold our breath for the rest of our lives. Sooner or later, our Eve will always end up gasping for air. She just can't do it. That's because the powerful desires living inside her won't be denied. They're part of the legacy inherited by all the children of God.

But we've got to remember that things drastically changed when each of us personally experienced the Fall. The moment we died spiritually, we found ourselves trapped—not in an Eden-like state but one chock-full of sinfulness, selfishness, sadness, and suffering. A spiritual deadness slowly overtook our hearts and left us with an extremely frustrating problem. Though our core desires still pulsed feverishly inside us, we've found ourselves unable to satisfy those desires in a way that is truly fulfilling.

Yes, we needed life, but because of the Fall, our inner man now felt restlessness, bored, apathetic, numb, or lifeless. Yes, we needed joy, but because of the Fall, we now experienced trials and afflictions that devastated, damaged, and depressed us. Yes, we needed love, but because of the Fall, we now battled rejection, disappointment, abandonment, betrayal, or abuse. Is it any wonder we spent our time seeking out other lovers? Our spiritual death caused such a nagging void inside us that we were willing to reach for almost anything if it would help us escape the emptiness for a little while.

So our turning to counterfeit lovers hasn't just been about instant gratification—*it's been our attempt to cope with all the torturous consequences of the Fall.* It's understandable, really. In our spiritual deadness, we struggled to feel loved, alive, and happy, so we scraped together whatever we could to help us survive. In fact, the weight of our wounds and sins and unmet needs often made our Eve so desperate for relief that she willingly turned to things that would eventually enslave her. That's one reason so many of us continue to binge on food or romance novels or TV or social media or shopping or pornography or any number of substitute lovers. It isn't because we lack willpower—it's because our Eve is desperate to find the love, life, and joy she's been denied through the Fall and its accompanying spiritual death.

In essence, our lovers represent our attempt to return to the celestial paradise where we lived before we were born. It's the very thing we lost in the Fall, and subconsciously we're desperate to find a way to get it back. So we turn to other lovers because they give us a small taste of the transcendent life we were made for. As unhealthy as some of our aprons and escapes may be, we have to remember that they *do* work—not in the long run and not all the time, but they *do* satisfy our Eve for a little while. And because they fulfill our most poignant and pressing desires (albeit briefly), our heart clings to them with all the passion of a woman in love. As a result, our willpower-driven efforts to give them up are no match for our Eve's urgent insistence that she needs them, that she'll die without them, and that everything will feel lifeless and barren if she leaves them behind.

However, we often forget that clinging to our lovers has had another alarming side effect: it's placed us in bondage. It's that addiction thing we were just talking about. In fact, if we go back to the book of Hosea, we'll find that that's exactly what happened to Gomer in the end (see Hosea 3:1–3). Though our captivity is often more mental and emotional than physical, our chains are still very real. We're captive in that we're trapped with a perpetual lack of satisfaction. We run again and again to our favorite things, yet we battle a gnawing feeling of never being truly fulfilled, of always wanting more, of yearning for the good life but never really being able to find it. Hosea 4 describes it this way: "For [my people] shall eat, and not have enough: they shall commit whoredom, and shall not increase: because they have left off to take heed to the Lord" (Hosea 4:10).

To put it plainly, our Eve has become a prisoner of her *lust*. Like Paul said, we've all pursued "the lusts of our flesh, fulfilling the desires of the flesh and of the mind" (Ephesians 2:3). But don't forget that lust is simply defined as any passionate or overmastering desire or craving. Think about that definition and the various desires and cravings that flood your fallen heart. There's a reason these cravings overpower us so easily. Because our counterfeit lovers can't fill us long term, our Eve is forced to keep going back for more. Then some more. Then just a little bit more. In this way, the lusts (or desires and cravings) of our fallen heart begin to master us and drive us back again and again to the same old sinful patterns.

When that happens, sin actually begins to "reign" or have "dominion" over us (Romans 6:12, 14)—so much so that we become "the *servants* of sin" (Romans 6:17; emphasis added). In other words, our "deceitful lusts" (Ephesians 4:22) place us in bondage in that they continually manipulate us and demand that we fulfill their every whim and wish. And unfortunately, our journey has showed us that we've spent a ton of time doing exactly that. All things considered, we got ourselves into quite a predicament when we followed the lusts and longings of our fallen heart.

I'll admit that for me, the most frustrating part about all of this is that I really hated being like Gomer. I didn't want to act like her at all. At times the guilt and shame were enough to swallow me whole. As I watched myself cling to all kinds of seductive suitors, I knew deep down that I wanted to be different. To break free from those seemingly unbreakable chains. But I'd tried and failed so many times that I felt not only powerless but hopeless—like I'd been betrayed by my own desires and there was no way out. Because my Eve's messed-up lusts fought so hard against my longing to be free, at times I wondered if my only choice was to accept my bondage and leave it at that.

In short, my "heart [was] divided" just like the book of Hosea said (Hosea 10:2). Part of me desperately wanted everlasting life, but another part of me still clung to my favorite aprons and escapes. Yet as I sat there staring at all the baggage my heart had accumulated over the years, it finally hit me that I was *done*—done wearing the same old fig leaves, done looking for happiness I could never quite find, and done running off into hiding. Like the Lord said, I had "labour[ed]" and was "heavy laden" (Matthew 11:28). At last, my heart buckled in surrender. I began to feel a yearning growing within me to experience the deliverance of Christ for myself. It was a hunger more intense than anything I'd ever felt. I wanted to know Him . . . to learn from Him . . . to be *saved* by Him!

I recalled the many scriptural travelers who had pressed on to find such deliverance, and I found myself desperately wanting to follow their same path. Like Enos, I wanted to be made whole (see Enos 1:8). Like King Benjamin's people, I wanted to taste the exquisite joy of spiritual rebirth (see Mosiah 5:7). Like those in Alma's story, I wanted my soul to be "illuminated by the light of the everlasting word" (Alma 5:7). I knew that could only happen if I took the time to find Jesus Christ for myself (see Jeremiah 29:13). Yet I'd already proven time and time again that I couldn't overcome my messed-up desires on my own. I needed help. But after all I'd done, I wasn't sure if the Lord would even want to help me.

If you find yourself battling the same feelings of frustration and hopelessness, this is the part where Gomer's story really starts to shine. We need to remember that the point of the narrative wasn't that Gomer was unfaithful—the point was that *she had a Redeemer.* I think the most beautiful moment in the story is the part where even after all her adultery and unfaithfulness, Hosea came to bring Gomer home. Despite all her terrible choices, he was willing to pay the price to redeem her from bondage. And he offered her a place, not just as his servant but as his very own (see Hosea 3:2–3).

I can just picture Hosea pulling Gomer's ragged form into his arms and tipping her weary, tear-streaked face up to his. In a quiet moment that only the two of them would share, he whispered words that were no doubt music to her ears: "Thou shalt abide for me many days; thou shalt not play the harlot, and thou shalt not be for another man: so will I also be for thee" (Hosea 3:3). I'm sure his forgiveness and love made Gomer's heart soar with overflowing feelings of wonder, gratitude, and adoration.

Amazingly, Gomer's story is our story too, for Jesus Christ is our beloved Hosea. He's our one and only Redeemer. Just like the compassionate prophet, He too was willing to pay the price—by shedding His own blood—to redeem us from bondage. Like Hosea, He's simply waiting for us to reject our other lovers and turn our hearts to Him, for He alone can satisfy our Eve's deepest longings. Nothing and no one else can come close . . . especially all our favorite fig leaves and hiding places. The answer is and has always been for we Gomers to turn to Jesus Christ and find *life* that is "eternal" (Doctrine and Covenants 14:7), *joy* that is "unspeakable and full of glory" (Helaman 5:44), and *love* that is "the most joyous to the soul" (1 Nephi 11:23). If we'll just open our eyes, we'll see that our Savior really is our true Deliverer—the healer of our hearts, restorer of our minds, and rescuer of our souls.

Are you beginning to grasp the depth of love our Redeemer has offered us through His infinite Atonement? Incredibly, He doesn't just promise us forgiveness for our sins and redemption from the Fall; He promises us a relationship of love that will surpass anything we've ever experienced. Just turn to Hosea 2 and you'll hear Him offer the same promise to us that Hosea whispered to Gomer:

> And it shall be at that day, saith the Lord, that thou shalt call me Ishi [or *husband*]; and shalt call me no more Baali [or master]. . . .
>
> And I will *betroth thee unto me for ever*; yea, I will *betroth thee unto me* in righteousness, and in judgment, and in lovingkindness, and in mercies.
>
> I will even *betroth thee unto me* in faithfulness: and thou shalt *know* the Lord. (Hosea 2:16, 19–20; emphasis added)

Notice that He used the very same analogy Paul used in Ephesians 5. Christ truly seeks to "betroth" us unto him—meaning He wants us to turn to Him and "know" Him as fully as a husband seeks to know his wife. It's a mind-blowing invitation for those of us who have spent so much time pursuing other lovers. Even after all our spiritual adultery and unfaithfulness, all the Lord wants is for us to turn our hearts fully to Him. If we do so, He's offered us a place—not just as servants in His house but as His very own. I think it's one of the most beautiful and stirring pictures of love ever recorded in the pages of scripture.

So tell me: are you ready to take Him up on His extraordinary offer? Are you ready to set down all your baggage and look up to see His eyes shining with forgiveness, understanding, and love? Are you ready to turn your back on all the other suitors that have been fighting for your attention and submit yourself to Him? Are you ready to open your heart once and for all to the love story that really does end all love stories? Are you ready to give yourself wholly to the One who holds the key to all the happiness and fulfillment of your fallen heart?

If so, our goal on the next leg of our journey is simple. We must detach ourselves from all the other lovers that have kept us distracted and distanced from the Lord. I know you may wonder like I did how we'll ever succeed when we've failed so many times in the past. How in the world can we change the messed-up desires of our heart for good?

Fortunately, we've got some powerful answers waiting for us on the path ahead. We're about to uncover some life-changing truths that will not only help us find freedom from bondage but also the life, love, and joy our Eve was created for.

Readings & Reflections

I found a quote from Elder Neal A. Maxwell that really sparked some personal pondering. Speaking of those in Sodom and Gomorrah, he said they spent their time "[seeking] some fresh sensation, some new sensual experience that would still assure them they were still alive."[94]

I think each of us could ask ourselves: In my spiritual deadness, how have I turned to counterfeit lovers for "some fresh sensation" that would assure me I was "still alive"? Like those in Sodom and Gomorrah, have I relied on "sensual" experiences to try to ignite my inner flame? Write down your thoughts about this topic.

---

94. Neal A. Maxwell, *Look Back at Sodom: A timely account from imaginary Sodom* (Salt Lake City, UT: Deseret Book Co., 1975), 16–17.

We talked in this chapter about the "lusts of our flesh." Consider the following quote from Dr. Chauncey C. Riddle, a former Brigham Young University professor, where he describes the different forms our personal lusts may take:

> What are the rocks of lust in our lives? One is the desire to eat too much, to eat the wrong things, and to eat when we should not. Another is the inability to get to bed on time, to get up on time, or to be where we are supposed to be on time. Rocks of lust are the habits of being absorbed in television or reading when we should be working with our family or doing our [ministering]. They are hunger for a new car when the old one would serve as well or better; the desire to have it known to everyone when we have done some good deed; the need to retaliate when someone has hurt us. They are anger, selfishness, loud laughter, and self-indulgence. They are the powers of Satan exercised on us through our own flesh. We can be rid of these things only by yielding to the enticings of the Holy Spirit.[95]

What thoughts came to mind as you read his words? How do you think these types of lusts affect the love and worship of our heart?

95. Chauncey C. Riddle, "Becoming a Disciple," *Ensign,* Sept. 1974; emphasis added.

For more on how the Lord feels about our fleshly lusts, look up the following passages:

- Romans 13:14 (I love how we're told to "put on" Christ in this verse)
- 1 Peter 2:11
- Mormon 9:28

How do you think these references could apply to you personally?

The prophet Brigham Young offers this powerful insight that I believe applies perfectly to our counterfeit lovers:

> If I were to ask you individually, if you wished to be sanctified throughout, and become as pure and holy as you possibly could live, every person would say yes; yet if the Lord Almighty should give a revelation instructing you to be given wholly up to Him, and to His cause, you would shrink, saying, "I am afraid he will take away some of my darlings." That is the difficulty with the majority of this people.[96]

96. Brigham Young, in *Journal of Discourses*, 2:134.

What are some of your personal "darlings"? Why do you think we "shrink" at the thought of laying them down when we're actually being offered something even better?

In his 1982 general conference talk, Elder Ronald E. Poelman reviewed the story of Hosea and Gomer and offered these reassuring words:

> Portraying God to ancient Israel as a loving, forgiving father, Hosea foreshadowed, more than most Old Testament prophets, the spirit and message of the New Testament, the Book of Mormon, and modern revelation.
>
> In these latter days the Lord has said: "For I the Lord cannot look upon sin with the least degree of allowance; Nevertheless, he that repents and does the commandments of the Lord shall be forgiven" (Doctrine and Covenants 1:31–32).
>
> By disobeying the laws of God and breaking his commandments, we do offend him, we do estrange ourselves from him, and we don't deserve his help and inspiration and strength. But *God's love for us transcends our transgressions. . . .*
>
> I know of no greater inducement to repentance and reconciliation with our Father in Heaven than an awareness of his love for us personally and individually. That such awareness may increase within each of us is my prayer, to which I add my personal witness to you individually that Jesus of Nazareth is the Son of God, the Savior of all mankind, and the Redeemer of each of us individually.[97]

---

97. Ronald E. Poelman, "God's Love for Us Transcends Our Transgressions," *Ensign*, May 1982, 28; emphasis added.

At this point, how has the story of Hosea and Gomer impacted you personally? Do you really believe, as Elder Poelman said, that "God's love for [you] transcends [your] transgressions" (even in the times when you've acted like Gomer)?

Let's conclude this chapter by meditating on the Lord's love for us even in our sinfulness and weakness. Read through the following verses and write down any impressions that come to mind:

- Isaiah 1:18
- Mosiah 26:30
- Doctrine and Covenants 58:42

RESPONSE

In what ways are you feeling prompted to respond to the concepts found in this chapter?

12

The Invitation

The grand question bearing down on us right now is this: how can we exchange the messed-up lusts of our Eve for desires that are cleansed, transformed, and purified? Or as Alma put it, how can we truly experience this "mighty change in [our] hearts" (Alma 5:14)? I'm guessing you already know how it can happen. In fact, the Lord has told us multiple times what we need to do. His invitation can be summed up in these simple words: "repent, and come unto me with full purpose of heart, and I shall heal [you]" (3 Nephi 18:32). It's a call that's open to anyone who will listen.

Over and over in the scriptures, Christ continues to plead with us: "I will be merciful unto [you] . . . if [you] will *repent* and *come unto me*" (2 Nephi 28:32; emphasis added). "Now this is the commandment: *Repent,* all ye ends of the earth, and *come unto me*" (3 Nephi 27:20; emphasis added). "Therefore, whoso *repenteth* and *cometh unto me* as a little child, him will I receive" (3 Nephi 9:22; emphasis added). For "if ye will *come unto me* ye shall have eternal life" (3 Nephi 9:14, emphasis added; see also Doctrine and Covenants 45:5).

If the Lord values us enough to keep extending this invitation, perhaps we should take a closer look at His request. First, notice again that He isn't inviting us to *do* religious things but to *come to Him as a person*. I know this may be new territory for some of us, especially if our church experience has centered mostly around the "doing" part of our culture—the busy activities and the hours of service in our different callings. But it's a key step we can't miss if we want to move forward on this path.

Note too that it isn't our Heavenly Father we're turning to in this instance but Jesus Christ Himself. I know that may seem like a small distinction, but it couldn't be more critical. That's because we've reached the part of our journey where we're searching for *redemption*, meaning we're seeking the One who can change us into an entirely new person. And for that, it's Christ alone we must turn to.

Like we've been talking about for the last several chapters, we must take the time—perhaps for the first time in our lives—to draw close to the Lord and nurture a personal relationship with Him, for it's "only in and through Christ [we] can be saved" (Mosiah 16:13; see also 2 Nephi 31:21; Alma 38:9; Helaman 5:9). That's why in all those scriptural invitations, we're commanded to come unto Jesus, not the Father.

Also notice in the verses I quoted that the Lord didn't just ask us to come to Him—He asked us to *repent.* So we better make sure we know exactly what that process entails. While the most common meaning for the word repent is "a turning of the heart and will to God" (Bible Dictionary, "Repentance"), my favorite definition comes from the original Greek word for repentance, *metanoeo.* This word "denotes a change of mind, i.e., a fresh view about God, about oneself, and about the world" (Bible Dictionary, "Repentance"). Isn't that exactly what we're after on this part of our journey? Don't we desperately need to have our minds changed and renewed? Don't we want to see the Lord, ourselves, and the world in a fresh new way?

I love the way President Russell M. Nelson captured this deeper level of repentance:

> The doctrine of repentance is much broader than a dictionary's definition. When Jesus said "repent," His disciples recorded that command in the Greek language with the verb *metanoeo.* This powerful word has great significance. In this word, the prefix *meta*

> means "change." The suffix relates to four important Greek terms: *nous*, meaning "the mind," *gnosis,* meaning "knowledge," *pneuma,* meaning "spirit," and *pnoe*, meaning "breath." Thus, when Jesus said "repent," He asked us to change—to change our mind, knowledge, and spirit—even our breath.[98]

Now add to that inspiring definition this perspective on *metanoeo* from Elder Theodore M. Burton—a perspective that forever changed the way I look at repentance:

> In the New Testament . . . the Greek writers used the Greek word *metaneoeo* to refer to repentance. *Metaneoeo* is a compound word. . . . In the context in which *meta-* and *-neoeo* are used in the New Testament, the word *metaneoeo* means a change of mind, thought, or thinking so powerful that it changes one's very way of life. . . .
>
> Confusion came, however, when the New Testament was translated from Greek into Latin. Here an unfortunate choice was made in translation; the Greek word *metaneoeo* was translated into the Latin word *poenitere.* The Latin root *poen* in that word is the same root found in our English words *punish, penance, penitent,* and *repentance.* The beautiful meaning of the Hebrew and Greek words was thus changed in Latin to a meaning that involved hurting, punishing, whipping, cutting, mutilating, disfiguring, starving, or even torturing! It is no small wonder, then, that people have come to fear and dread the word repentance, which they understand to mean repeated or unending punishment.[99]

Have we previously looked at repentance as an opportunity to beat ourselves up mentally for all our sins? We can't allow the Latin root word to mislead us! In the words of Elder Richard G. Scott, "Repentance is not punishment. It is the hope-filled path to a more glorious future."[100] It's the path where we turn to the Lord with all

---

98. Russell M. Nelson, "Repentance and Conversion," *Ensign* or *Liahona*, May 2007, 103.

99. Theodore M. Burton, "The Meaning of Repentance," *Ensign*, Aug. 1988; emphasis in original.

100. Richard G. Scott, "Personal Strength through the Atonement of Jesus Christ," *Ensign* or *Liahona*, Nov. 2013, 84.

our heart, might, mind, and strength. As Elder Burton said, it's the path where we experience "a change of mind, thought, or thinking so powerful that it changes [our] very way of life." Pretty amazing invitation if you ask me. It should make us want to run into the arms of our Savior as fast as we possibly can.

In the scriptures, the Lord is also very clear about how we turn to Him, meaning in what attitude and mindset we need to come. In 3 Nephi, He outlined the conditions: "And ye shall offer for a sacrifice unto me *a broken heart and a contrite spirit.* And whoso cometh unto me with a broken heart and a contrite spirit, him will I baptize with fire and with the Holy Ghost" (3 Nephi 9:20; emphasis added). And again: "Ye shall repent of your sins, and come unto me with a broken heart and a contrite spirit" (3 Nephi 12:19).

Here we learn that His invitation is only open to those who are willing to come to Him in absolute humility. False pretenses and insincere attempts won't cut it at this point in our quest. Instead, He asks that we bow down before Him in an entirely broken and contrite state.

If you're wondering what it means to be broken, I think it looks exactly like it sounds. At last, our Eve's hard shell of pride, denial, and blindness has cracked, splintered, and given way. In its place, we now feel an overwhelming sense of our spiritual poverty—a sense of truly being "poor in spirit" (3 Nephi 12:3). In other words, we're finally aware of our utter nothingness and unworthiness before the Lord (see Mosiah 4:11; Alma 38:14). Like the publican in the parable of the Pharisee and the publican, we've reached the point where all we can do as we come to Christ is to smite our breast and say, "God be merciful to me a sinner" (Luke 18:13).

Many scriptural writers recorded similar feelings as they reached this point in their journey. The closer they drew to Jesus Christ, the more overwhelmed they were by their sinfulness compared with His holiness, and they fell at His feet with exclamations of utter humility and contrition. For example, after encountering Jesus's incomparable power at the sea of Galilee, Peter simply cried out, "Depart from me; for I am a sinful man, O Lord" (Luke 5:8). And the brother of Jared echoed a similar plea on the mount: "Now behold, O Lord, and do not be angry with thy servant because of his weakness before thee; for we know that thou art holy and dwellest in the heavens, and that we are unworthy before thee" (Ether 3:2). Both men show us what it looks like to humble ourselves "even in the depths of humility" (Mosiah 4:11).

In this state of wholehearted brokenness, we'll find that we no longer want to rationalize or excuse our Gomer-like behavior. We no longer want to pretend we're better than we are. We no longer want to justify or deny the depth of our personal sin and weakness. Instead, we're willing to come to Christ exactly as we are so He can heal, redeem, and transform us.

With that said, I want to throw out a quick caution before we travel any further, because there's one fear that may paralyze us and keep us from moving forward on our journey. We may worry that after all the sinful things we've done, the Lord will be disappointed with us or reject us when we reach out to Him. After all, there may have been others in our life who withheld their love when we did something wrong, or who went cold and silent when they were upset with us. But Jesus Christ isn't like that at all. In fact, John reassures us that "God sent not his Son into the world to *condemn* the world; but that the world through him might be *saved*" (John 3:17; emphasis added). As our Redeemer, Christ isn't going to belittle us or reject us or shake His finger at us over all our failures and mistakes. Instead, He only wants to save us and rescue us and deliver us from all our sin, sorrow, and shame.

If you need further evidence of this, think about the way Jesus dealt with the many kinds of sinners He encountered during His earthly ministry. The woman at the well had been through five different husbands and was now living with a new partner (see John 4:18). Another woman accused of adultery was caught "in the very act" (John 8:4). Paul (as Saul) had "[breathed] out threatenings and slaughter against the disciples of the Lord" (Acts 9:1), making it his sole purpose to wipe out all Christians. And the great Apostle Peter denied three different times that he even knew the Lord (see Mark

14:66–72). Yet all these and many others were not only forgiven but invited to draw near to Him and partake of the blessings of salvation.

It's clear then that the Lord's invitation isn't just for those who are "good enough" but for every single one of us, no matter how unclean, sinful, or dysfunctional our past may be. In the Book of Mormon, Nephi reminds us of this with these undeniable words:

> Behold, doth he cry unto any, saying: Depart from me? Behold, I say unto you, Nay; but he saith: Come unto me all ye ends of the earth, buy milk and honey, without money and without price. . . .
>
> Hath he commanded any that they should not partake of his salvation? Behold I say unto you, Nay; but he hath given it free for all men; and he hath commanded his people that they should persuade all men to repentance.
>
> Behold, hath the Lord commanded any that they should not partake of his goodness? Behold I say unto you, Nay; but all men are privileged the one like unto the other, and none are forbidden. (2 Nephi 26:25–28)

Jesus Himself also offers us a similar promise: "Will ye not now return unto me, and repent of your sins, and be converted, that I may heal you? . . . Behold, mine arm of mercy is extended towards you, and *whosoever will come, him will I receive*; *and blessed are those who come unto me*" (3 Nephi 9:13–14; emphasis added).

I don't think He could put it any clearer than that. *All* who come to Him will not only be received but also blessed for exercising the faith to reach out to Him for redemption.

If you think about it, when Jesus was on the earth, there was only one group of people who sparked His anger and received His unadulterated wrath. It was the scribes and Pharisees, or those who didn't think they needed saving—those who "trusted in themselves that they were righteous" (Luke 18:9). Amazingly, even they were initially invited to come along with everyone else (see Matthew 23:37). But because their hearts were not broken, and because they were unwilling to admit their sinfulness (and thus their need for Christ), the invitation to come was withdrawn, and in the Lord's own words, their "house [was] left unto [them] desolate" (Matthew 23:38).

So if we think He's waiting for us to get our act together or to reach some imagined standard of worthiness before we can "earn" the right to His Atonement, we've got it completely backwards. In our fallen state, that's something we can never, ever do. The beautiful thing about the gospel is that just like He did in ancient times, Jesus invites us to come to Him exactly as we are. In other words, *right in the middle of our mess*. All He asks for in return is full and complete honesty about every single part of that mess and the true condition of our heart.

There's one prophet who did this exceptionally well, so we're going to use him as our example as we continue along this path. You may assume it's someone like Alma the Younger or Paul, or at least a prophet who had a pretty messed-up past. However, this particular man isn't one we often associate with sinfulness or brokenness. In fact, most of us tend to think he was so valiant that he never made a mistake his entire life. But by his own hand, he admits that that wasn't the case at all.

The prophet we're going to focus on is Nephi.

I'll never be able to thank him enough for writing what many have called the Psalm of Nephi—or 2 Nephi 4:15–35—because it gives us a glimpse into his own struggle with his fallen, sinful, and spiritually dead heart. The section begins with some poignant verses where he deeply laments his personal sins and iniquities. Listen to his soul-wrenching confession and let it stir up memories of times when you've had the very same thoughts and feelings:

> Nevertheless, notwithstanding the great goodness of the Lord, in showing me his great and marvelous works, my heart exclaimeth: O wretched man that I am! Yea, my heart sorroweth because of my flesh; my soul grieveth because of mine iniquities.
>
> I am encompassed about, because of the temptations and the sins which do so easily beset me.
>
> And when I desire to rejoice, my heart groaneth because of my sins. (2 Nephi 4:17–19)

I don't think I've ever heard someone confess their sins with more humility and brokenness than that. In fact, a few verses later, Nephi specifically mentions that his "heart is broken and [his] spirit is contrite" (verse 32). He displays his brokenness by admitting the depth of his fallenness without even a hint of hesitation or a moment of reserve. It's the kind of confession David described in Psalms when he said, "I acknowledged my sin unto thee, and mine iniquity have I not hid. I said, I will confess my transgressions unto the Lord" (Psalm 32:5).

Notice that Nephi doesn't make one single excuse, even though he could have easily mentioned Laman and Lemuel's behavior and how that justified him in acting the way he did. But rather than pointing his finger in blame, Nephi took full responsibility for his own sinful behavior. In fact, he confessed it with a kind of candidness that's extremely rare in our modern-day world.

Notice too that he's not just talking about a few minor weaknesses or a couple of harmless mistakes. No, Nephi says he feels *beset* with sin, which is a word that means "to surround or attack on all sides."[101] He also says he's *encompassed about*, which paints a picture of his sin and temptation closing in all around him.[102] It's as if he feels totally overwhelmed and completely overcome by his fallen nature. We know this because he goes so far as to call himself a "wretched man" (verse 17), which means despicable, pitiful, or miserable.[103]

To me, this is exactly the kind of honesty we've been talking about. Nephi's confession isn't just genuine—it's also incredibly straightforward. And it's the same thing we need to do at this point in our quest. Remember, our Savior has said, "By this ye may know if a man repenteth of his sins—behold, he will *confess* them and *forsake* them" (Doctrine and Covenants 58:43). We'll deal with the second part of that verse later, but for now, the time has come for each of us to *confess*—to ourselves, to the Lord, and even to a priesthood authority if

101. *Dictionary.com*, s.v. "beset," accessed Apr. 1, 2023, https://www.dictionary.com/browse/beset.

102. *Dictionary.com*, s.v. "encompass," accessed Apr. 1, 2023, https://www.dictionary.com/browse/encompass.

103. *Dictionary.com*, s.v. "wretched," accessed Apr. 1, 2023, https://www.dictionary.com/browse/wretched.

needed—that we too have been "beset" and "encompassed about" by all kinds of different sins and iniquities.

If you don't mind another definition, I'll tell you that the word *confess* comes from the Greek word *homologeo*, which means to "speak the same thing," to "agree with," or to "declare openly by way of speaking out freely."[104] So when we confess, what we're really doing is "agreeing" with the Lord about our lost and fallen state. We're "declaring openly" and "freely" our sins and acknowledging our false worship before Him.

One of the biggest threats to this process is our human tendency to downplay our personal weakness and remain blind to our individual sins and shortcomings. For this reason, President Dieter F. Uchtdorf gives us this bold but much-needed warning:

> None of us likes to admit when we are drifting off the right course. Often we try to avoid looking deeply into our souls and confronting our weaknesses, limitations, and fears. Consequently, when we do examine our lives, we look through the filter of biases, excuses, and stories we tell ourselves in order to justify unworthy thoughts and actions.
>
> But being able to see ourselves clearly is essential to our spiritual growth and well-being. If our weaknesses and shortcomings remain obscured in the shadows, then the redeeming power of the Savior cannot heal them and make them strengths. Ironically, our blindness toward our human weaknesses will also make us blind to the divine potential that our Father yearns to nurture within each of us.[105]

That's why I believe it's crucial that we ask for the Lord's help in facing and confessing our sins and weaknesses. There are times when only He will be able to remove our stubborn blindness. When only He can help us move past the "biases, excuses, and stories we tell ourselves to justify unworthy thoughts and actions." While we may think we truly know ourselves, Christ can see into the deepest shadows of our

---

104. W. E. Vine, *Vine's Complete Expository Dictionary of Old and New Testament Words* (Nashville, TN: Thomas Nelson, 1984), 120.

105. Dieter F. Uchtdorf, "Lord, Is It I?," *Ensign* or *Liahona*, Nov. 2014, 58.

souls far better than we can, so we must ask for His discernment and insight to help us see—and confess—all the inner baggage that will keep us from moving forward on our quest.

Now, I know Nephi's confession only consisted of a few short verses, but we're going to go a lot deeper than that. Basically, our goal is to explore every last corner of our heart and get absolutely everything off our chest. We've uncovered quite a bit of baggage along the paths of this journey, so the time has come for us to own every single bit of it. Not only that, but we must make sure the Lord *knows* we own it by confessing all of it in true brokenness and humility.

In the October 2011 general conference, Elder D. Todd Christofferson emphasized the importance of confession, pointing out that it should be "more than a casual 'I admit it; I'm sorry.'" He continued:

> Confession is a deep, sometimes agonizing acknowledgment of error and offense to God and man. Sorrow and regret and bitter tears often accompany one's confession, especially when his or her actions have been the cause of pain to someone or, worse, have led another into sin. It is this deep distress, this view of things as they really are, that leads one, as Alma, to cry out, "O Jesus, thou Son of God, have mercy on me, who am in the gall of bitterness, and am encircled about by the everlasting chains of death" (Alma 36:18).[106]

Like Elder Christofferson said, "deep distress" may play a part in our personal confession. We know Nephi experienced this because he said that he grieved and sorrowed and groaned over his personal sins (see 2 Nephi 4:17, 19). I'll admit that I also struggled with these same difficult emotions as I hauled all my personal baggage out into the open. As I stared at the enormity of who I'd become as a result of the Fall, it was agonizing to look at the depth of my sinfulness, especially once I understood how big and wide and deep it really was. To be honest, it wasn't just painful—at times I felt completely overwhelmed and hopeless at the prospect of dealing with such a complicated mess.

---

106. D. Todd Christofferson, "The Divine Gift of Repentance," *Ensign* or *Liahona*, Nov. 2011, 40; emphasis added.

And yet, as odd as it may sound, this type of emotional pain can be a good thing. For example, Elder Marion D. Hanks referenced Nephi's "sweet psalm of contrition and faith" and pointed out an important distinction about the prophet's sorrow that will help us deal with our own uncomfortable emotions: "Nephi understood that *true remorse is a gift from God, not a curse, but a blessing.* True remorse involves sorrow and suffering; but *the sorrow is purposeful, constructive, cleansing*, the 'godly sorrow' that 'worketh repentance to salvation,' and not the 'sorrow of the world' (2 Corinthians 7:10)."[107]

I think it helps to remember that godly sorrow is "purposeful, constructive, [and] cleansing" and always leads us to repentance. Though difficult, it always moves us in the right direction. In contrast, when we're caught up in worldly sorrow, we're just sad that we can't continue living in ignorance, or that we can't escape the negative consequences of our choices. If those consequences went away, so would our desire to repent. To make sure our confession is genuine, then, we need to evaluate the motive lying underneath our feelings of sorrow and distress. I like the way author Matt Chandler captures it:

> All the crying and carrying on can make for some dramatic, sincere-sounding confessions. *But raw emotion alone does not equal repentance.* That's because emotions are truly the bouncy-houses of the human organism. They go up, they come down. Roll out, roll around. Can't walk a straight line or keep their balance for more than a few minutes. So once the show's over and the aspirin has started to kick in, those energized feelings—the ones that had you promising all those heartfelt "never-agains"—won't be anywhere to be found, no matter how much you seemed to mean it when you said it.
>
> Whenever the main driver of recovery is emotional zeal alone, the fuel will always burn up once the passion has played out. *The difference between changing our ways and being stuck in the same old*

107. Marion D. Hanks, "He Means Me," *Ensign*, May 1979, 76; emphasis added.

stuff is often the same difference between wanting to be whole and just wanting to feel better again.[108]

Yes, we may experience some difficult emotions during this part of our journey. Like Chandler said, it may bring tears and anguish and uttered promises of "never again." But the true test of our confession isn't just that we're feeling those kinds of emotions. The true test is whether, deep in our hearts, we're really ready to change. So it's important to ask ourselves: Do I just want to feel better in the moment? Or do I truly want to be made whole? Am I still blaming other people or circumstances or even God for my failures? Or have I taken responsibility for my own personal sins? Am I continuing to rationalize my behavior? Or am I completely open about all my sins, no matter the pain this confession causes me? If any red flags pop up while you're pondering these questions, it may be time to push a little deeper into your confession and see if any additional baggage comes spilling out.

Another way we can evaluate our true motives is by going back to the example Nephi set for us in his psalm. When we're experiencing true godly sorrow, we understand like Nephi how much we've been "beset" and "encompassed about" by all kinds of different temptations and sins. We understand how deeply our heart has been mired in false beliefs. We accept once and for all that we too are in a "wretched" state and in desperate need of repentance. If we've reached this point as Nephi did, we can rest assured that we're motivated by godly sorrow and not the shallow, fleeting sorrow of the world.

Now, you've probably guessed that this type of confession is a deep and multi-layered process that will take some time to work through completely. But please don't let that scare you. I promise: confessing your sins will feel incredibly liberating and therapeutic in the end. So I'm begging you not to give up. You've come too far to turn back now. If you'll press forward with me to the end of this path, you'll eventually find yourself standing on a spectacular summit, one that really will

---

108. Matt Chandler and Michael Snetzer, *Recovering Redemption: A Gospel Saturated Perspective on How to Change* (Nashville, TN: B&H Books, 2014), 70; emphasis added.

change your life forever. All the pain and discomfort you're feeling right now will totally be worth it in the end.

If you're willing, then, the best thing you can do at this point is to slow down your pace and take the needed time to acknowledge all your aprons, escapes, and attempts to blame. One thing that helped me was to write down everything I'd learned about my personal sin in either a notebook or journal (I used both but you could use a computer or your phone if that works better for you). For many of us, writing and journaling are incredibly cathartic. Often things come out through this method that we didn't even know were buried inside us. As you do this, go back through the different paths on our journey and look again at everything you've uncovered along the way. Then write about (or at least summarize) each of those things one by one. (If the thought of this much writing is giving you hives, maybe you could just jot things down in an outline or make some notes. The important thing isn't writing a novel but getting it all down in some kind of written form.)

You may wonder why I would suggest such a lengthy and complicated process. I mean, why not just spend some time on our knees confessing and call it good? There are actually several reasons. When we take time to write everything down, it shows that we're taking the Lord's injunction to confess very seriously. It requires us to peel away all our excuses and justifications and helps us see things more clearly, perhaps for the first time in our entire lives. It allows us to better understand the many sins that have ruled our thoughts, feelings, and actions. And it forces us to acknowledge what's going on deep inside us and how big the mess really is. Perhaps most importantly, writing things down helps us remember all our aprons and escapes so the Lord can help us sort out each issue when the time is right.

For instance, in my own journal I wrote about my problem with people-pleasing and my desperate need for others' approval. I wrote about my addictions to certain kinds of escapes and how I used them to try to fill my emptiness. I wrote about grudges I was holding on to and my sometimes harsh and critical judgment of others. I wrote about moments of worldliness, laziness, selfishness, pride, and gossip and about my struggle with thoughts of fear and unbelief. I wrote about my self-righteousness, or times I thought I was better than others because they sinned differently (or more publicly) than me. I wrote about days I served so I could subconsciously pat myself on the back. I wrote about the countless things I'd done to draw attention to myself, about times of prayerlessness and completely forgetting the Lord, and about sins in both my marriage and my parenting. And I also wrote about many things that are far too personal to share in this setting.

I know some may think I'm crazy to confess this much of my baggage for all the world to see. But the truth is, I have no interest in wearing a "good girl" mask. No desire to hide my struggles and have others think I'm all that. I'm not all that. Underneath my church-going facade, I'm no different than any other sinner in the scriptures. And I've found it's very freeing to be real and authentic about that.

In addition, I'm hoping that confessing my baggage publicly will earn me enough credibility to say one very important thing: *if I can do it, so can you.* I know this kind of confession is daunting. I know you may worry that the pain and anguish will be too much to bear. But remember, this is the part of our quest where you'll really start to make some breakthroughs. Where you'll begin to see yourself and your heart in a whole new way. Where you'll better understand the whys and hows of your various obsessions and addictions. Yes, it can be a challenging trail, but don't forget how close you are to the summit. Even though you'll continue the practice of confession throughout your life, you'll hopefully never have to experience it on this level ever again. So have courage. Or pray for it if you don't feel like you have any. Let the Lord's love surround you as you face this difficult process and take things at your own pace, one small step at a time.

If it helps, I'll share a beautiful passage from the book of James where he describes this part of our quest with some profound and poignant words: "Draw nigh to God, and he will draw nigh to you. Cleanse your hands, ye sinners; and purify your hearts, ye double minded. Be afflicted, and mourn, and weep: let your laughter be turned to mourning, and your joy to heaviness. Humble yourselves in the sight of the Lord, and he shall lift you up" (James 4:8–10; see also Joel 2:12–13).

I believe that last phrase—"he shall lift you up"—is incredibly important. Put simply, *it's the very thing that will enable us to get through the pain of our confession*. Isn't it comforting to know that as we bow down before the Lord and confess everything to Him in humility, He will be there to lift us up? We know Nephi understood this because he did something specific after mentioning his sorrow over his personal sins. Rather than getting caught up in feelings of self-pity, embarrassment, or shame, he turned his thoughts immediately to the Lord. Watch how quickly he changed the focus of his mind from the agony of his fallen state to the mercy, love, and tenderness of his Savior:

> And when I desire to rejoice, my heart groaneth because of my sins; nevertheless, I know in whom I have trusted.
>
> My God hath been my support; he hath led me through mine afflictions in the wilderness; and he hath preserved me upon the waters of the great deep.
>
> He hath filled me with his love, even unto the consuming of my flesh.
>
> He hath confounded mine enemies, unto the causing of them to quake before me.
>
> Behold, he hath heard my cry by day, and he hath given me knowledge by visions in the night-time.
>
> And by day have I waxed bold in mighty prayer before him; yea, my voice have I sent up on high; and angels came down and ministered unto me.
>
> And upon the wings of his Spirit hath my body been carried away upon exceedingly high mountains. And mine eyes have beheld great things, yea, even too great for man; therefore I was bidden that I should not write them. (2 Nephi 4:19–25)

Tell me, how can Nephi wallow in sorrow when he knows he has a God like that? And how can we? The prophet's words are an amazing reminder that if we turn to Him, the Lord really will lift us up. In fact, I'd like to suggest that we follow Nephi's example and end our confession by writing down everything our Savior has done for us as well. If you need a little inspiration, spend some time in Psalms and let the beautiful words of praise wash over you in a fresh, new way. Then turn to your journal and take the time to pen your own lines of gratitude and adoration. Pour out your thanks in written form for all the Lord has meant to you over the years. It really will fill you with all the hope and faith you'll need to move forward on our quest. Jesus Christ loves you. And He's ready to not only heal and transform your heart but to lift you out of all the sorrow and sadness you may be feeling as a result of the Fall.

Once your confession is complete, it's time to turn our steps to the other half of the repentance process: that of *forsaking* our personal sin. I hope you're ready because we're about to see some pretty big changes in our Eve—changes that will hopefully last not just a day but an entire lifetime.

Readings & Reflections

One of my favorite passages on repenting and coming to Christ is found in Mosiah 4. First, read verses 5–12 and see what correlations you can find with the Psalm of Nephi. Then answer the following questions:

- In verse 11, what are the people told to "always retain in remembrance"?

- What else does King Benjamin ask them to do in that verse?

- What promises are they then given in verse 12?

____

____

____

____

- How do you think this counsel applies to our current path on our journey?

____

____

____

____

Next, consider this counsel from Elder Richard G. Scott:

> I invite each one of you to thoughtfully review your life. Have you deviated from the standards that you know will bring happiness? Is there a dark corner that needs to be cleaned out? Are you now doing things that you know are wrong? Do you fill your mind with unclean thoughts? When it is quiet and you can think clearly, does your conscience tell you to repent?
>
> For your peace now and for everlasting happiness, please repent. Open your heart to the Lord and ask Him to help you. You will earn the blessing of forgiveness, peace, and the knowledge you have been purified and made whole. Find the courage to ask the Lord for strength to repent now.[109]

Notice how Elder Scott described direct communication with the Lord—where we're asking Christ specifically for His help and strength. Is that a new concept for you? How do you think that echoes Alma's experience in Alma 36:18?

109. Richard G. Scott, "Finding Forgiveness," *Ensign*, May 1995, 77.

We also talked in this chapter about coming to the Lord with a broken heart and a contrite spirit. Read 2 Nephi 2:6–7 and note what you learn from those verses and how it can apply to you.

Continuing with that idea, ponder the following from Elder D. Todd Christofferson and Sister Neill F. Marriott:

> In ancient times when people wanted to worship the Lord and seek His blessings, they often brought a gift. For example, when they went to the temple, they brought a sacrifice to place on the altar. After His Atonement and Resurrection, the Savior said He would no longer accept burnt offerings of animals. The gift or sacrifice He will accept now is "a broken heart and a contrite spirit" (3 Nephi 9:20). As you seek the blessing of conversion, you can offer the Lord the gift of your broken, or repentant, heart and your contrite, or

obedient, spirit. In reality, it is the gift of yourself—what you are and what you are becoming.[110]

What is our heart condition today? Paradoxically, in order to have a healed and faithful heart, we must first allow it to break before the Lord. "Ye shall offer for a sacrifice unto me a broken heart and a contrite spirit," (3 Nephi 9:20), the Lord declares. The result of sacrificing our heart, or our will, to the Lord is that we receive the spiritual guidance we need.

With a growing understanding of the Lord's grace and mercy, we will find that our self-willed hearts begin to crack and break in gratitude. Then we reach for Him, yearning to yoke ourselves to the Only Begotten Son of God. In our brokenhearted reaching and yoking, we receive new hope and fresh guidance through the Holy Ghost.[111]

What further insights are we given through the words of these great souls?

____

____

____

____

____

____

____

Look up the following scriptures and see what they teach us about having a broken heart:

- 3 Nephi 12:19–20
- Moroni 6:2
- Doctrine and Covenants 20:37
- Doctrine and Covenants 56:18

---

110. D. Todd Christofferson, "When Thou Art Converted," *Ensign* or *Liahona*, May 2004, 12.

111. Neill F. Marriott, "Yielding Our Hearts To God," *Ensign* or *Liahona*, Nov. 2015, 32.

How can we tell if our heart is truly broken? Why do you think there's such a strong connection between the concept of repentance and having a broken heart and a contrite spirit?

Read Alma 13:27–30, focusing especially on verse 30. How do you think the Lord can "grant you" repentance? (You can turn to Alma 24:10; Alma 34:17; Helaman 12:24; and Mormon 3:3 for further study on this idea.)

This description of repentance from Elder F. Enzio Busche touched my heart in a very personal way. Take some time to ponder his words and think about where you are in your own journey into the depths of brokenness, repentance, and humility. Speaking of coming to Christ in brokenness, he says the following:

> In the depths of such [feelings], we may finally be led to that lonesome place where we suddenly see ourselves naked in all soberness. Gone are all the little lies of self-defense. We see ourselves in our vanities and false hopes for carnal security. We are shocked

> to see our many deficiencies, our lack of gratitude for the smallest things. We are now at that sacred place that seemingly only a few have courage to enter—because this is that horrible place of unquenchable pain in fire and burning. This is that place where true repentance is born. This is that place where the conversion and the rebirth of the soul are happening. . . . This is the place where sanctifications and rededications and renewal of covenants are happening. This is the place where suddenly the atonement of Christ is understood and embraced.[112]

Are you beginning to experience what Elder Busche was talking about? How has your confession of sin helped you better understand and embrace the blessings of the Lord's Atonement?

____

____

____

____

____

____

____

____

112. F. Enzio Busche, "Truth Is the Issue," *Ensign*, Nov. 1993, 26.

RESPONSE

In what ways are you feeling prompted to respond to the concepts found in this chapter?

13

Awake to Grace

Imagine you're spending one of your free Saturdays cleaning out a messy, overstuffed closet. Most of us have done something like that before, and we know it takes several steps to work through completely. The first step, of course, is the initial purge where we pull everything out of the closet so we can see all the junk that's been hiding in there. While the closet is now clean and empty and beautiful, the room is still piled with all the clutter that we just removed from those shelves. Though it's good that the junk has been brought out of hiding, the job is only half finished. The only way for us to complete it is to deal with each item that we pulled out in our purge. Otherwise, we'll just end up cramming it all back in once again and we'll be left with the same old frustrating mess.

You can probably see where I'm going with this analogy. If the last chapter was our purge where we pulled all our Eve's baggage out into the open, then this is the part where we begin to clean up the mess. Where we figure out what to do with all that stuff so it doesn't continue to clutter up the corners of our minds and hearts. It's like the scripture we quoted from Doctrine and Covenants 58:43—our repentance first requires that we *confess*, and then it's time for us to *forsake*. In other words, it's time for us to take all that junk we purged and deal with it one small step at a time.

Compared to the confession part, I'll admit that the forsaking part is a lot more complicated. Since the word *forsake* means "to quit or leave entirely; abandon; [or] desert,"[113] that means this is the part where we abandon our fig leaves, hiding places, and finger-pointing once and for all. But like I've been saying throughout our journey, that's a whole lot easier said than done. Rather than dealing with our junk, most of the time we've just left it stacked on a side table or kicked into a corner on the floor. Or perhaps we shoved our baggage back in the closet with the rationalization that we'll deal with the whole chaotic mess some other day.

This time around, we don't want to get caught in that trap. This time, we want to learn how to forsake our sins in such a way that they really do *stay* forsaken. But how can we cast out all our complicated baggage once and for all? How can we keep our closets (or hearts) from attracting the same endless clutter again and again? How can we de-junk our shelves so there's finally room for Christ to dwell there and ignite the space with His glorious lamp of everlasting life?

If you'll let your eyes drift to the trail ahead, you'll see that we've actually reached a crossroads. It's a place where the road diverges in two opposite directions. Thankfully, there are some road signs that designate the different paths we can take to find our way. Upon further discovery, we see that the road on our right is marked "Faith in Christ's Grace," while the left-hand path is labeled "Relying on My Works." Although both roads appear to lead us to the spiritual rebirth and eternal life we've been longing for, there's only one path that will really enable us to find it.

I'll admit that the minute I looked to the left, I knew I'd been down that road many times before. In my past efforts to repent, I'd often taken the path of "Relying on My Works" in the hopes of finally overcoming my personal sins once and for all. When simply

---

113. *Dictionary.com*, s.v. "forsake," accessed Apr. 1, 2023, https://www.dictionary.com/browse/forsake.

walking didn't work, I tried running or even sprinting down that path. Summoning all the willpower I could muster, I made lists, offered myself rewards, and worked and reworked my goals. I even asked others to help keep me on track. But despite all those ambitious efforts, sooner or later I always ended up right back where I began. Suddenly, it occurred to me that the left-hand road—the path where I relied on my own willpower to find freedom from sin—actually formed a circle. Try, fail, try, fail . . . around and around I went. No wonder I never got anywhere!

Thankfully, Jesus Christ understands our inability to truly forsake our sins for good. In fact, He gave His life because He knew we could never succeed by relying on our own efforts. He knew that because of the Fall, we're chained to our natural man and its frustrating appetites and passions, no matter how hard we try to work ourselves free. Amazingly, the Lord suffered and died to pave a new road, one based solely on His grace. And it's a road that will allow us to forever leave behind that useless circle of works.

It shouldn't surprise us, then, that the scriptures are packed with the words of prophets and apostles who boldly point to the path of "Faith in Christ's Grace." For instance, when Enos received a remission of his sins, he revealed exactly which road got him there: "And I said: Lord, how is it done? And he said unto me: *Because of thy faith in Christ . . . thy faith hath made thee whole*" (Enos 1:7–8; emphasis added). Standing as a second witness, Paul also directed his listeners solely to the Lord's empowering grace: "*For by grace are ye saved through faith*; and that not of yourselves: it is the *gift of God*: *Not of works*, lest any man should boast" (Ephesians 2:8–9; emphasis added). Joseph Smith also retranslated another of Paul's verses in a way that leaves no doubt: we are "justified *only* by his grace through the redemption that is in Christ Jesus" (Romans 3:24, footnote *a*; see also Doctrine and Covenants 20:30–31). Over and over, the Lord's servants remind us that placing our faith in Christ's grace is the only way we'll be able to clean out our cluttered hearts once and for all.

I came across an analogy from author Rick Warren that helps illustrate why we'll never get anywhere by relying on our own works or willpower. It goes like this:

> Imagine riding in a speedboat on a lake with an automatic pilot set to go east. If you decide to reverse and head west, you have two possible ways to change the boat's direction. One way is to grab the steering wheel and physically *force it* to head in the opposite direction from where the autopilot is programmed to go. By sheer willpower you could overcome the autopilot, but you would feel constant resistance. Your arms would eventually tire of the stress, you'd let go of the steering wheel, and the boat would instantly head back east, the way it was internally programmed.[114]

The picture he paints is a vivid one. The automatic pilot on the boat represents the strong pull of our natural man. We know our hearts have been deceived because of the Fall, and our Eve continues to turn to her various aprons, hiding places, and finger-pointing. The tendency to run to these things has become our default setting, or the underlying motivation that subtly influences our heart from day to day. As the analogy points out, we can try on our own to change that internal setting, but all we'll end up doing is pulling on that inner steering wheel until our willpower gives out. Left to ourselves, the power of our natural man (and its corrupted appetites, desires, and passions) is simply too strong for us to resist.

Happily, this is where the good news of the gospel comes in—the news that there *is* a way to change the direction of our automatic pilot. It comes as we exercise "Faith in Christ's Grace." This road works so well because the Lord's grace is an "enabling power," or "a divine means of help and strength" (Bible Dictionary, "Grace"). But let's not assume that this enabling power only provides a little help here and there after we've worked as hard as we can on our own. Jesus Christ is "the author *and* the finisher of [our] faith" (Moroni 6:4; emphasis added), not just the finisher! He is the "Alpha *and* Omega, the

---

114. Rick Warren, *The Purpose Driven Life: What On Earth Am I Here For?* (Grand Rapids, MI: Zondervan, 2002), 181; emphasis in original.

beginning *and* the end" (Doctrine and Covenants 84:120; emphasis added).

When it comes to grace, I think we often get stuck on Nephi's oft-quoted verse, "It is by grace that we are saved, after all we can do" (2 Nephi 25:23). Many of us hear that last phrase and assume it means we have to work as hard as we can on our own before grace can kick in. To do our very best and *then* He'll make up the rest. But let's stop and take a second look at what Nephi was actually saying in 2 Nephi 25. President Dieter F. Uchtdorf offers this much-needed counsel in his epic talk, "The Gift of Grace":

> I wonder if sometimes we misinterpret the phrase "after all we can do." We must understand that "after" does not equal "because."
>
> We are not saved "because" of all that we can do. Have any of us done all that we can do? Does God wait until we've expended every effort before He will intervene in our lives with His saving grace?
>
> Many people feel discouraged because they constantly fall short. They know firsthand that "the spirit indeed is willing, but the flesh is weak." They raise their voices with Nephi in proclaiming, "My soul grieveth because of mine iniquities."
>
> I am certain Nephi knew that the Savior's grace allows and enables us to overcome sin. This is why Nephi labored so diligently to persuade his children and brethren "to believe in Christ, and to be reconciled to God."
>
> After all, that is what we can do! And that is our task in mortality![115]

I love how he says all we can do is "believe in Christ, and . . . be reconciled to God" so the Savior's grace can then enable us to overcome our sin. And how are we reconciled to God? We don't have to earn it. All we have to do is *come to Him*. To reach for His grace with all our hearts. To join our weakness with His magnificent power. Then, as the Apostle Paul points out, "through the grace of the Lord Jesus Christ we shall be saved" (Acts 15:11).

---

115. Dieter F. Uchtdorf, "The Gift of Grace," *Ensign* or *Liahona*, May 2015, 110.

Like President Uchtdorf, I too believe that Nephi understood this principle very well. Going back to 2 Nephi 4, look at what the prophet does after he praises all that the Lord has accomplished in his life. First, he gives himself a little pep talk and cries out, "Awake, my soul!" (verse 28). But he doesn't then gear up for a new round of goal setting. He doesn't promise the Lord he'll try harder to do better. And he doesn't attempt to muster up more resolve to stop sinning either. No, Nephi does the very thing we've been talking about this entire time: *he places all his hope and trust not in his own works but in the enabling power of Jesus Christ.* Listen carefully to the way he expresses it:

> Rejoice, O my heart, and cry unto the Lord, and say: O Lord, I will praise thee forever; yea, my soul will rejoice in thee, my God, and the rock of my salvation.
>
> O Lord, *wilt thou* redeem my soul? *Wilt thou* deliver me out of the hands of mine enemies? *Wilt thou* make me that I may shake at the appearance of sin?
>
> May the gates of hell be shut continually before me, because that my heart is broken and my spirit is contrite! O Lord, *wilt thou* not shut the gates of thy righteousness before me, that I may walk in the path of the low valley, that I may be strict in the plain road!
>
> O Lord, *wilt thou* encircle me around in the robe of thy righteousness! O Lord, *wilt thou* make a way for mine escape before mine enemies! *Wilt thou* make my path straight before me! *Wilt thou* not place a stumbling block in my way—but that *thou wouldst* clear my way before me, and hedge not up my way, but the ways of mine enemy. (2 Nephi 4:30–33; emphasis added)

Looking at all his "wilt thou" phrases, we can tell that Nephi truly believed Christ was the only one who could change him. The only one who could redeem his soul. The only one who could deliver him from his enemies. The only one who could remove all stumbling blocks. And the only one who could make him shake at the very appearance of sin. Because of this belief, Nephi doesn't promise the Lord that he'll try harder not to get angry or that he'll do all he can not to give in to the temptation to sin. He doesn't attempt some version of "all he can do." Instead, he goes straight to the true source of power because he knows that's the only thing that can produce such a mighty change deep in his heart.

In fact, Nephi makes it clear in the final verses of his psalm that he refuses to trust in his own works or willpower (or as he calls it, "the arm of flesh"): "O Lord, I have trusted in thee, and I will trust in thee forever. I will not put my trust in the arm of flesh; for I know that cursed is he that putteth his trust in the arm of flesh. Yea, cursed is he that putteth his trust in man or maketh flesh his arm" (verse 34).

He then closes his plea with an inspiring declaration of trust in the Lord and His ability (and willingness) to change him. Take a minute to let his words penetrate the depths of your mind and heart: "Yea, I know that God will give liberally to him that asketh. Yea, my God will give me, if I ask not amiss; therefore I will lift up my voice unto thee; yea, I will cry unto thee, my God, the rock of my righteousness. Behold, my voice shall forever ascend up unto thee, my rock and mine everlasting God. Amen" (verse 35).

I think this is one of the most profound testimonies of grace in all of scripture. Though Nephi doesn't use the actual word in his passage, every sentence sings of his belief in the Savior's ability to redeem him. In short, Nephi's soul really does awake just like he talked about in his prayer. But the amazing thing is what he actually awakes to. He awakes to the astonishing, life-changing power of Christ. He awakes to the indescribable strength available to him through his "everlasting God," the "rock of [his] righteousness." In short, *he awakes to grace*—to his desperate and all-encompassing need for the Lord's Atonement. With eyes wide open, Nephi is completely focused on Jesus as the only one who can make the desperately needed changes in his life.

Now, the kind of change we're talking about isn't just a cleaner, better version of our old self. No, the only way we can "walk in newness of life" (Romans 6:4) is to ask the Lord to give us a "*new heart*" and a "*new spirit*" (Ezekiel 36:26). Once we "put on the new man" (Ephesians 4:24), we won't just *act* differently—we'll *feel* differently and *think* differently than we ever have before. As Elder David A. Bednar explains, this kind of transformation is "mighty, not minor—a spiritual rebirth and fundamental change of what we feel and desire, what we think and do, and what we are."[116] It's the point where we'll have "no more desire to do evil" (Alma 19:33) and no more "disposition" to return to our same old sins anymore (Mosiah 5:2).

I want you to imagine what it would be like to lose all your "desire" and "disposition" for sin. Maybe the best way to visualize such a change would be to contemplate the opposite. So for just a moment, think about what it's felt like to suffer the consequences of your sin. Like the times you've lost your temper, for instance. Picture the look on the other person's face or the hurt you saw in their eyes. Or remember the guilt that flooded you over those inappropriate thoughts, the ones you're thankful no one else knows about. Feel again the embarrassment of being caught in a lie, or the humiliation of that binge you just gave way to, whether it was with a credit card at the mall or the ice cream in your freezer. Reflect on the shame, the lack of control, and the humiliation you've felt over your addictions, your obsessions, and your sins.

Now tell me: what it would feel like to put an end to all that torment? To be freed from all the sin that has haunted you? Wouldn't the relief—and the joy—be almost indescribable? At the very least, such a miracle would feel like a dream come true. But it's not a dream. It really *is* possible—and it's possible for *you*, not just the men and women in the scriptures. Remember, we've each been promised that we can be "partakers of the divine nature [once we've] escaped the corruption that is in the world through lust" (2 Peter 1:4). But that promise can only be fulfilled if, like Nephi, we place all our faith and trust in the Lord Jesus. Only He can help us "give away all [our] sins" (Alma 22:18) and grant us a "remission of [our] sins by fire and by the Holy Ghost" (2 Nephi 31:17). "Being then made free from sin," we'll become "the servants of righteousness," and our lives will finally show "fruit unto holiness, and the end everlasting life" (Romans 6:18, 22).

Let's wrap up this discussion by addressing what may be the most important question of all. While we understand a little better how

---

116. David A. Bednar, "Ye Must Be Born Again," *Ensign* or *Liahona*, May 2007, 20.

the Lord's grace works in our lives, we may not know how to *access* that power. How do we receive our Savior's grace? How do we get this life-changing transformation started? There's only one way to do it. Like Nephi did, the key is to *ask* (and *keep on asking*) for the gift of grace, for without the Lord's power filling and strengthening us from this moment on, we won't even move an inch on this new road. Instead, we'll automatically find ourselves right back to "Relying on Our Works" and its never-ending circle. Right back to our same old sinful habits, behaviors, and addictions. If you remember, that's exactly what Christ told the woman at the well. He said, "If thou knewest the gift of God, and who it is that saith to thee, Give me to drink; *thou wouldest have asked of him*, and he would have given thee living water" (John 4:10; emphasis added).

Please note: this isn't your typical "Heavenly Father, please help me with this or that today." This is a cry *directly to the Lord Himself.* It's the very thing Nephi did in his psalm and what many others in the Book of Mormon did when they found themselves in desperate need of their Savior's grace. For instance, listen to Alma's cry: "O Jesus, thou Son of God, have mercy on me" (Alma 36:18). The prophet even told his son, "Never, until I did *cry out unto the Lord Jesus Christ for mercy*, did I receive a remission of my sins. But behold, I did *cry unto him* and I did find peace to my soul" (Alma 38:8; emphasis added). And the same is true for each of us.

Put simply, we need to reach out to Jesus Christ. Remember, Brigham Young encouraged us earlier to not only "cling to him" and "make friends with him" but also to "keep open communication with . . . our Savior."[117] So open up your heart and—just like Alma did—cry out to Jesus. Ask for His help. Beg for His life-giving grace, forgiveness, and mercy. For He promises us in scripture, "If you will *ask of me*, you shall receive; if you will knock, it shall be opened

117. Brigham Young, in *Journal of Discourses*, 8:339. See also page 163 of this book.

unto you" (Doctrine and Covenants 11:5, emphasis added; see also Doctrine and Covenants 6:21–23).[118]

While this kind of cry doesn't have to be fancy, it does need to come from an authentic place deep in our heart. I love how Dr. Chauncey C. Riddle explains it:

> True prayer begins with a yearning in the soul of man. . . . Its essence is a feeling of the heart. The measure of a prayer is the intensity and the depth of that feeling. . . . Does that feeling wholly fill his soul? Is he oblivious to everything else but the fact that he is in the presence of his beloved Master? Does he cry out from anguish at the realization of his own nothingness contrasted with the goodness of God? . . .
>
> If these things take place, the child of God is achieving and experiencing what the scriptures call "mighty prayer." . . . What poverty of soul entraps one who has never felt the fire of mighty prayer! Having achieved full worship even once would color and heighten every prayer thereafter, for the remainder of one's life.[119]

With these stirring words in mind, think back through the various prayers you've offered over the years. Can you say that you've experienced what Dr. Riddle just described? Like Lamoni's father in the Book of Mormon, have you ever fallen on your face and cried out to the Lord? Have you ever begged like he did for the "wicked spirit" to be "rooted out of [your] breast" (Alma 22:15)? If not, then the moment has now arrived. In the soul-igniting words of Beth Moore, "*Cry out.* Open your mouth, say, 'God, help me!' and mean it. Not as a figure of speech. Not with half a heart. With everything you've got, look up and cry out. Bring heaven to a standstill. Get some attention."[120]

---

118. I know some may question the idea of reaching out to Jesus personally because we're told in scripture to pray to the Father. (I also had this same concern.) But after an extensive study on the subject, I actually found a mountain of scriptural evidence that supports direct communication with the Lord Himself. If you'd like to learn more, you can find a link to my research on the bottom of my Favorites page at jaciwightman.com.

119. Chauncey C. Riddle, "Prayer," *Ensign*, Mar. 1975.

120. Beth Moore, *Get Out of That Pit: Straight Talk about God's Deliverance* (Nashville, TN: Thomas Nelson, 2007), 120, 123; emphasis in original.

You may be wondering why it's so crucial for us to offer such an all-encompassing prayer of the heart. I mean, the Lord already knows about our need, so why does He make us go to all the trouble? Beth Moore continues:

> I think He usually waits for us to cry out so He can remove all doubt about who came to our rescue. . . .
>
> Further, God sees great advantage in awaiting our cry because He is unequivocally driven by relationship. . . . Never lose sight of the fact that God will forever be more interested in your knowing your Healer than experiencing His healing, and knowing your Deliverer than knowing your deliverance. The king of all creation wants to reveal Himself to you. His highness is willing to come to us in lowness. *Our cries . . . voice openness. Readiness. That's what God is after.*[121]

Story after story in the scriptures shows Christ's amazing response to those who cry out from the depths of their heart. Enos and Alma got such a response (see Enos 1:1–8; Alma 36:18–23). So did Lamoni, his wife, and his father (see Alma 18–22). And let's not forget the people of King Benjamin (see Mosiah 4) or our beloved role model Nephi (see 2 Nephi 4). The Lord's grace is there for the asking. But the only way we can receive it is to fall on our knees and cry out.

With that said, we're finally ready to set our feet on the wonderfully empowering road of "Faith in Christ's Grace." I've already spent some time walking this life-altering path. Would you like to hear what happened as I journeyed? Trust me when I tell you that you're now on a road that will lead to some very dramatic changes in your fallen Eve.

Readings & Reflections

Let's turn to Alma 5 so we can study the prophet's beautiful description of salvation in verses 7–9. After reading these verses, note the critical questions Alma offers in verse 10: "And now I ask of you *on what conditions* are they saved? Yea, *what grounds* had they to hope

121. Moore, *Get Out of That Pit*, 122–23.

for salvation? *What is the cause* of their being loosed from the bands of death, yea, and also the chains of hell?" (emphasis added).

How does Alma answer his own questions in verses 11–13? What *is* the specific cause of the people's redemption? Is it through their works or their faith?

Carefully reread Ephesians 2:8–9. How would you put these verses into your own words? How do you feel about what Paul teaches here about grace?

Now look up Romans 3:20–28 where Paul offers a similar testimony. We already read one verse from this section, but we need to see it in context. What further light does this passage shed on your understanding of the doctrine of grace? Does Paul leave you with any new questions to study?

Turn to Alma 7:3. What does Alma hope the people have done with regards to grace? (If it helps, review the definition of the word *supplicate.* Also notice the use of the word *continued* in this verse.) How often have you asked the Lord specifically for the gift of His grace? How can you "continue" to do so as Alma encouraged his people?

Read Hebrews 4:14–16. In these verses, what are we promised to be given "in time of need"? Can you think of any examples of how the Lord has helped you or blessed you through His grace? Does this promise change the way you'll face future challenges, fears, and struggles?

In this chapter, we discussed how we access Christ's grace by crying out to Him with all our heart. Why do you think the scriptures use the word *cry* when referring to this type of prayer? Read the following scriptures that discuss this vital concept:

- Psalm 88:1–3
- Enos 1:4
- Mosiah 4:1–2
- Alma 34:17–27 (note specifically who we're supposed to "cry" to in verse 27)

Do you think there's a difference between the concept of crying out and how you've been praying lately? How so?

Finally, read Mosiah 29:20. What is the Lord's promise "in all cases" to those who "[cry] mightily unto him" for deliverance? How do you think this verse relates to receiving our Savior's empowering grace?

RESPONSE

In what ways are you feeling prompted to respond to the concepts found in this chapter?

A Soul Ignited

"The light of everlasting life was lit up in his soul."

(Alma 19:6)

14

Lighting Our Inner Flame

Have you ever been so excited that your heart feels like it's doing cartwheels inside your chest? It's quite a sensation—and it's exactly what happens to me every time I reach this part of the journey. I'm feeling this way because you've finally learned everything you need to know for the Lord to ignite your heartlight. I promise it's unlike anything you've ever experienced. Even if you picture the best day or best moment you've ever had on earth, I'm here to tell you that the lamp of everlasting life is better than that. A thousand times better. We're talking about a light breaking forth inside you that's so illuminating that your heart will come alive with more radiance and passion than you can even imagine. I love this perspective from Adam Miller:

> Life in Christ has a certain feel. It's not just an idea. It doesn't just change how I think. Life in Christ goes deeper than this. It's in my body, my heart, my lungs, my muscles and blood and bones. It glows like a burning coal in my belly. *Life in Christ feels like being alive. It feels—in all its ordinary sensitivity, difficulty, and complexity—like what being alive feels like.*[122]

---

122. Adam Miller, *An Early Resurrection: Life in Christ Before You Die* (Salt Lake City, UT: Deseret Book, 2018), 224–29, Kindle edition; emphasis added.

That's what you'll experience if you'll continue your walk down the road of grace. Slowly but surely, you'll begin to feel alive. *Ignited.* Lit up with a supernatural light that will fill you and saturate you and consume you continually throughout the day. Through Christ, your spiritually dead heart will be brought back to life. You'll finally be "born again" through the redeeming power of our Savior (see 3 Nephi 9:20; Mosiah 27:25).

At this point, I hope you've spent time confessing all your personal aprons, hiding places, and finger-pointing. And I hope you've cried out and asked the Lord to help you repent and forsake those things once and for all. So if your Eve is truly awake and you're ready to experience some drastic and much-needed changes, it's time to let the Lord ignite your fallen heart. I know He'll do this for you. I know because He's already worked this glorious miracle inside of *me.* To put it plainly, once I placed my faith in Christ's grace, something amazing happened to my heart. My Eve was lit up with the light of everlasting life.

Let me share a little more of my story. As I set my feet firmly on this new road of grace, I could sense the Lord inviting me to set down all the baggage I'd been carrying around my entire life. I could feel Him say to me, "Jaci, I want you to take all the things you've used to try to fill your soul hunger and lay them at My feet. That includes your cookie dough ice cream, your shopping habit, and your hours on social media. It also includes your need for approval, your people-pleasing, and your pharisaical attempts to live the gospel. In short, it's time to untie your aprons and leave your favorite hideouts. 'Go and sell that thou hast, . . . and come and follow me' (Matthew 19:21)."

This prompting made me think, as Elder Jeffery R. Holland once taught, of "the covenant we make in the temple—our promise to obey and sacrifice, to consecrate unto the Father, and His promise to empower us with 'a great endowment.'"[123] I could sense that my Savior was calling me to make greater sacrifices than I ever had in order to

123. Jeffrey R. Holland, "Keeping Covenants: A Message for Those Who Will Serve a Mission," *New Era*, Jan. 2012, 4.

come to know Him. When I was endowed in the temple, I'd promised to do exactly that: to consecrate myself and my life to His purposes alone. As Elder Holland pointed out, "That is precisely what we go to the temple to do—to bind ourselves to the Lord."[124] So it was easy to see why Christ was asking me to set aside all other distractions and devote myself fully and completely to Him.

It also brought to mind Jesus's direction to His disciples in ancient times: "He who seeketh to save his life shall lose it: and he that loseth his life for my sake shall find it" (Matthew 10:39, footnote *a*; see also Matthew 16:25; Mark 8:35; Luke 9:24; Luke 17:33). But I actually learned something intriguing about these references. There are two main Greek words in the New Testament that can be translated "life." One is *zoe,* which refers to our general spiritual or physical life,[125] but that's not the word Jesus used in these verses. Instead, every single time He chose the Greek word *psyche*, which literally means "soul" or "heart."[126] It's exactly what the Lord was trying to teach me. Only in "losing" my heart would I ever be able to find it. The sanctification I was seeking would only come by truly "yielding [my heart] unto God" (Helaman 3:35).

In essence, He was asking me to quit trying to self-medicate through all my aprons and escapes and instead take my spiritual deadness to Him for healing. Yes, I could keep trying to ignite my Eve's pilot light through my favorite coping mechanisms, but I could now see that that was a frustrating and fruitless endeavor. The choice was up to me. The only way I could come to know Christ and His sweet lamp of everlasting life was by voluntarily turning over my Eve—and all her fervent desires—to my blessed Savior.

I'd like to say that, as soon as He asked, I immediately tossed aside all my aprons and escapes and ran to Him with abandon. But I didn't.

---

124. Jeffrey R. Holland, "Keeping Covenants," 5.

125. James E. Strong, *The Strongest Strong's Exhaustive Concordance of the Bible* (Grand Rapids, MI: Zondervan, 2001), 1614.

126. Strong, *The Strongest Strong's Exhaustive Concordance of the Bible*, 1654. I used this resource to find the original Greek word for *life* that Jesus used in each of those references.

My favorite comforts and hiding places had carried me through thick and thin, and my Eve wasn't so sure she could survive without them. After all, these were the treasures my heart truly loved. They were the things that helped me cope from day to day. As I considered giving them up, I didn't think I could handle life without them.

Take my sugar habit, for instance. To be honest, I couldn't imagine the thought of not grabbing a bowl of ice cream or some thick, rich brownies at the end of a long, hard day. While the idea sounded nice in theory, when it actually came down to it, surrendering one of my favorite escapes almost felt like a death of sorts, as if my heart, and not just my mouth, would be left empty and desolate. I know it may sound ridiculous that I was so emotionally dependent on something so trivial. But maybe you can relate if you imagine giving up the activity, hobby, or habit that feeds your soul the most. Could you just lay that thing down on the side of the road and walk away? Our attachments go much deeper than we want to admit.

To make things worse, my enemy was anxious to keep me clinging to my favorite escapes. His whispers began to flood my mind: "Jaci, you don't need to let go of your comforts. In fact, deep down you know you don't want to. Those things are your joy! They've fed your Eve again and again. You know you need them to be happy." It was difficult not to give in to his arguments because in a way, he was right. Deep down, a part of my Eve was still imprisoned. It was the part of me that didn't really *want* to let go. Though I desperately wanted the Lord to be my only God, and I desperately wanted the everlasting life He offered, underneath that yearning, my Eve also wanted to hang on to her beloved obsessions—her other lovers—for a little longer.

That left me with only one alternative. Digging down to the depths of my soul, I began to cry out to the Lord. I pleaded with Him to pour out His grace on my efforts to let go. I begged with all I had, not only for the ability to leave behind my aprons and escapes but also for power to overcome the intense desire that kept me attached to them. While I knew my heart had been manipulated by the adversary, my Eve was having a hard time letting go, and I needed help. At last, in answer to my cry, I felt empowered to take the first small step.

Trembling with uncertainty, while at the same time feeling waves of grace infiltrating my stubborn heart, I thought about my most addictive escape. I'd set up camp in this hiding place for a very long time, and I loved what it felt like to live there. But I knew it was time to step out of the shadows once and for all. So, drawing on the enabling power I could feel growing within me, I gave it one last look, then I turned my back on that spot and began to walk into the light.

To be honest, the first few steps out of my comfort zone were pretty rough. I'd run to this place whenever I was stressed, tired, sad, restless, or even bored. Without it, I felt exposed and insecure. While I knew the Lord was with me, I had no idea how to lean on someone I couldn't see. For most of my life, I'd relied on my aprons and escapes to calm my troubled heart, but now I was being asked to look beyond those counterfeit comforts and journey to a new place. Leaving this hiding place initially felt very daunting and difficult.

I was also surprised at the feelings of loss that began to wash over me—like I'd experienced the death of a friend I dearly loved. While I knew this escape had only temporarily sheltered me, I'd spent so much time hiding there that I felt a huge sense of barrenness and emptiness when I left it behind. It reminded me of a few verses of imagery from Hosea where the Lord, in trying to win Gomer back from her adulterous lovers, explained His plan to redeem His wayward daughter: "And I will visit upon her the days of Baalim, wherein she burned incense to them, and she decked herself with her earrings and her jewels, and she went after her lovers, and forgat me, saith the Lord. Therefore, behold, *I will allure her, and bring her into the wilderness, and speak comfortably unto her*" (Hosea 2:13–14; emphasis added).

Those words really resonated with me because it seemed like my Redeemer was also drawing me into the wilderness—into a stark emotional place that was devoid of everything but Him. Yet as difficult as it was to experience those desolate feelings, I knew deep down that the Lord wasn't doing it to torture me but to transform my fallen heart.

If you think about it, the concept of a wilderness experience is found in many places throughout the scriptures. Elijah, Abraham, David, Moses, and John the Baptist all spent many influential years in the desert. So did Lehi, Nephi, and their families. Even Jesus was drawn into the desert for forty days, where He not only communed with God but battled and overcame the temptations of the enemy.

Jehovah also kept the children of Israel circling for forty years in the wilderness when they could have reached Canaan in just a few short weeks. Obviously, there was something crucial that they could only learn while in the desert. Simply put, they could only enter the Promised Land by exercising great faith in the Lord, and it took time in the school of the wilderness—where Christ used things like manna and quail and water from a rock—for them to learn how to trust Him. And the same thing was true for me too. I also needed to learn some very poignant, personal lessons that could only come by having the courage to face what felt like a very dry and barren desert.

Listen to the way Dr. Gerald G. May describes this wilderness experience and how vital it is to our quest:

> The desert is where the battle with attachment takes place. The saga of the desert tells of a journey out of slavery, through the desert, toward the garden that is home. But it is much more than a journey; it is the discovery of the depths of weakness, the power of grace, and the price of both. Moreover, what takes place in the desert is not simply difficult travel and adventurous learning; it is repentance and conversion, the transformation of mixed motivations into purified desire, the greening of desert into garden through the living water of grace. There is no geographic journey here; it all takes place within our hearts. And what happens is not only purgation and purification, but also a loving courtship, a homemaking between the human soul and its Creator.[127]

His poignant words definitely calmed my heart. And they inspired me to keep praying with even greater intensity. As I pushed forward and allowed the Lord to continue to draw me out of hiding and closer to Him, an astonishing thing began to happen: *a small flame started to flicker inside my heart.* Over time, this flame inside me grew, filling me with an inner sense of energy and vitality—an inner sense of *life.*

---

127. Gerald G. May, *Addiction and Grace: Love and Spirituality in the Healing of Addictions* (New York, NY: HarperOne, 1988), 134.

As the days went by, I was amazed to find this feeling growing steadily stronger. My Eve's pilot light had never been lit like this. Slowly but surely, my wilderness began to transform into a lush and vibrant promised land.

Yes, I'll admit there were moments when the difficulty of the wilderness overwhelmed me, and I was tempted to run back into hiding. My escapes continued to call to me like an oasis in the desert, and at times I gave in to their seductive voices. But I quickly learned an important lesson about my heartlight: every time I looked back toward my favorite escapes, the flicker began to dim. And if I gave in to the temptation to run back to them, the flame completely blew out. At last, I knew it was time to choose. Which one did I want more: my hiding places . . . or the Lord's sweet everlasting life?

Actually, the decision was easy. I was so enamored with my heart's new flame that my favorite spots soon lost their appeal. The escapes I'd so dearly loved could no longer feed my heart like they used to—not after I'd tasted the lamp of everlasting life. Finally, I was able to run down the road of grace without looking back. It was then that I realized the addictive power was broken. Those counterfeit comforts no longer held me prisoner.

As my journey continued, I had another "aha" moment that rocked me to the very core. It was the realization that the warm glow I now carried in my heart was actually coming *from the Lord Himself*—from His presence living in me through the power of the Spirit. And He felt so close that He knew every thought, feeling, and desire of my heart. It was such a profound sensation that I began to seek Him constantly as I moved throughout the day. I couldn't get enough of His inner presence within, of His light and life and grace that were continuing to grow and swell within my heart.

One of the things I loved most about having Christ in me was the way I began to sense His unique personality. It struck me that I'd often believed Jesus was so stiff and formal and holy that He wasn't really relatable. But now I was getting to know a person who wasn't just loving but also warm, energetic, charming, creative, and even fun. This was someone I *wanted* to spend time with. Someone I *wanted* to get to know and turn to and talk to every single chance I could get. Someone who was much more alive and real and wonderful than I'd ever imagined.

In the end, I learned that my trek through the wilderness wasn't just about finding the lamp of everlasting life—it was about coming to know Jesus Christ for myself. It was about learning to love and be loved by Him. It was my chance to, as Mormon said, "taste and know of the goodness of Jesus" (Mormon 1:15). Soon, nothing mattered to me but being as close to Him as possible. And it motivated me to continue abandoning all my fig leaves and hiding places as quickly as my time and energy would allow.

As my journey progressed, I was relieved to learn that I didn't need to give up all my aprons and escapes at once. The process felt more like peeling an onion, with layer after layer being shed as each thing was slowly left behind. I found I needed time to prepare for the deeper, more difficult layers. These were the fig leaves that were intricately woven into the thoughts and emotions of my Eve and the habitual behaviors of my Adam. If you're curious how we untangle such a knotted mess, the road of grace holds the answer. Just like we're taught in Doctrine and Covenants 50, our goal is to "grow in grace and in the knowledge of the truth" (verse 40). These two things will be our secret weapons as we continue our walk down this path. We need *grace*, or the Lord's power, to give us the strength to break free from our attachments. And we need *truth*, or the Lord's words, to purify our minds from the lies and deception of the enemy.

To be free of the adversary's lies, our aim is to identify all false beliefs still living inside us and let the Lord strip away those toxic thoughts so that He has a clean slate on which to write. If it will help, I'll share how this happened on my own personal journey. Through the Lord's tutoring, I discovered that the aprons and escapes I'd gathered over the years fell into three general categories: *things, people,* and *belief systems*. In each area, Satan had beguiled me, and I'd allowed myself to be seduced. So a great deal of my repentance involved recognizing and removing the lies lurking in each of these three areas. Here are some examples of what the adversary's voice sounded like inside my heart and head:

- "Jaci, if you'll pursue this *thing* . . . (eat some chocolate, binge watch your favorite show, buy a new pair of shoes, escape into that novel, spend time on social media, take a vacation, etc.) . . . it will bring you the joy you're hungering for."
- "If you'll focus on that *person* . . . (get more attention, love, or romance from my spouse; continue being a people pleaser; find a way to control another person's behavior; etc.) . . . you'll experience greater love and happiness."
- "If you'll follow this *belief system* . . . (any one of the countless worldly philosophies on how to find success and happiness in life) . . . all your needs will finally be fulfilled."

Satan especially loved whispering these lies whenever I felt restless, unhappy, stressed, or any other negative emotion. In my attempts to cope, I'd suddenly feel the urge to munch on something, disappear into a good book, or go shopping. I'd get lost in social media or turn on my favorite chick flick. Or I'd look to others for some extra validation or attention. In these moments, it never occurred to me that I'd been tempted by the adversary; instead, I viewed these things as perfectly harmless escapes. But living this way wasn't harmless at all. I say that because every time I accepted and acted on Satan's suggestions, I was turning from the Lord to find comfort in temporal things, in those around me, or in the belief systems of the world. But despite all my efforts to escape, I never found that inner flame I was looking for. I knew it was time for me to eradicate the lies and "[rely] wholly upon the merits of him who is mighty to save" (2 Nephi 31:19)

The onion-peeling process was actually pretty straightforward. First, the Lord would spotlight a lie I was believing in a certain area of my life. Then He would show me the truth about that situation—or "things as they really are" (Jacob 4:13). If I was willing to cast out that lie and adopt His truth into my belief system, He'd then move on to the next lie, thus showing me how to tear down, one by one, the deceitful fig leaves I'd sewn. This step-by-step process enabled me to take apart my more complicated aprons while still allowing my heart time to assimilate new ways of thinking.

Nephi explained the progression beautifully: "For behold, thus saith the Lord God: I will give unto the children of men line upon line, precept upon precept, here a little and there a little; and blessed are those who hearken unto my precepts, and lend an ear unto my counsel, for they shall learn wisdom; for unto him that receiveth I will give more" (2 Nephi 28:30).

It was difficult because certain lies had lived inside my mind for decades. Mentally, I'd rehearsed these lies so many times that they'd become like deep ruts inside my head, trapping my thoughts in the same distracting and destructive patterns. To teach my mind to travel in a new direction, I had to learn to create new thought patterns with the help of the Lord's enabling grace and truth.

To do this, He taught me some strategies to use whenever I felt stuck in those same mental ruts. One was to jot down (or print out) various scriptures that spoke the truth I needed to hear. I kept these verses close by and reviewed them while in the car or doing the dishes or even walking down the aisle at the store. In addition, I memorized some of my favorites and repeated them to myself over and over whenever I was tempted to give in to feelings of fear, discouragement, or frustration.

It's important to note that this wasn't about repeating positive affirmations of the *self*—it was about directing my mind to the mercy, goodness, and faithfulness of *Christ*. It's the very thing King Benjamin counseled his people to do when he said, "Remember, and always retain in remembrance, *the greatness of God*, and *your own nothingness*, and his goodness and long-suffering towards you, unworthy creatures" (Mosiah 4:11; emphasis added). Then came the promise: "If ye do this ye shall always rejoice, and be filled with the love of God, and always retain a remission of your sins; and ye shall grow in the knowledge of the glory of him that created you, or in the knowledge of that which is just and true" (verse 12). Meditating on Christ's greatness rather than my own was what I needed most to move further and further down the road of grace.

When Satan whispered, "It's too hard. It can't be done. You can never change," I would remind myself that "with God nothing shall be impossible" (Luke 1:37), or that the Lord "will not fail [me], nor forsake [me]" (Joshua 1:5). If I felt overwhelmed or depressed, I studied verses where He'd promised to be with me (see Doctrine and Covenants 39:12), to fight my battles (see Doctrine and Covenants 105:14), or to give liberally to all who ask (see James 1:5). This wasn't just about repeating scripture but about soaking in the faithfulness and power of Christ until it finally began to feel real to me. It was about reviewing those words so often that they started to lift off the page and plant themselves firmly into the furthest reaches of my heart.

As I continued this routine, I felt the lamp of everlasting life growing stronger and stronger within me. Again and again, the Lord showed me the truths I needed most, not only from the scriptures and the words of prophets and apostles but also from other sources He led me to study (depending on which issue I was dealing with at the time). As I relied on His secret weapons of grace and truth, the enemy's lies slowly began to unravel one by one, and I discovered new ways of thinking, a new level of trust in the Lord, and, as the Bible Dictionary's definition of *metanoeo* emphasizes, a "fresh view about God, about [my]self, and about the world" (Bible Dictionary, "Repentance").

Now, I know some may be thinking, "Yes, Jaci, I'm sure this process worked for you, but you don't know how bad my problems are. You don't know how many times I've tried to change. You don't know how deep my issues go, or how ugly my personal baggage is." Perhaps you've lived with certain aprons and escapes for so long that they feel absolutely impossible to overcome. (Of course, that in and of itself is just one more big lie.)

I'll acknowledge that the further I progressed down the road of grace, the deeper the Lord began to delve into the hidden corners of my heart. And He unearthed some fig leaves there that, to me, seemed much too big and complicated to ever untangle. I noticed that many of these coping mechanisms were put in place by my subconscious mind to protect me from further pain and suffering. And they'd worked well enough that my heart was fighting desperately to keep them firmly in place. In fact, a few of these wayward habits and desires hung on with such stubbornness that I thought I'd never be able to break free.

Perhaps you've felt that same kind of unyielding spirit reigning inside your heart. Perhaps, like me, your Eve has decided at times that she simply *refuses* to give something up, no matter how many times you pray or how many verses of scripture you read. It could be feelings of unwillingness to forgive someone who hurt you. It could be compulsive eating or shopping or time on social media. It could be immoral thoughts or temptations that keep plaguing your mind no matter how hard you try to distract yourself. It could be anything really. All you know is that your Eve is putting up a fight the likes of which you've never experienced. Her fierce intention to hold on is causing an internal struggle that feels like a brutal tug-of-war inside your heart. Back and forth you swing, between wanting to let go and wanting to cling to your favorite sins. You may even be tempted like I was to give in to your obsessive cravings just to relieve the tension from the tug-of-war for a little while.

I remember one particular stretch of road where I faced an incredibly rebellious desire in my heart that wouldn't relent. To make matters worse, Satan seemed to be doing all he could to get me to give up. Temptations to succumb overwhelmed me, and I found myself surrendering to those temptations again and again. The battle in my mind was so intense that I really thought I'd be captive in this area forever.

During this time, I often wondered why the Lord wasn't applying His grace and making that sinful desire disappear. He had done that for me in other areas of my life, but this time He seemed to be holding back. Over and over, I begged Him to dissolve the grasp this thing held on my heart, but months went by and the struggle remained. It was hard to see any purpose in continuing the fight.

Then I learned that the Apostle Paul had experienced the same kind of ongoing struggle. Surprisingly, he too had something he couldn't overcome—something he wanted very much to conquer but which continued to linger. In 2 Corinthians 12, he begged like I did for that thing to be taken away: "And lest I should be exalted above measure through the abundance of the revelations, there was given to me a thorn in the flesh, the messenger of Satan to buffet me, lest I should be exalted above measure. For this thing I besought the Lord thrice, that it might depart from me" (verses 7–8).

But it didn't happen. The thorn wasn't removed. That's just the way the grace road works sometimes. Some fights aren't immediately won. Some struggles persist. Some temptations continue to plague us. But I believe there's a very specific reason for that. Christ explained it when he told Paul, "My grace is sufficient for thee: *for my strength is made perfect in weakness*" (2 Corinthians 12:9; emphasis added).

You may wonder how His strength can be made perfect in the midst of these kinds of intense mental battles. I know it may sound odd, but when He chooses not to remove certain thorns in our lives, He's actually offering us an incredibly precious gift, for *that struggle is the very thing that will teach us to rely on Him in a whole new way*. It won't be because our weakness has been taken away but because we're still very much in the throes of it. You see, when the thorn remains, it creates a need for Him that wouldn't be there if our trial was removed. Because these kinds of struggles are often constant and unrelenting, we need the Lord with a desperation that drives us to His feet again and again. We reach the point where we must learn to rely on His power from minute to minute or else we'll remain stuck in our captivity forever. Either we learn to have Christ dwelling in us continually or we move no further in our walk down the road of grace.

Paul understood this, and it actually led him to *rejoice* in his thorn instead of begging for it to be taken away. He said, "Most gladly therefore will I rather *glory* in my infirmities, that the power of Christ may rest upon me. Therefore I *take pleasure* in infirmities, in reproaches, in necessities, in persecutions, in distresses for Christ's sake: *for when I am weak, then am I strong*" (2 Corinthians 12:9–10; emphasis added). Like him, we too are being invited to see the miracles—the infusion of life and light—that can happen when the Lord adds His strength to our personal weakness.

So how do we move to this deeper level where we're abiding in Christ and relying on His grace from moment to moment? Let's continue to break down the process step by step. First, I want you to picture that stubborn thorn that you feel like you just can't overcome. It may be thoughts you can't seem to control—the ones that enter your mind again and again. Or the sinful behavior you keep trying to stop—that thing that keeps popping back up just when you think you've gotten rid of it. Or negative feelings you keep pushing down for someone who has hurt, abandoned, or abused you. Now, instead of seeing that thorn as a source of hopelessness or failure, try seeing it as a catalyst that drives you to Jesus Christ.

Every time that obsessive thought or temptation returns—even if it's a hundred times a day—immediately cry out in your heart, no matter what else is going on around you. Don't suppress the issue and think it will impress Him. Don't sweep it under the rug and hope it will go away. Face it head-on with your Savior by your side. Bring it out into the open and let Him hold your hand as you look at that thorn from every angle. Try to identify what's actually fueling it. Take an honest look at what your Eve is really longing for when she clings to that apron or escape. Then ask the Lord how He can fill your need in a way that not only calms your cravings and helps you withstand the addictive pull of temptation but also heals and soothes your heart through His soul-igniting grace.

In other words, use your thorn as an opportunity to "grow in grace" just like we talked about earlier. Here's how Christian philosopher Dallas Willard explains it: "To 'grow in grace' means to utilize more and more grace to live by, until everything we do is assisted by grace. . . . The greatest saints are not those who need *less* grace, but those who consume the *most* grace, who indeed are *most in need of grace*—those who are *saturated by grace* in every dimension of their being. *Grace to them is like breath.*"[128]

128. Dallas Willard, *Renovation of the Heart: Putting on the Character of Christ* (Colorado Springs, CO: NavPress, 2002), 93–94; emphasis added.

We'll talk more in the next few chapters about how the Lord can meet our Eve's core needs by saturating us with His grace. But for now, just know that as we lean more and more on our beloved Savior, even the most stubborn thorns will slowly, carefully begin to work their way free. With our hand clinging tightly to His, we really will find healing—even from deeply damaging and painful brokenness. It will come as we learn more and more how to trust Him and experience His renewing, redeeming love.

But here's the thing: to know Christ on this personal of a level, *we have to come to Him with everything we've got.* Jesus made it clear that "ye shall seek me, and find me, when ye shall search for me *with all your heart*" (Jeremiah 29:13; emphasis added). At the risk of stating the obvious, "all your heart" really does mean *all* your heart. It means we must "bow down before him, and worship him with all [our] might, mind, and strength, and [our] whole soul" (2 Nephi 25:29). It means we must follow Alma's counsel and "let all thy doings be unto the Lord" and wherever we go "let it be in the Lord; yea, let all thy thoughts be directed unto the Lord; yea, let the affections of thy heart be placed upon the Lord forever" (Alma 37:36). *All* our thoughts. *All* our doings. *All* our affections placed on Him in a way we've most likely never done before.

It reminds me of the tenacity many New Testament believers displayed as they pursued their blessed Savior. One group pulled a section of roof off a house to gain access to His healing (see Mark 2:4). Another man climbed a tree simply to get a glimpse of Him (see Luke 19:2–6). Yet another woman pushed through a heavy crowd just to touch of the hem of His garment (see Luke 8:43–48). The persistence of these followers was remarkable to say the least. And it's that same persistence we need to have if we truly want to know Him and experience His healing on this kind of a level. As President Russell M. Nelson explains:

> When you reach up for the Lord's power in your life *with the same intensity that a drowning person has when grasping and gasping for air*, power from Jesus Christ will be yours. When the Savior knows you truly want to reach up to Him—when He can feel that *the*

> *greatest desire of your heart is to draw His power into your life*—you will be led by the Holy Ghost to know exactly what you should do.[129]

I hope you can see that this isn't just a nice, gentle stroll down the road of grace. This is the point where we're running headlong into the arms of our loving Savior. Where we're "seek[ing] this Jesus" (Ether 12:41) with single-minded focus, with a hunger that eclipses all other interests and a determination to find Him no matter the cost. If we do this, He'll begin to take up residence in our heart through the power of the Spirit. As He begins to live in us every moment of the day, He'll teach us how to abandon the lies we've been believing and embrace new ways of thinking, feeling, and behaving. He'll teach us how to act through His grace and not be acted upon by our obsessions and addictions. He'll teach us how to heal all the pain, suffering, and wounds of our past. And He'll teach us how to leave behind all our stubborn baggage once and for all.

Best of all, He'll fan our heart's flame into a huge, roaring bonfire. As President Ezra Taft Benson taught, once we're "committed to Him, centered in Him, and consumed in Him," we'll finally be "made alive in Christ."[130] And nothing in this world will rival being born again through the blessed grace of our Savior. Having our spiritually dead heart ignited so brightly that our emptiness is filled and our soul's needs are satisfied is almost beyond our comprehension. As we abide in Him and He in us, He'll light up our heart in a way that eclipses anything we've ever experienced.

I believe this kind of radical change—this massive, life-altering conversion—was exactly what happened to Nephi. I don't think it's any coincidence that right after he wrote his humble psalm of faith and repentance, the Lord instructed him to leave Laman and Lemuel behind and depart into the wilderness to start a new life (see 2 Nephi 5:5). In this new place, Nephi said, "The Lord was with us; and we did

---

129. Russell M. Nelson, "Drawing the Power of Jesus Christ into Our Lives," *Ensign* or *Liahona*, May 2017, 42; emphasis added.

130. Ezra Taft Benson, "Come Unto Christ," *Ensign*, Nov. 1987, 85.

prosper exceedingly" (verse 11). In this place, he said they "lived after the manner of happiness" (verse 27). And the same thing awaits all who walk the road of grace. As we learn what it's like to truly dwell in Christ and He in us, we'll find a wondrous new home for our heart to live in for the rest of our light-filled, grace-infused life. I promise you: once we've experienced the thrilling new world of spiritual rebirth, we'll never want to go back to our old ways of living ever again.

Readings & Reflections

I love this quote from Brent Curtis and John Eldredge that sums up the aim of our entire journey: "Sanctification is an awakening, the rousing of our souls from the dead sleep of sin into the fullness of their capacity for life."[131]

At this point, do you feel like you're beginning to experience an awakening? How are you personally leaving behind the "dead sleep of sin" and coming to understand the "fullness of [your] capacity for life" (or in other words, *eternal* life)? (See Alma 5:7–9 for more on this.)

President Nelson counseled us that when we reach for Christ, we must do it "like a drowning person grasping and gasping for air." Have you ever experienced this kind of intense desire to connect with the Lord? How could you begin to reach for Him like that *continually* rather than just occasionally or sporadically?

131. Brent Curtis and John Eldredge, *The Sacred Romance: Drawing Closer to the Heart of God* (Nashville, TN: Thomas Nelson, 2001), 201.

Many of us are familiar with the following statement from the Prophet Joseph Smith, but I think it'd be helpful to read it with a fresh pair of eyes:

> Let us here observe, that a religion that does not require *the sacrifice of all things* never has the power sufficient to produce the faith necessary unto *life* and salvation; for, from the first existence of man, the faith necessary unto the enjoyment of *life* and salvation never could be obtained without *the sacrifice of all earthly things.* It was *through this sacrifice, and this only,* that God has ordained that men should enjoy *eternal life.*[132]

How exactly does Joseph say we obtain eternal life? How do you think that ties in with the onion-peeling process of repentance we discussed in this chapter? How does it tie in with the covenants we make in the temple?

132. *Lectures on Faith* (1985), 69; emphasis added.

Just in case we think spiritual rebirth will bring us to a state of total sinlessness, take a moment to read 1 John 3:6, 9 and 1 John 5:18. Make sure to examine the footnotes and compare the original version of each verse with the Joseph Smith Translation.

In these scriptures, John teaches that even after being quickened, we'll still occasionally give way to sin. But the difference is that once we're born again, we "cannot *continue* in sin" (1 John 3:9; emphasis added). Imagine what a joy it will be to finally put an end to our continuous, daily battle with sin and the shame, guilt, and despair that go along with it!

____

____

____

____

____

____

____

____

To conclude, I want to share one final thing that surprised me as I moved through the transformation process. It's that not everyone in my life was supportive of my choice to discard my various aprons and escapes. I found there were some who preferred the old me, and I quickly lost their favor because I wouldn't wear the same counterfeit clothing or run to the same hiding places anymore.

Perhaps these individuals thought I was casting them away with the baggage I was leaving on the side of the road. That wasn't how I felt at all, and it pained me to see certain interactions end in misunderstanding and hurt feelings. Unfortunately, a few of my relationships didn't survive my walk down the road of grace. But the Lord gently reminded me that even the closest of associations are at times affected by our choice to follow His lead. As He said in Matthew 10:34–36, "Think not that I am come to send peace on earth: I came not to send peace, but a sword. For I am come to set a man at variance against his father, and the daughter against her mother, and the daughter in law against her mother in law. And a man's foes shall be they of his own household."

In addition, I found the words of Elder Neal A. Maxwell and President Ezra Taft Benson comforting:

> When the determination is first made to begin to be more spiritually settled, there is an initial vulnerability: it is hard to break with the past. But once we begin, we see how friends who would hold us back spiritually are not true friends at all. Any chiding from them reflects either resentment or unconscious worry that somehow they are being deserted. In any attempt to explain to them, our tongue is able to speak only 'the smallest part' (Alma 26:16.) We continue to care for them, but we care for our duty to God more. Brigham Young counseled candidly: "Some do not understand duties which do not coincide with their natural feelings and affections. . . . There are duties which are above affection."[133]

> The Lord said, "He that loveth father or mother more than me is not worthy of me: and he that loveth son or daughter more than me is not worthy of me" (Matt. 10:37). One of the most difficult tests of all is when you have to choose between pleasing God or pleasing someone you love or respect—particularly a family member. Nephi faced that test and handled it well when his good father temporarily murmured against the Lord (see 1 Ne. 16:18–25). Job maintained his integrity with the Lord even though his wife told him to curse God and die (see Job 2:9–10). The scripture says, "Honour thy father and thy mother" (Ex. 20:12; see also Mosiah 13:20). Sometimes one must choose to honor Heavenly Father over a mortal father.[134]

For me, it all came down to the fact that I knew I was on the right path. Eternal life was lit up inside of me! All I could do was pray that someday those who did not understand would finally be able to

---

133. Neal A. Maxwell, "Settle This in Your Hearts," *Ensign*, Nov. 1992, 66.

134. Ezra Taft Benson, "The Great Commandment—Love the Lord," *Ensign*, May 1988, 5.

pursue this glorious journey for themselves. I offer this insight in case you face similar misunderstandings in your experience as well.

Note: If you're still having trouble shedding some of your more stubborn aprons and escapes, I'd highly recommend the Church's twelve-step addiction recovery program. We often assume this program is only for those addicted to drugs, alcohol, or pornography, but it's actually designed to help us overcome *any* deeply entrenched behavior, craving, or habit. I promise: the twelve steps are powerful and they work. They're the very steps the Lord used to help me shed some of my more difficult personal baggage. If you feel prompted to check it out, you can find everything you need online at addictionrecovery.ChurchofJesusChrist.org.

Finally, for any who are dealing with the intensely damaging effects of various kinds of trauma or abuse, I've come to cherish the work of Dr. Dan B. Allender. His profound insights on the healing path, especially how Christ can transform a deeply wounded soul, are truly life-changing. His website is theallendercenter.org, and you can find his books many places online. (Rather than recommending one book in particular, I trust the Lord will lead you to those that will best speak to your personal situation.)

RESPONSE

In what ways are you feeling prompted to respond to the concepts found in this chapter?

15

INFUSED WITH JOY

AS WE CONTINUE TO EXPLORE THE EXPANSIVE VIEW OPENING UP ON the path before us, our journey will lead us back to another deep desire of the heart: *joy*. To capture the full vision of where we're heading, listen first to these ecstatic words from Ammon in Alma 26:

> Behold, my joy is full, yea, my heart is brim with joy, and I will rejoice in my God. . . .
>
> Therefore, let us glory, yea, we will glory in the Lord; yea, we will rejoice, for our joy is full; yea, we will praise our God forever. Behold, who can glory too much in the Lord? Yea, who can say too much of his great power, and of his mercy, and of his long-suffering towards the children of men? Behold, I say unto you, I cannot say the smallest part which I feel. (verses 11, 16)

Doesn't the joy in Ammon's heart jump right off the page when you read those words? I turn to this chapter all the time to drink it in. I can just picture the exuberant missionary with a look of delight on his face. Ammon seems to gush with joy, not only in those two verses but throughout the entire chapter. Every time I read his words, I want my heart to be "brim with joy" too. Don't you?

The prophet Enos joins us in our desire for joy and happiness. When he remembers what his father Jacob (and probably his uncle

Nephi) taught him "concerning eternal life, and the joy of the saints" (Enos 1:3), he desperately wanted to obtain these things for himself. I think it's interesting that Enos specifically mentions two core desires of the heart. In addition to eternal life, he wants to taste the inner joy other Saints had experienced as well.

When it comes to joy, a search of the Book of Mormon reveals almost seventy chapters that have something to say on the subject. But to truly understand what happens when we learn to abide in Christ, you need to know that several of those chapters speak of a very specific kind of joy—a joy that leaves normal, everyday happiness in the dust. For instance, Alma declared that "the Lord doth give me *exceedingly great joy* in the fruit of my labors" (Alma 36:25; emphasis added). Also, in Lehi's dream, the fruit of the tree of life "filled [his] soul with *exceedingly great joy*" (1 Nephi 8:12; emphasis added). And when King Benjamin's people experienced a mighty change of heart, their "mouths [were] stopped that [they] could not find utterance, so *exceedingly great was [their] joy*" (Mosiah 4:20; emphasis added).

The Book of Mormon also contains many other verses that capture this same joy, only by using different words. Here are just a few examples:

- "This is the account of Ammon and his brethren . . . and their incomprehensible joy" (Alma 28:8).
- "My soul is carried away, even to the separation of it from the body, as it were, so great is my joy" (Alma 29:16).
- "There can be nothing so exquisite and sweet as was my joy" (Alma 36:21).
- "[The people] were filled with that joy which is unspeakable and full of glory" (Helaman 5:44).
- "Their hearts were swollen with joy, unto the gushing out of many tears" (3 Nephi 4:33).
- "No one can conceive of the joy which filled our souls at the time we heard him pray for us unto the Father" (3 Nephi 17:17).

- (Also, note how in Alma 19:12–14 and 27:17, Ammon, Lamoni, and others lose consciousness because they're so overcome with this soul-filling joy.)

I'm sure you can see that we're not just talking about an ordinary, run-of-the-mill type of joy here. Let's break down *exceeding great joy* word by word so we can better understand this incredible concept. For starters, *exceeding* means "extraordinary," "to surpass," or "to go beyond the bounds or limits of."[135] Next, there's the word *great,* which means "unusual in degree, power, [or] intensity"[136] or "notably large in size, huge."[137] Finally, synonyms for *joy* include delight, bliss, happiness, satisfaction, and elation. Put those three definitions together and exceeding great joy becomes elation beyond normal limits. Satisfaction that is notably large in size. Extraordinary happiness that surpasses the usual. Just the thought of such a possibility can make our hearts yearn for this amazing joy just like Enos did.

And that leads me to my next question: why in the world would the Book of Mormon go to such great lengths to portray such a powerful, electric sense of joy? Is it just so we can admire what happened to a handful of people hundreds of years ago? Is it just so we can rejoice for Ammon or Lamoni's good fortune? I'm sorry, but if that's all it is, then it's torture—because we *all* want this kind of happiness. We *all* want to experience it just like the ancient Saints did.

Thankfully, the scriptures reveal that exceeding great joy isn't reserved for prophets alone, but there *are* conditions as to who obtains it. "Behold," the Book of Mormon tells us, "this is joy which none receiveth save it be the truly penitent and humble seeker of happiness" (Alma 27:18). In fact, the "happiness which is prepared for the saints" is actually "hid" from "the wise and the prudent" (2 Nephi 9:43),

---

135. *Dictionary.com,* s.v. "exceeding," accessed Apr. 1, 2023, https://www.dictionary.com/browse/exceeding. Also *Dictionary.com,* s.v. "exceed," accessed Apr. 1, 2023, https://www.dictionary.com/browse/exceed.

136. *Dictionary.com,* s.v. "great," accessed Apr. 1, 2023, https://www.dictionary.com/browse/great.

137. *Merriam-Webster.com Dictionary,* s.v. "great," accessed Apr. 1, 2023, https://www.merriam-webster.com/dictionary/great.

from those who are "puffed up because of their learning, and their wisdom, and their riches" (verse 42). But if we will "cast these things away, and consider [our]selves fools before God, and come down in the depths of humility" (verse 42), then God will open to us the experience of exceeding great joy.

I'm guessing C. S. Lewis would have loved those verses because he said something similar when writing about this extraordinary kind of joy:

> Indeed, if we consider the unblushing promises of reward and staggering nature of the rewards promised in the Gospels, it would seem that our Lord finds our desires not too strong but too weak. We are half-hearted creatures, fooling around with drink and sex and ambition when infinite joy is offered us, like an ignorant child who wants to go on making mud pies in a slum because he cannot imagine what is meant by the offer of a holiday at the sea. We are far too easily pleased.[138]

Those distracting mud pies are just another way to describe our favorite aprons and escapes. See why we had to "cast them away"? Only as we leave the "slum" behind can we take God up on His offer of a "holiday at the sea," a holiday that Lewis describes as "infinite joy." By the way, if you look up the word *infinite*, you'll find it means "unlimited, unmeasurable, boundless, or endless."[139] So by using this term, Lewis joins Book of Mormon prophets in proclaiming that joy in Christ isn't just exceeding, great, and incomprehensible—it's also "everlasting" (2 Nephi 8:11). Imagine that. Just like the lamp of eternal life we already discovered, *unending* joy can also be ours once we've left our aprons and escapes behind and learned to truly abide in our Savior.

One of the most important things to understand about exceeding great joy is that it can only come to us as a gift from the Lord. In other words, it's not something we can muster up on our own. The

---

138. C. S. Lewis, *The Weight of Glory and Other Addresses* (San Francisco: HarperSanFrancisco, 1980), 26.

139. *Dictionary.com*, s.v. "infinite," accessed Apr. 1, 2023, https://www.dictionary.com/browse/infinite.

Apostle Paul clearly states in Galatians that this joy is a "fruit of the Spirit" (Galatians 5:22), not a fruit of our own efforts to make ourselves happy.

A favorite author of mine named Sarah Young, who writes as if Christ is speaking in first person, captures this scriptural truth with this inspiring prose: "I am creating something new in you: a bubbling spring of joy that spills over into others' lives. Do not mistake this Joy for your own or try to take credit for it in any way. Instead, watch in delight as My Spirit flows through you to bless others. Let yourself become a reservoir of the Spirit's fruit."[140] In a later entry, she builds on the same theme: "Open wide your heart and mind to receive more and more of Me. When your Joy in Me meets My Joy in you, there are fireworks of heavenly ecstasy. This is eternal life here and now: a tiny foretaste of what awaits you in the life to come."[141]

I love how she describes the joy we can experience through Christ as "eternal life here and now." Doesn't that add a beautiful dimension to the lamp of everlasting life? As the Lord lives in us and pours exceeding great joy into our hearts, it will intensify our inner flame in a whole new way. Through Him, our Eve will finally find the joy she's so desperately been searching for.

Our Savior has actually been telling us all along about this life-changing gift of joy. Think about verses like this one: "In this world your joy is not full, but in me your joy is full" (Doctrine and Covenants 101:36). Or the invitation to "call on the Lord thy God . . . that your souls may be joyful" (Doctrine and Covenants 136:29). Or the Lord's words, "I will impart unto you of my Spirit, which shall enlighten your mind, which shall fill your soul with joy" (Doctrine and Covenants 11:13).

Maybe the reason this joy has been so rare in our lives is because we've never taken the time to purposefully seek it or ask for it. If you're ready to begin that search, here's some wonderful counsel from

140. Sarah Young, *Jesus Calling: Enjoying Peace in His Presence* (Nashville, TN: Thomas Nelson, 2004), 172.

141. Young, *Jesus Calling*, 199.

President Russell M. Nelson: "How, then, can we claim that joy? We can start by 'looking unto Jesus the author and finisher of our faith' (Hebrews 12:2) 'in every thought' (Doctrine and Covenants 6:36). We can give thanks for Him in our prayers and by keeping covenants we've made with Him and our Heavenly Father. *As our Savior becomes more and more real to us and as we plead for His joy to be given to us, our joy will increase.*"[142]

Coming to know Christ and abiding in Him really is the only path to tasting the exquisite sweetness of exceeding great joy. As His grace saturates the depths of our heart, we'll find ourselves filled with an inner happiness we didn't even know was possible in this life—a perpetual sense of joy that will calm our restlessness, soothe our anxiety, and remind us that through the grace of the Lord, everything will be okay.

With that said, we need to return to the scriptures because there's one thing that may hamper our ability to experience exceeding great joy. It's that we live in a fallen world where things often feel like they're not going to be okay *at all*—not even close. While at times the Lord uses His miraculous power to save, heal, and deliver His faithful Saints, sometimes He does exactly the opposite, meaning He places His servants right into the very heart of affliction—in situations that seem to be the very antithesis of exceeding great joy. Rather than living happily ever after, even His most beloved disciples often encounter circumstances that seem destined to send them spiraling right back into despair, frustration, or even all-out hopelessness. Elder Jeffrey R. Holland illustrates it well:

> For every infirm man healed instantly as he waits to enter the Pool of Bethesda, someone else will spend 40 years in the desert waiting to enter the promised land. For every Nephi and Lehi divinely protected by an encircling flame of fire for their faith, we have an Abinadi burned at a stake of flaming fire for his. And we remember that the same Elijah who in an instant called down fire from heaven to bear witness against the priests of Baal is the same Elijah who

142. Russell M. Nelson, "Joy and Spiritual Survival," *Ensign* or *Liahona*, Nov. 2016, 82; emphasis added.

> endured a period when there was no rain for years and who, for a time, was fed only by the skimpy sustenance that could be carried in a raven's claw. By my estimation, that can't have been anything we would call a "happy meal."[143]

These contradictory stories reveal that life doesn't come with any guarantees. Even after our heart is spiritually reborn and lit up with everlasting life, it seems we'll still have to endure some difficult, soul-wrenching trials. So how can we live in perpetual joy when such an unpredictable future lies waiting for us on the road ahead?

To answer that, let me share some good news we haven't yet received—a nugget of truth that will completely shift the way we view our various challenges and trials. It comes to us carefully encapsulated in the words of Alma: "And now, my brethren, I desire that ye shall plant this word in your hearts, and as it beginneth to swell even so nourish it by your faith. And behold, it will become a tree, springing up in you unto everlasting life. And then may God grant unto you that your burdens may be light, through the joy of his Son. And even all this can ye do if ye will. Amen" (Alma 33:23).

This verse tells us that once "everlasting life" is "springing up" inside our heart, something will also happen to our personal burdens—they'll be made light "through the joy of his Son." In fact, two chapters earlier, Alma demonstrated this when he said that the Lord gave their group "strength, that they should suffer no manner of afflictions, *save it were swallowed up in the joy of Christ*" (Alma 31:38; emphasis added).

Let's pause for a moment because I don't want you to miss this life-changing truth. In these verses, we learn that the "joy of Christ" doesn't only exist to make us endlessly happy, although it definitely does just that. In addition, this joy is of such immense power that it can swallow up all the pain of our struggles and afflictions. Even when life is at its lowest. Even when the world is falling apart around us. Even when happiness is the absolute *last* thing we should be able

143. Jeffrey R. Holland, "Waiting on the Lord," *Ensign* or *Liahona*, Nov. 2020, 116.

to feel. Once "the light of everlasting life" ignites our fallen heart, it will "[infuse] such joy into [our] soul" that all our pain, misery, and anguish will be swept by the wayside, and like Lamoni, we'll find ourselves "overcome" and "carried away" in the joy of our God (see Alma 19:6). In other words, our Adam's outward life will no longer have the ability to rule over our Eve's passions and emotions. Through the power of Christ, we'll begin to taste an entirely new way of experiencing life.

In President Nelson's conference talk that I quoted earlier, he gave us a stirring example of what it looks like to be infused with joy while in the midst of intense difficulty. He highlighted Eliza R. Snow's story of having to flee Missouri in the winter of 1838 after the famous Extermination Order was issued by Governor Boggs. One night, the only shelter that her group of refugees could find was an old, run-down cabin where all the chinking between the logs had already been used for firewood. Eighty people crammed into the tiny space, with most having to stand or sit all night to try to stay warm.

Despite the trying circumstances, Eliza noted that "not a complaint was heard—all were cheerful, and judging from appearances, strangers would have taken us to be pleasure excursionists rather than a band of gubernatorial exiles." President Nelson then remarked, "Eliza's report of that exhausting, bone-chilling evening was strikingly optimistic. She declared: 'That was a very merry night. None but saints can be happy under every circumstance.' That's it! *Saints can be happy under every circumstance.* We can feel joy even while having a bad day, a bad week, or even a bad year!"[144]

He then concluded with what would become my favorite quote from the talk—one that I've noticed has been shared again and again on social media. I believe it perfectly captures the exceeding great joy available to us through Jesus Christ:

> My dear brothers and sisters, *the joy we feel has little to do with the circumstances of our lives and everything to do with the focus of our lives.* When the focus of our lives is on God's plan of salvation . . .

144. Russell M. Nelson, "Joy and Spiritual Survival," 82; emphasis added.

> and Jesus Christ and His gospel, we can feel joy regardless of what is happening—or not happening—in our lives. *Joy comes from and because of Him. He is the source of all joy.* We feel it at Christmastime when we sing, "Joy to the world, the Lord is come." And we can feel it all year round. For Latter-day Saints, *Jesus Christ is joy*![145]

Did you notice that he's describing a whole new way of looking at the world? In the past, our Eve's happiness was almost always dependent on our Adam's outward circumstances—on our kids behaving, our bank account overflowing, or our marriage thriving. But once we learn to dwell in Christ and He in us, we'll experience something far greater than that. As President Nelson said, even if we're having a bad day, a bad week, or a bad year, the Lord will lift us up and infuse our hearts with a joy that will defy all description.

Latter-day Saint author Colleen Harrison provides compelling testimony that supports this magnificent doctrinal truth. After receiving her own personal spiritual rebirth, she found herself experiencing a deep infusion of joy during an extremely tragic event. She writes, "Through the sudden and potentially devastating experience of opening my door to a highway patrolman bearing the news of my oldest daughter's violent automobile accident which left her body so mangled that she had to be identified by birthmarks, through the closed casket funeral at which He gave me strength to speak, *I was suspended in a state of joy, not shock, like most people thought.*"[146]

That's the unbelievable point our journey has brought us to—a place where even "the sting of death is swallowed up in Christ" (Mosiah 16:8)!

Like Sister Harrison, I too have felt exceeding great joy fill me from the top of my head to the soles of my feet. And like she said, it's often come in difficult moments when I shouldn't have been able to feel any happiness at all. The experience reminds me of a day I spent driving through a snowy, blustery blizzard. From my vantage point,

---

145. Russell M. Nelson, "Joy and Spiritual Survival," 82; emphasis added.

146. Colleen G. Harrison, *He Did Deliver Me From Bondage* (Hyrum, UT: Windhaven, 2002), 18; emphasis added.

the freezing winds swirled furiously around me and the drifts piled high on the road, but because I was tucked safely inside my car, I felt no impact whatsoever from the powerful storm. Rather than being taunted by the piercing wind or immobilized by the bone-numbing cold, my body was warm and my heart was peaceful as I drove through the snow with surprising ease. To me, the scenario perfectly captures what it has felt like to "enter into the joy of [the] Lord" (Doctrine and Covenants 51:19).

It really is like living in a whole new reality. Once Christ lives continually inside our hearts, the tempests of life will still swirl around us, but we'll no longer be ravaged by the weight of that terrible storm. Instead, we'll remain "suspended in a state of joy" just like Sister Harrison said. In essence, His joy will live in us because *He* lives in us, no matter what else is going on in our daily lives. Just like I felt in my car during that snowstorm, we'll feel insulated. Sheltered. Wrapped snugly in the unending joy and delight of our Savior. Even in the worst of circumstances, the hardest of challenges, and the most wrenching of situations, an underlying happiness will fill the depths of our heart.

But I've also learned another solemn truth about this powerful inner joy: if we're not careful, it's possible to lose it. To find out how, all we need to do is think back to my experience driving through that blizzard. Tell me: what would have happened if I chose to step outside the comfort of my car? The protection would have immediately ended. My leaving the car meant it could no longer give me sanctuary from that vicious storm. And the same holds true in my daily life. If I let my heart drift away from my connection with my Savior, He can no longer offer me the benefits of living in His presence. Just like Peter trying to walk on the water (see Matthew 14:29–31), if we take our focus off the Lord to glance at the raging winds and threatening waves, the gift of joy will quickly evaporate and we'll sink as fast as Peter did, right back into that old emotional blackness. But if we keep our gaze locked on the eyes of our Savior, our heart will continue to dwell in "greater happiness and peace and rest" (Abraham 1:2) than we've ever known.

Of course, experiencing the joy of the Lord doesn't mean we'll never feel sorrow or fear or other kinds of emotional distress. All those feelings are—and will continue to be—a regular part of mortality. But as President Nelson testified, we'll be able to find joy on the bad days simply because Christ is with us. Paul summed this up beautifully when he said we can be "sorrowful, yet alway[s] rejoicing" (2 Corinthians 6:10) and "exceeding joyful in all our tribulation" (2 Corinthians 7:4).

And if you think about it, our ability to find joy amid suffering is one of the greatest ways the Lord will demonstrate His power to those around us. For what bigger miracle could there be than for others to see us still happy even in incredibly difficult circumstances? What better display of grace than for them to see Him carrying us joyfully through even the hardest of trials and most agonizing of afflictions? It truly is one of the sweetest secrets of having our Savior dwelling in us, for only He can fill us so full of joy and happiness that nothing—and I mean *nothing*—can cause us to despair ever again.

Every time I contemplate the miraculous, soul-filling joy available through our Savior—a joy that really does swallow up any sorrow, adversity, or stress life can throw our way—I simply want to echo the words of Ammon: "I cannot say the smallest part which I feel" (Alma 26:16). Joy in Christ is more magnificent, more expansive, and more captivating than I ever thought possible. It truly is "unspeakable and full of glory" (Helaman 5:44), a richness we must experience for ourselves to comprehend. But it *is* real—and it's an abundant blessing available to all those who come to know and abide in their blessed Savior.

Readings & Reflections

Read the following scriptures and take notes on how exceeding great joy is experienced in different ways:

- 2 Samuel 6:13–15
- Isaiah 44:23
- Zephaniah 3:14

- 2 Nephi 22:5–6
- Doctrine and Covenants 136:28

Has a spiritual experience ever made you want to dance, sing, or shout? How would you describe what exceeding great joy feels like to you?

I love how Psalm 45:7 tells us that the Lord was "anointed . . . with the *oil of gladness* above [His] fellows" (emphasis added). The New International Version translates it as the "oil of joy." Now look up Isaiah 61:3. How do you think this description of Christ adds to what we just discussed?

We need to remember that Satan offers his own counterfeit version of joy. Here are some examples you can study:

- Job 20:5
- 3 Nephi 27:11

How can we make sure we're not deceived or distracted by this fleeting, short-term counterfeit?

Return to 2 Nephi 9:42–43 and ponder the connection between humility and joy. Why would a loving Father want you to consider yourself a "fool" before Him? How do you think bowing down before God ultimately lifts our hearts up?

Have you ever personally experienced great joy amid extreme suffering? Read Luke 6:22–23 and 1 Peter 3:14 and note any thoughts or impressions that come from these verses.

Now turn to Hebrews 12:2. What was it that enabled even Jesus Christ Himself to endure the agony of the Atonement?

Going back to the Gospel of John, we'll hear Jesus speak yet again of the gift of joy that's available through Him: "These things have I spoken unto you, that *my joy* might remain in you, and that your joy might be full" (John 15:11; emphasis added). In His Intercessory Prayer, He also says to the Father, "And now come I to thee; and these things I speak in the world, that they might have *my joy* fulfilled in themselves" (John 17:13; emphasis added). After everything we've discussed, what does that phrase "my joy" mean to you? Can you see any ways these verses can apply to you and not just a few of His disciples?

To conclude, note what we learn about joy in the following verses:

- Psalm 132:16
- Doctrine and Covenants 52:43
- Doctrine and Covenants 136:29

Evaluate how your view of joy has changed as you've walked the various paths of our journey. What more do you think you need to learn about the joy of the Lord?

____

____

____

____

____

____

____

____

RESPONSE

In what ways are you feeling prompted to respond to the concepts found in this chapter?

16

Abiding in His Love

After all the steep and rocky paths we've traveled throughout our journey—after all the difficult baggage and all the blood, sweat, and tears—I'm thrilled to tell you that we've finally reached the summit. Join me as we take a deep breath and soak in the view. At long last, our nagging feelings of emptiness and deadness are starting to fade. In their place, the Lord is making us "a new heart" (Ezekiel 18:31)—one that shimmers with everlasting life and throbs with unspeakable joy. Not only can we feel ourselves being cleansed and purified through our Savior's grace, but we're experiencing a closer relationship with Him than we ever thought possible. As His presence within us sets our hearts ablaze, we're beginning to feel the ever-present glow of the lamp of eternal life. With all these awe-inspiring blessings in hand, would you be surprised if I told you this summit has an even greater view waiting to be discovered?

To take in the full expanse of this glorious landscape, we need to go back to the very beginning. As we started out on this journey, what did we say were our heart's most profound and influential desires? Deep down, our Eve hungers for three key things: *life, joy,* and *love.* So far, we've learned how Christ can ignite our fallen hearts with the lamp of everlasting life, causing our inner man to come alive in Him.

We've also learned how He can fill our souls with indescribable joy that transcends even our most difficult trials and afflictions. So what core desire remains? Love. Will the Lord be able to provide our Eve with the deep and meaningful love she so desperately needs? Most definitely.

To my great delight, I found a quote from Elder Jeffrey R. Holland where he links all three core desires of Eve to a very familiar scriptural symbol:

> One image that has at least three variations in the Book of Mormon is the tree, a symbol through which Christ is seen as restoring and redeeming the human family by the fruitfulness of his love.
>
> The reader finds the first manifestation of the symbolic Christ in the vision of the Tree of Life. . . . As the Spirit revealed to Nephi the explanation of the vision his father had seen, the Spirit made explicit that the Tree of Life and its precious fruit are symbols of Christ's redemption. . . . *The images of Christ and the tree [are] inextricably linked. . . .*
>
> Thus, at the very outset of the Book of Mormon, . . . Christ is portrayed as the source of *eternal life* and *joy,* the living evidence of divine *love,* and the means whereby God will fulfill his covenant with the house of Israel and indeed the entire family of man, returning them all to their eternal promises.[147]

If Jesus Christ is the tree of life, then He offers us fruit from His branches that Nephi says is "most sweet, above all that [we have] ever before tasted" (1 Nephi 8:11). And what is this fruit? "Yea, it is the *love of God*, which sheddeth itself abroad in the hearts of the children of men; wherefore, it is *the most desirable above all things* . . . and *the most joyous to the soul*" (1 Nephi 11:22–23; emphasis added). As Elder Holland explained, the Lord really does restore and redeem us "by the fruitfulness of his love."

Now, I know that in our day and age, it's often *human* love that is celebrated as "most desirable above all things" and "most joyous

---

147. Jeffrey R. Holland, *Christ and the New Covenant: The Messianic Message of the Book of Mormon* (Salt Lake City, UT: Deseret Book, 1997), 159–60, 162; emphasis added.

to the soul." That message is embedded in a million different ballads and chick flicks and romance novels. We're told that all we need to be truly fulfilled is to find the one person who "completes" us—the one who will meet our every need and make us live happily ever after. And that's a completely understandable conclusion. Falling in love really does throw us headlong into a jumble of exhilarating, heady emotions. For months on end, we can think of nothing else but the object of our affections. Consumed with feelings of adoration, this love lifts us and inspires us and makes us want to be a better person.

And yet as intoxicating as human love may be, Lehi's vision just revealed something even more life-changing and powerful. The prophet taught us that the most soul-renewing, joy-producing thing we can experience in this life isn't human love . . . it's *Christ's* love. Think what that means for us personally. It means that tasting the Lord's love will be the Mount Everest of our mortal experience. It means the bestowal of His love will surpass every other affection we've ever known. And it means even one bite of this delectable fruit will send our heart leaping and dancing with unending joy.

While the idea of this kind of love may seem inspiring, I know the actual experience of it may not be anywhere near our current reality. What if, unlike Lehi's vision, Christ's love *hasn't* been the most transcendent thing we've ever tasted? What if it really is human love that has captured our sweetest memories and holds the greatest place of significance in our heart? If that's the case, we need to realize that we've missed something incredibly profound. In fact, it's the most astonishing gift available to us through the gospel of Jesus Christ. And yet we may wonder what kind of love could be bigger and better than the intoxicating rush of romance. What could Christ offer us that's more desirable than finding a life partner who completes us? That's more amazing than one who holds us and kisses us and whispers words of love to our heart? How can someone we can't even see or hear love us more intensely than that?

Actually, it's not hard to imagine once we realize that the Lord's love is ignited in the same place where we learned to abide in Him—deep in the recesses of our mind and heart. While in the past we may have known *intellectually* of His love for us (and perhaps even taught and testified of it), once we learn to dwell in Him and He in us, we'll finally enter into the full *experience* of Jesus's boundless love. Like Nephi who was "filled . . . with his love, even unto the consuming of [his] flesh" (2 Nephi 4:21), we too will find our Eve swept up into His arms and wrapped in the sweetness of His embrace. At last, we'll know what it feels like to be "encircled about eternally in the arms of his love" (2 Nephi 1:15).

You need to know that the love I'm describing here isn't just a warm fuzzy feeling or a quickly fleeting moment. It's a very real awareness that will completely overtake our consciousness. The rush, the joy, the intensity we feel with human love—it will all still be there, only a hundred times stronger and deeper. In the words of Elder Dieter F. Uchtdorf, it's a love that "enters our hearts when we awake in the morning, stays with us throughout the day, and swells in our hearts as we give voice to our prayers of gratitude at evening's end."[148] The taste of this fruit won't just mimic human love . . . it will far outshine anything we've ever experienced.

I say this because Christ can love us in a way no mortal person ever could. Because He can live in our heart, the Lord can soothe us on the inside, not just hug us on the outside. He can be with us every minute of the day or night to calm and strengthen us the moment we need it. He can bend time (see Joshua 10:13), change our circumstances (see 2 Kings 7:1–16), or soften hearts to come to our aid (see Doctrine and Covenants 104:80). He never gets grouchy or tired or caught up in His own plans. He never ignores us or misunderstands us or dismisses our efforts to reach out to Him. Most importantly, because He is omniscient and omnipotent, He knows exactly what we need and how to satisfy our hearts to the very utmost.

I know many of us are familiar with the scriptural verses on charity—that it's the "pure love of Christ" and that it "suffereth long" and is "not easily provoked," and especially how it "never faileth" (see Moroni 7:45–47). And we often quote these verses as an example of

---

148. Dieter F. Uchtdorf, "Believe, Love, Do," *Ensign* or *Liahona*, Nov. 2018, 48.

the way we need to love others. While this is very true and important to understand, just for a minute consider this unique perspective on charity from the pen of Elder Holland:

> The greater definition of "the pure love of Christ" . . . is not what we as Christians try but largely fail to demonstrate toward others but rather *what Christ totally succeeded in demonstrating toward us*. . . . It is *his love for us* that is not "puffed up . . . , not easily provoked, thinketh no evil." It is *Christ's love for us* that "beareth all things, believeth all things, hopeth all things, endureth all things." It is *as demonstrated in Christ* that "charity never faileth." It is that charity—his pure love *for us*—without which we would be nothing, hopeless, of all men and women most miserable. Truly, those found possessed of the blessings of his love at the last day—the Atonement, the Resurrection, eternal life, eternal promise—surely it shall be well with them. . . .
>
> With that divine gift, that redeeming bestowal, we have everything; without it we have nothing and ultimately are nothing, except in the end "devils and angels to a devil" (2 Ne. 9:9).[149]

Are you suddenly seeing "charity never faileth" in a whole new light? Looking at it through this lens, the phrase means something very different. It means that even though human love may dim or change or grow dull over time, Christ's love for us never will, for His love truly is "everlasting" (Jeremiah 31:3; Moroni 8:17). In fact, Paul makes it clear that nothing can ever separate us from our Savior's all-consuming love: "Who shall separate us from the love of Christ? shall tribulation, or distress, or persecution, or famine, or nakedness, or peril, or sword? . . . For I am persuaded, that neither death, nor life, nor angels, nor principalities, nor powers, nor things present, nor things to come, Nor height, nor depth, nor any other creature, shall be able to separate us from the love of God, which is in Christ Jesus our Lord" (Romans 8:35, 38–39).

I can't think of a more comforting or reassuring scripture than that. Truly we need the Lord's love more than we need air to breathe. In fact, I believe the soul-deep longing to be loved that we've carried

149. Jeffrey R. Holland, *Christ and the New Covenant*, 336–37; emphasis added.

our entire lives was ultimately put there to drive us to Him—to a love that heals every wound, fills every void, softens every blow, and erases every sin. Can you imagine what will happen to our heart once we know without a doubt that we're adored and cherished by our Savior? Being loved like that does something to our Eve. It makes her come alive with a beauty and radiance that will transcend any human love story that's ever been told. The fruit of the tree of life really is everything Nephi and Lehi described it to be. Not only is it "desirable above all other fruit," but it really will "[fill our] soul with exceedingly great joy" (1 Nephi 8:12).

What's even more astonishing about this fruit is the fact that we don't have to be content with one bite—or even one piece—of this rapturous delicacy. Alma promised us that we can "feast upon this fruit *even until [we] are filled*, that [we] hunger not, neither shall [we] thirst" (Alma 32:42; emphasis added). As unbelievable as it sounds, once we learn to abide in Christ and He in us, we'll be able to feed our hearts *continually* on His love, meaning we can bask in it and revel in it *every single day for the rest of our lives*. Surely nothing will make us happier than to "[know] of [Christ's] goodness and [taste] of his love" (Mosiah 4:11)

In Ephesians 3, Paul records what I believe is one of the most beautiful prayers in all of scripture. And it centers specifically on the Lord's extraordinary, life-altering love, a love that comes once Christ "dwell[s] in [our] hearts by faith" (verse 17). While the King James Version is inspiring in its own right, the Message translation phrases this passage in such a poetic way that I can't help but share it. Listen in as Paul prays in Ephesians 3:17–19: "I ask him that with both feet planted firmly on love, you'll be able to take in with all followers of Jesus *the extravagant dimensions of Christ's love*. Reach out and experience the breadth! Test its length! Plumb the depths! Rise to the heights! Live full lives, full in the fullness of God" (emphasis added).

If you're wondering how we experience the "extravagant dimensions of Christ's love"—how we "test its length" and "plumb the depths" and "rise to the heights," like Paul said—I believe the answer is simple. If we begin to look for the different ways our Savior expresses His love to us, we'll recognize it more and more in our daily lives. Just by opening our eyes to see it, we'll notice His love being poured out in small and simple ways—and at times in gestures that are so miraculous that they'll take our breath away.

For instance, He may show His love for us through a brilliant sunrise streaking across the sky that instantly takes the stress out of our daily commute. He may show it through a palpable sense of support that fills us the very moment we need it. Or He may show it by reminding us of His nearness when we're feeling lost and alone. He may even show it by pointing us to the lyrics of an inspirational song or by whispering reminders of His affection to our minds with words only we can understand. Again, all we have to do is look for it, and we'll see that our Savior displays His love for us in many different ways—ways that can be intimate, tender, whimsical, funny, or even thrilling and exciting.

I remember one day when the Lord's love so overwhelmed me that I was left speechless at the depth of His tender care. At the time, we were trying to finish our basement, and we'd hired a contractor to help us complete the work. However, right when things were starting to come together, several unforeseen costs sapped our budget and we ran out of money to buy the carpet. In frustration, all I could think of to do was scrounge up some used carpet somewhere to throw down on the concrete until we could find a way to pay the several-thousand-dollar bill ourselves.

But just as I was about to move forward with this plan, the phone rang. To my utter shock and amazement, the carpet store told me that someone (a dear friend who remains anonymous to this day) had just paid the cost to carpet our entire basement. All we had to do was go in and pick out what we wanted. I'll never forget how I sat on the basement stairs that day and cried sweet tears of joy at the miracle we'd just experienced. I felt completely wrapped in the Lord's love—in the knowledge that He knew my needs and had just provided for them in an absolutely mind-blowing way. Through the astonishing generosity of a friend, I was swept up in the love of my Savior and knew without a doubt that He truly loved and cared for me on an amazingly personal level.

While Christ won't always use big miracles like that to display His love for us, it won't matter because His small gestures will be just as meaningful and sweet.

I recall another time when a simple rainstorm was so magical and captivating that I knew it had His signature written all over it. Our family had spent the day at Lagoon Amusement Park in Farmington, Utah, and even though it was near closing time, we decided to squeeze in one last ride on what was then their fastest and coolest roller coaster, Wicked. As we were waiting in line, it started to rain. But rather than ruining our fun, we found ourselves laughing and cracking jokes and throwing our arms around each other to keep ourselves warm. Our joy rose to new heights when it was announced that the ride would stay open despite the weather. Once we boarded the coaster, we soared through the air as the droplets soaked our clothes and sprayed our faces. Exhilarated, we jumped off the ride and ran through the deserted streets of Lagoon, splashing in puddles and hollering and having a completely wonderful time.

Of course, you could try to convince me that it was just a simple rainstorm, or that all families have fun when they go to an amusement park. But I'll never believe you because something was different that night. That entire evening, I could feel the Lord's smile igniting the depths of my heart, and I knew that His joy had become our joy, and that He was celebrating right along with us. Wrapped in His love, that wet and wonderful night became a cherished memory our family will never forget.

If you peek inside the back cover of my scriptures, you'll find a long, handwritten list with phrases like *the strawberries* and *that day at the cabin* and *Boston's story* and *Luke 1:45*. (You'll also find *the basement carpet* and *Lagoon and the rain* there too.) I know those words won't mean anything to anyone else, but they mean a great deal to me because they're special moments between the Lord and me, moments when I knew without a doubt that He loved me. I wrote them down so I could always remember the tender relationship we share and the many priceless ways He satisfies the deepest desires of my heart.

If you're frustrated because you haven't yet experienced your Savior's love on that personal of a level, I'll let you in on a little secret. If you want to feel His love washing over you and flooding every corner of your weary heart, there's only one thing you need to do. *Ask Him for it.* Tell Him you want to know His love more than anything else in the entire world. As Moroni encouraged us in the Book of Mormon, "pray unto the Father with all the energy of heart, that ye may be filled with this love, which he hath bestowed upon all who are true followers of his Son, Jesus Christ" (Moroni 7:48). It's a promise that's offered to every single one of us. If we'll just ask "with all the energy of heart"—and keep on asking—a miraculous thing will start to happen inside our Eve. A very real and tangible awareness of Christ's love will begin to sing inside our souls. Eventually, we'll be able to say for ourselves that we've personally tasted the sweetness of the fruit of the tree of life.

What's more, when we ask with that kind of passion and persistence, we won't just experience our Savior's love *for us*—our heart will also be filled to overflowing with a very powerful and personal love *for Him*. He'll be the first thing we think about in the morning. Thoughts of Him will wake us up smiling in the middle of the night. Filled with feelings of adoration for our beloved Savior, we really will "love the Lord [our] God with all [our] heart, [and] with all [our] might, mind, and strength" (Doctrine and Covenants 59:5).

The love we'll feel for the Lord reminds me of the conversation Jesus had with Peter about *phileo* and *agape* love. Yes, like Peter, we may have felt an appreciative, *phileo*-level love for Him in the past. But once the Lord's love begins to blaze like fire in our hearts, we'll finally experience a deep level of *agape* love for Him that will eclipse anything we've ever felt. In short, we'll want to sacrifice every earthly thing just for the privilege of being close to Him. We'll want to consecrate all we have and all we are to His purposes and the growth of His earthly kingdom. In the words of Elder F. Enzio Busche, "With this fulfillment of love in our hearts, we will never be happy anymore just by being ourselves or living our own lives. We will not be satisfied until we have surrendered our lives into the arms of the loving Christ, and until He has become the doer of all our deeds and . . . the speaker of all our words."[150]

Have you ever noticed how the scriptures speak of "the song of redeeming love" (Alma 5:26; see also Alma 26:13)? This particular melody is the song of *agape*. It's the song that dances in our souls once we're spiritually reborn through Christ (see Psalm 40:3; Isaiah 30:29; Revelation 14:3). Professor Robert L. Millet gives a wonderful explanation of this rapturous song:

> To sing the song of redeeming love is to joy in the matchless majesty of God's goodness, to know the wonder of his love. It is to sense and know, by the power of the Holy Ghost, that the Lord is intimately involved with his children, and that he cares, really cares, about their well-being; it is to relish and cherish that fruit which is most joyous to the soul. . . .
>
> *But it is also to love Christ purely, to partake of a quality and depth of soul-love for Him which knows no earthly or temporal counterparts. It is to love and honor and worship and praise the Lord as God with feelings and emotions which are unspeakable.*[151]

Once this "unspeakable" love for Christ overtakes us, our covenants (especially our temple covenants) will suddenly become even more precious to us. No longer will we feel obligated to keep them out of duty or because that's what a good Church member does. Instead, we'll begin to cherish them because there's nothing we'll want more on this earth than to give ourselves completely to Him, and to do so *by covenant*. When we love a mortal person, we seek to bind ourselves to that person by covenant, so the same thing will be true of Christ, the supreme object of our love.

What's more, with this love shining brightly in our hearts, we'll find ourselves feeling things for the Lord that we never realized we could feel for Him in this life. My favorite characterization of this

150. F. Enzio Busche, "Truth is the Issue," *Ensign*, Nov. 1993, 26.

151. Robert L. Millet, *By Grace We Are Saved* (Salt Lake City, UT: Bookcraft, 1989), 106–7; emphasis added.

is found in the book of Psalms. There David gives us an inspiring glimpse of what a heart looks and sounds like when it's completely wrapped up in an *agape* love for the Lord. As you read David's moving and emotional words, notice the different ways he displays his love for His blessed Savior.

First, David continually *praises* Him: "I will praise thee, O Lord, with my whole heart . . . I will be glad and rejoice in thee: I will sing praise to thy name, O thou most High" (Psalm 9:1–2). "Because thy lovingkindness is better than life, my lips shall praise thee" (Psalm 63:3). "Let my mouth be filled with thy praise and with thy honour all the day" (Psalm 71:8). "My tongue also shall talk of thy righteousness all the day long" (Psalm 71:24).

He constantly *longs* for the Lord: "As the hart panteth after the water brooks, so panteth my soul after thee, O God. My soul thirsteth for God, for the living God" (Psalm 42:1–2). "O God . . . my soul thirsteth for thee, my flesh longeth for thee. . . . My soul followeth hard after thee" (Psalm 63:1, 8). "My soul longeth, yea, even fainteth for the courts of the Lord: my heart and my flesh crieth out for the living God" (Psalm 84:2).

Christ has become *his only desire*: "One thing I have desired of the Lord, that will I seek after; that I may dwell in the house of the Lord all the days of my life, to behold the beauty of the Lord, and to inquire in his temple" (Psalm 27:4). "My heart is fixed, O God, my heart is fixed: I will sing and give praise" (Psalm 57:7). "There is none upon earth that I desire beside thee" (Psalm 73:25). "I had rather be a doorkeeper in the house of my God, than to dwell in the tents of wickedness" (Psalm 84:10).

Finally, David receives *deep and lasting satisfaction* from the relationship: "How excellent is thy lovingkindness, O God! therefore the children of men . . . shall be abundantly satisfied with the fatness of thy house; and thou shalt make them drink of the river of thy pleasures" (Psalm 36:7–8). "My soul shall be satisfied as with marrow and fatness; and my mouth shall praise thee with joyful lips" (Psalm 63:5). "For he satisfieth the longing soul, and filleth the hungry soul with goodness" (Psalm 107:9). "How sweet are thy words unto my taste! yea, sweeter than honey to my mouth!" (Psalm 119:103).

I believe we can use David's touching words to measure our own personal feelings for the Lord. Once we're filled with *agape*, won't we also feel compelled to praise Him continually? Won't we also thirst for Him and long to feel Him close? Won't we also desire no other earthly thing but Him? Won't we also receive abundant satisfaction from the relationship? After all, He really is our truest love—our one and only Redeemer. He died in our place to rescue us from the awful effects of sin, sorrow, and shame. He's reached down into the depths of our souls and showed us how to overcome our insecurity, worthlessness, and fear. He's given us power to overcome our natural man and filled us with an unending amount of life, joy, and love. For all that and more, our love for the Lord won't just burn brightly within us—it will overflow with such abundance that we'll be consumed with feelings of adoration, wonder, and devotion.

President Ezra Taft Benson captured it perfectly when he described what happens to those who are filled with this rapturous and all-encompassing love for the Lord:

> [Those] captained by Christ will be consumed in Christ. To paraphrase President Harold B. Lee, they set fire in others because they are on fire.
>
> Their will is swallowed up in his will. (See John 5:30).
>
> They do always those things that please the Lord. (See John 8:29).
>
> Not only would they die for the Lord, but, more important, they want to live for Him.
>
> They have Christ on their minds, as they look unto Him in every thought. (See Doctrine and Covenants 6:36).
>
> They have Christ in their hearts as their affections are placed on Him forever. (See Alma 37:36). . . .
>
> In Book of Mormon language, they "feast upon the words of Christ" (2 Nephi 32:3), "talk of Christ" (2 Nephi 25:26), "rejoice in Christ" (2 Nephi 25:26), "are made alive in Christ" (2 Nephi 25:25), and "glory in [their] Jesus" (2 Nephi 33:6).
>
> In short, *they lose themselves in the Lord and find eternal life.*[152]

---

152. Ezra Taft Benson, "Born of God," *Ensign*, July 1989; emphasis added.

That last phrase is the key to our entire quest.

Once we lose ourselves in the Lord, we'll find eternal life.

Once we lose ourselves in the Lord, we'll find a love that will ignite our Eve with more fire than we've ever imagined.

Once we lose ourselves in the Lord, our hearts will never be the same ever again.

I feel like I could shout it from the rooftops! Because truly, every other experience in my life has paled in comparison to being "clasped in the arms of Jesus" (Mormon 5:11). The taste of His soul-filling love has been so overpowering, so breathtaking, and so intoxicating that I simply want to wrap my arms around the tree of life and never let go. Because I've found the Lord's love to be so deeply intimate and personal, and so completely satisfying and fulfilling, I think I finally understand why Nephi affectionately calls Him "my Jesus" (2 Nephi 33:6).

Believe it or not, there's also another glorious side effect of being filled with this immense and life-changing love. Not only will it overflow inside our hearts and fill us with all the happiness and joy we could ever need—it will also spill over into the lives of everyone else we encounter, from strangers and work acquaintances to our closest and most cherished loved ones. As Elder Dieter F. Uchtdorf explains:

> The love Jesus spoke about . . . isn't a gift-card, throwaway, move-on-to-other-things love. It isn't a love that is spoken of and then forgotten. It is not a "let me know if there is anything I can do" sort of love. . . . It is this endless compassion that allows us to more clearly see others for who they are. Through the lens of pure love, we see immortal beings of infinite potential and worth and beloved sons and daughters of Almighty God. Once we see through that lens, we cannot discount, disregard, or discriminate against anyone.[153]

Simply put, once we taste the fruit of the tree of life—once we truly know in the depth of our souls that we're beloved by our Savior—we'll be empowered to view others through that same vision-changing, life-transforming love. Without a second thought, we'll treat them

153. Dieter F. Uchtdorf, "Believe, Love, Do," 48.

as He treated them, befriend them as He befriended them, and serve them as He served them. Finally, we'll understand why Nephi said the "tree of life, whose fruit is most precious and most desirable above all other fruits . . .[is] *the greatest of all the gifts of God*" (1 Nephi 15:36; emphasis added).

While we take our last few minutes to gaze on the awe-inspiring love of Christ and all it means in our hearts and lives, I wonder if you'd join me one final time as we return to the story of the woman at the well. That story has become so precious to me, I can't help but linger there a moment longer and review the beautiful truths we learned in those few short verses.

Only this time, I want you to use your mind to enter the scene. Sit and rest against the edge of the well, close to where the Samaritan woman is letting down her pitcher. Watch as Jesus strolls over and sits nearby, His eyes surveying the woman with joyful anticipation. You hear Him ask her for a drink and see the shock quickly register on her face. As she questions His intent, He leans in and—in the most warm and unassuming way—offers her the deal of the century: "If thou knewest the gift of God, and who it is that saith to thee, Give me to drink; thou wouldest have asked of him, and he would have given thee living water" (John 4:10).

I'm hoping that by now, Jesus's words mean a great deal more to you. Because now you know exactly what He's talking about when He speaks of "living water." Now you know what He means when He says, "The water that I shall give [you] shall be *in [you]* a well of water springing up into everlasting life" (verse 14; emphasis added).

As our journey comes to a close, the question I most want to ask is this: has this story now become personal to you? Like this woman, has an encounter with Jesus begun to change you? Like her, are you filled with desire to tell everyone you know about His miraculous power to save? I believe our quest will have meant nothing until you've come to know Jesus Christ for yourself—until you've truly learned to abide in Him and He in you. Only by nurturing this intimate relationship can you enjoy the transcendent gift of "abid[ing] in [His] love" (John 15:10).

It's exactly what He's been hoping for all along. More than anything, the King of the Universe wants to live in you and ignite you with the lamp of everlasting life. He wants to infuse your soul with exceeding great joy. He wants to shower you again and again with His heart-stopping love.

But you have to turn to Him and receive it.

You have to open your heart and let Him in.

Only then will you "taste and see that the Lord is good" (Psalm 34:8). Only then will you be "made rich" with "eternal life" (Doctrine and Covenants 11:7). Only then will you experience the "fruit [that is] desirable to make one happy" (1 Nephi 8:10)—happier, in fact, than you've ever been in your entire life.

As one who has finally found Him, as one who has been released from seemingly unbreakable chains, as one whose soul hunger has been filled to overflowing with life, joy, and love, may I simply say this: Christ stands waiting to give you everything your heart desires. If you haven't already done so, perhaps it's time to find Him for yourself.

Readings & Reflections

Let's take a minute to tie in our earlier discussion on the difference between *phileo* (affection or high regard) and *agape* (the pure love of Christ). Ponder the following questions.

How would you characterize your own love for Jesus Christ? Is it mainly a *phileo* type of love? Or has it transitioned to the deeper *agape*?

Have you ever specifically prayed to be filled with this kind of love? If so, what effect did that have on you?

Like Peter in John 21:15–17, what more could be possible in your personal relationship with the Lord?

Read Matthew 22:37–38 (Jesus used the word *agape* in this verse) and Doctrine and Covenants 20:19. Could it be that reaching this deeper level of love for Christ is a commandment rather than just a helpful suggestion? What do you think about that?

Turn to Ether 12:33–34. How does this passage say the Lord displayed His *agape* for us? Once we are filled with this love, how can we follow His example and lay down our lives for Him in return?

For a fun little study project, read 1 John 1–5 and count the number of times the word "love" is used. (Every single time, the Apostle used the Greek word *agape*.)

Now let's focus on a few points from those epistles. Turn first to 1 John 4:19. What insight does this simple verse add to our discussion on love? Now look also at verse 16 and answer the same question.

Next, turn to 1 John 4:7–11. How will being filled with the love of Christ impact your love for your family? Your neighbors? Your friends?

Even your enemies? How do you think tasting the fruit of the tree of life will change the way you love others in your life?

Take some time to journal about the many ways Christ has communicated His love to you. Perhaps you could even make your own list in the back of your scriptures (or record it in whatever way works for you). Ponder how His tender love for you has increased your feelings of love for Him in return.

I found a story that perfectly captures the "extravagant dimensions of Christ's love" like Paul talked about in Ephesians 3. It was written by Elder Melvin J. Ballard in 1949 but thankfully was reprinted in the December 2014 *Ensign*. Ponder his words and the way they capture the poignant sweetness of Jesus's love:

> I found myself one evening in the dreams of the night in that sacred building, the temple. After a season of prayer and rejoicing I was informed that I should have the privilege of entering into one of those rooms, to meet a glorious personage, and, as I entered the

door, I saw, seated on a raised platform, the most glorious being my eyes have ever beheld or that I ever conceived existed in all the eternal worlds.

As I approached to be introduced, He arose and stepped towards me with extended arms, and He smiled as He softly spoke my name. If I shall live to be a million years old, I shall never forget that smile. He took me into His arms and kissed me, pressed me to His bosom, and blessed me, until the marrow of my bones seemed to melt! When He had finished, I fell at His feet, and, as I bathed them with my tears and kisses, I saw the prints of the nails in the feet of the Redeemer of the world. The feeling that I had in the presence of Him who hath all things in His hands, to have His love, His affection, and His blessing was such that if I can receive that of which I had but a foretaste, I would give all that I am, all that I ever hope to be, to feel what I then felt![154]

The amazing thing is, you don't have to have your own dream to experience the same thing Elder Ballard felt. You can taste it continually as you learn to abide in Christ and "feast upon his love" (Jacob 3:2).

One of the most moving descriptions I've ever read that connects eternal life to our Savior's love comes from A. W. Tozer's book *The Pursuit of God*, where he quotes Nicholas of Cusa, a German philosopher from the fourth century. As we close, soak in his poignant and luxurious words:

Nicholas was a true follower of Christ, a lover of the Lord, radiant and shining in his devotion to the Person of Jesus. His theology was orthodox, but fragrant and sweet as everything about Jesus might properly be expected to be. His conception of eternal life, for instance, is beautiful in itself and, if I mistake not, is nearer in spirit to John 17:3 than that which is current among us today.

Life eternal, says Nicholas, is "nought other than that blessed regard wherewith Thee never ceasest to behold me, yea, even the secret places of my soul. With Thee, to behold is to give life; 'tis unceasingly to impart sweetest love of Thee; 'tis to inflame me to love of Thee by love's imparting, and to feed me by inflaming, and

154. Melvin J. Ballard, "I Know That He Lives," *Ensign*, Dec. 2014, 80.

> by feeding to kindle my yearning, and by kindling to make me drink of the dew of gladness, and by drinking to infuse in me a fountain of life, and by infusing to make it increase and endure."[155]

Oh, that we each may taste for ourselves of the Lord's love and, by so doing, be infused and inflamed with the exquisite inner fountain of everlasting life.

155. A. W. Tozer, *The Pursuit of God* (Sunnyvale, CA: Loki's Publishing, 2017), 61–62.

Response

In what ways are you feeling prompted to respond to the concepts found in this chapter?

Epilogue: Come Home

Wavering with uncertainty, Eve stares at the luscious piece of forbidden fruit sitting in the palm of her hand. It looks so appetizing that her mouth begins to water. Oh, how she longs to taste this sweet-smelling delicacy! She wonders how something that feels so right could be wrong. Eve brings the tempting fruit closer, and its sweet, alluring fragrance intensifies her craving even more. She draws a deep breath . . . then sinks her teeth into its juicy flesh. As a sense of intoxicating pleasure overtakes her, she throws her head back and revels in the satisfaction of fulfilled desire. What an experience! The gratification is exactly as she imagined it would be!

But unbeknownst to Eve, the choice to indulge her cravings slowly begins to change her. At first, her yearnings grow stronger, driving her to eat even more of the forbidden fruit. As she does so, her desires gain greater control over her, causing her to feel more driven to satisfy her powerful physical appetites. Suddenly, her world begins to spin and she feels darkness closing in around her. Something cold and hard grabs at her arms and legs and a feeling almost like death itself overtakes her.

Later Eve awakes to find herself lying flat on her back, staring up into the dim light. She rubs her eyes, shakes the dust off, and stands up. Confused, she takes a minute to study her new surroundings. It's a small space. Confining. She sees imposing stone walls and bars over the tiny window. With a gasp, she looks down to discover chains clamped tightly onto her trembling limbs. At last, the reality hits her that she's imprisoned. And she's not sure what to do about it.

Locked in her heavy shackles, Eve begins to experience waves of confusion, frustration, and anger. Maddened over her inability to control her situation, she rages and strains against her constraints. Sharp, biting words come out of her mouth, things she never dreamed she would say. Struggling to comprehend the changes happening inside her, Eve is horrified at the person she's become. How did she get here? This wasn't supposed to happen when she took that bite. It's not at all how she thought things would be.

If all that wasn't bad enough, Eve panics when she suddenly realizes that she's naked. Desperate to cover herself, she rummages through her cell but finds nothing. When the prison warden throws some rags her way, she pieces them together to make an apron of sorts. She calms down a bit as she wraps its comforting weight around her quivering frame.

Feeling a little more settled, Eve decides to explore her new environment, and she soon learns that she's part of an entire ward of prisoners. To her surprise, the cell doors open for a time, which allows Eve to drag her chains to the common area. As the other prisoners gather around her, they offer all sorts of advice on how to deal with life in captivity. They introduce Eve to their favorite games and the songs they love to sing. They entertain her with a number of playful shows and melodramas. She finds these escapes really do lift her spirits and help her forget about her confinement for a little while.

Next, her fellow captives teach her about the elaborate trade and barter system they've set up inside the prison. Sporting a dizzying array of merchandise designed to make life in captivity more fashionable and comfortable, the inmates barter with each other in an attempt to obtain some exciting new possessions. One prisoner even invites Eve to look over his collection and choose a few items with the promise that she'll pay him in the future. But just as she's beginning to enjoy her shopping, the guards break up the activities and send the captives back to their cells. As the cell door slams behind Eve, she finds herself wondering over her place in this strange new world.

"Well," she thinks, "as long as I'm here, I might as well clean up a bit." Grabbing some rags, she wipes and dusts, she scrubs the grime and gathers the clutter, she washes her face and brushes the dirt out of her clothing. The busyness takes her mind off her chains, so Eve increases her activity even more. She works tirelessly, organizing the other prisoners and planning projects to improve their time spent in bondage. Again, her efforts help her forget about her shackles for a while, but the warden won't let her do that for very long.

"You'll never be free," he taunts as he comes walking by. "This is your life now, so you better just accept it." His words chill her soul, but Eve isn't willing to give up hope. "Somehow," she muses, "I've got to find a way out of here. There *must* be a way out of this awful prison cell." Such thoughts quickly spur Eve into action.

Grabbing her chains, she strains and struggles, twisting her arms and trying to slide her wrists out of the cold iron grasp. No good. Next, she finds a sharp rock on the floor and saws away at the links, but the attempt proves totally useless. Exasperated, Eve grabs the heavy chains and runs forward with all her might, but the force bungees her backward and sends her crashing to the floor. Lying in the dust, Eve is forced to admit that despite all her tireless efforts, her bonds remain as firmly attached as ever.

Thus resigned, Eve acts on the warden's suggestion to accept her life in captivity. She returns to the common room and chooses merchandise to decorate her cell and dress up her grungy appearance. She socializes with the other captives and attends their entertaining games and shows. She keeps up with her busyness and tries to maintain a good attitude. But underneath it all, Eve realizes that these distractions aren't really working. Deep down, she knows her life was meant for more than a paltry prisoner's existence. But what other choice does she have? "Is life, after all, just about surviving?" she wonders. "About getting through another day? *What am I doing here?*"

As her internal battle wages on, Eve suddenly remembers an old book she saw lying forgotten in the corner of her cell. She quickly grabs it, blows the dust off its cover, and begins leafing through its worn and yellowed pages. Immediately, her eyes fall on these simple words:

> I will . . . give thee my servant for a covenant of the people, . . .
>
> That thou mayest say to the prisoners: Go forth; to them that sit in darkness: Show yourselves. They shall feed in the ways, and their pastures shall be in all high places.
>
> They shall not hunger nor thirst, neither shall the heat nor the sun smite them; for he that hath mercy on them shall lead them, even by the springs of water shall he guide them. (1 Nephi 21:8–10)

"Freedom for prisoners?" she wonders. "No more hunger or thirst? And what's this covenant the book is referring to?" She flips the page and is struck again with the words: "Wherefore, he will bring them again out of captivity, and they shall be gathered together to the lands of their inheritance; and they shall be brought out of obscurity and out of darkness; and they shall know that the Lord is their Savior and their Redeemer, the Mighty One of Israel" (1 Nephi 22:12).

A faint glimmer of hope begins to stir inside Eve. Is there really a Redeemer—someone who can set all prisoners free? Who is He? Eve pores over the pages of the book, reading all day and into the night, her thirsty heart drinking in the promises of Jesus Christ. She's amazed to find that not only does He offer her freedom, but He has actually shed His own blood to purchase it. His death for her life. He calls to Eve through the pages of the book, offering her the very liberty that has seemed so out of reach. "He *has* to be real," she muses. "I think it's time to find out for myself."

With that, Eve feels driven to do something she's never done before. Rather than making aprons, trying to stay busy, or shopping through the prison wares, rather than escaping into the captives' entertaining games and shows, rather than struggling and straining to break her chains, Eve turns from all those things and chooses instead to *cry out.* As the dam breaks inside her, the words pour out like a torrent, leaving her crying with a desperation that echoes off the cold stone walls:

"O Jesus, thou Son of God, have mercy on me, who am in the gall of bitterness, and am encircled about by the everlasting chains of death" (Alma 36:18). "O Lord, have mercy; according to thy abundant mercy" (Alma 18:41). "If thou art God, wilt thou make thyself known unto me, and I will give away all my sins to know thee" (Alma 22:18).

As Eve pleads for deliverance, she feels drawn to confess her sins of false worship. She acknowledges that she's heeded the other captives' advice and sought out alternate sources of comfort and fulfillment. She admits that she's gotten lost in busyness and spent needless hours trying to free herself through her own efforts. Having now abandoned all that, her attention is directed to thoughts of her Redeemer, which fills her with a new sense of hope and faith. Having sacrificed all she has, Eve takes a deep breath, and then finally she waits.

At last, she hears it. A key turning in the lock. The creaking of the stubborn, rusty hinges. Suddenly, the door swings open and floods her cell with more radiance than its dingy walls have ever seen. As her eyes adjust to the brilliant light, she sees Him standing there. Smiling. Gazing at her with a love that pierces her with its sweet and intimate tenderness. Slowly He approaches her and grasps her shackles in His scarred hands. At His touch, the heavy chains clatter to the floor. Overcome with wonder, Eve reflects on all the time she spent trying to convince herself that freedom wasn't possible, that she could survive in the cell, that it wasn't all that bad. Rubbing her aching wrists, Eve looks up and her eyes meet those of her Deliverer. In that moment, her heart comes alive with a vibrant flame more glorious than anything she's ever felt. A childlike joy sweeps over her at the miracle of it all!

But her Redeemer isn't finished quite yet.

Next, He washes her face and wipes the grime from her hands. He clothes her in a luxurious new robe and puts soft slippers on her feet. He smooths back her hair and lays a crown on her head that gives Eve, for the first time, a full awareness of who she really is. She isn't a prisoner anymore. An intense love beyond all comprehension threatens to overtake her consciousness. In her Deliverer's marvelous presence, she feels wrapped in His glorious love, her heart about to explode with exceeding great joy.

He pauses to speak to her of total obedience, of the need to continue to sacrifice all worldly things and lay them at His feet, of His desire for her to be wholly consecrated to Him. She smiles because it seems like such a small price to pay to know Him and His tremendous, all-consuming love. Of course she's His—all her heart and soul.

At last, He leads Eve out of her cell, past the prison walls, and out into the bright sunshine. She breathes in the fresh, clean air and looks around. The freedom is more astonishing than she ever dreamt it would be! Yet as liberating as it feels to leave her prison cell, it dawns on Eve that the most amazing thing about her rescue is the One standing before her. He came for her. *He came.* His companionship is all she'll ever need and more. Overwhelmed with love for her Redeemer, she's consumed with desire to offer Him all her newly illuminated heart could ever give.

As her Deliverer beckons, Eve realizes that she now knows the true meaning of salvation. Her heart has finally *come home.*

> O give thanks unto the Lord, for he is good: for his mercy endureth for ever.
>
> Let the redeemed of the Lord say so, whom he hath redeemed from the hand of the enemy;
>
> And gathered them out of the lands, from the east, and from the west, from the north, and from the south.
>
> They wandered in the wilderness in a solitary way; they found no city to dwell in.
>
> Hungry and thirsty, their soul fainted in them.
>
> Then they cried unto the Lord in their trouble, and he delivered them out of their distresses.
>
> Oh that men would praise the Lord for his goodness, and for his wonderful works to the children of men!
>
> For he satisfieth the longing soul, and filleth the hungry soul with goodness.
>
> Such as sit in darkness and in the shadow of death, being bound in affliction and iron. . . .

He brought them out of darkness and the shadow of death, and brake their bands in sunder.

Oh that men would praise the Lord for his goodness, and for his wonderful works to the children of men!

For he hath broken the gates of brass, and cut the bars of iron in sunder. . . .

He sent his word, and healed them, and delivered them from their destructions. . . .

Then are they glad because they be quiet; so he bringeth them unto their desired haven.

Oh that men would praise the Lord for his goodness, and for his wonderful works to the children of men! (Psalm 107:1–10, 14–16, 20, 30–31)

About the Author

Jaci (JAY-see) Wightman is a Certified Health Coach, Mind-Body Coach, and Biblical Life Coach. The author of four books, she's created a Christ-Centered Wellness platform that includes a podcast, a YouTube channel, several faith-based online courses, and one-on-one coaching. She loves to speak to groups of all ages. With her seven children now grown, she's also relishing her role as Eema to an ever-growing crew of grandkids. Jaci's greatest passion lies in teaching and testifying of Jesus Christ's ability to transform us physically, mentally, emotionally, and spiritually—especially in the places where we struggle the most. You can visit her online at jaciwightman.com.

Scan to visit

www.jaciwightman.com